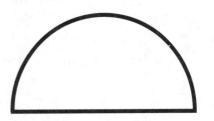

LIVING THE WORD

Scripture Reflections
and Commentaries
for Sundays and
Holy Days

by
Rev. Robert Duggan
and
Virginia Stillwell

LIVING THE WORD

Scripture Reflections
and Commentaries for
Sundays and Holy Days

Vol. 18   December 1, 2002—November 23, 2003

Published annually
Individual copy: $12.95
(2-9 copies: $9.95 per copy;
10-24 copies: $8.95 per copy;
25-99 copies: $7.95 per copy;
100 or more copies: $5.95 per copy)

Published with ecclesiastical approval.

Editor: Michael E. Novak
Copy Editor: Marcia T. Lucey
Typesetter and Cover Design: Tejal Patel
Editorial Director: Mary Beth Kunde-Anderson

Copyright © 2002 by World Library Publications,
a division of J. S. Paluch Company, Inc.
3825 N. Willow Road, Schiller Park, IL 60176-9936
1 800 566-6150; FAX 1 888 957-3291

Printed in the United States of America
(ISSN) 1079-4670
(ISBN) 1-58459-127-7

Introduction

Our renewed liturgy has generated a great deal of interest in sacred Scripture. In turn, a richer appreciation of the readings for Mass has done much for participation in our liturgical celebrations. It is this twofold deepening of the Christian life that *Living the Word* is intended to facilitate. It is our hope that individuals, homilists, catechumens, candidates, discussion groups, religious education classes, and similar gatherings will all benefit from the commentaries and reflections found on these pages.

The readings for each Sunday, holy day, and major celebration from December 2002 through November 2003, Year B of the liturgical cycle, are presented here, along with a brief passage intended to suggest a focus or approach to consider while reading them. Following the readings is a commentary that provides a context for understanding them, incorporating both biblical scholarship and the Church's age-old wisdom. A reflection section develops the initial focus and ties it together with the commentary. The discussion questions and suggestions for responses that follow offer help in moving from reflection to action, inviting those who use this volume to go about truly "Living the Word."

Whether reflecting on the Scriptures in a group setting or individually, it is best to do so in the context of prayer. Consider creating an atmosphere that will foster prayerful reflection when you are using this book. In a quiet space, perhaps with lit candles and simple seasonal decoration (incense or soft music may also be appropriate), begin with a prayer and reading aloud of the Scriptures for that day, even if you are alone. Groups can encourage members to focus on one word or idea that speaks to them from each reading. Participants might want to share these ideas with one another before continuing.

After listening to the readings, ask yourself how they have changed you, enlightened you, moved you. Proceed to the commentary, reflection, and response. Use the discussion questions to shape your conversation or as a springboard for your own questions. Does the "Responding to the Word" section speak to you this week? How might your own response be the same or different?

Having started with prayer, perhaps once you have spent time in reflection or discussion it will be appropriate to lift up someone or something in a prayer that is related to the readings or your reflections. Pray spontaneously as you think about the texts' meaning for you or invite people in the group to offer prayers informally.

Finally, what action will you take this week that grows out of your prayerful reflection on this week's Scriptures? You may propose your own prayer for help to do something in response to the readings or simply stand and pray the Lord's Prayer. If you are in a group, offer one another a sign of peace before departing. If alone, extend yourself to another in a gesture of peace later in the day or week, in person, by phone, or by offering a simple prayer.

Repeating this pattern over time can help your prayerful reflection to deepen your appreciation for and commitment to God's Word every day of your life.

Table of Contents

Prayers Before Reading Scripture

Lord Jesus,
we give you praise.
Speak to us as we read your word,
and send your Spirit into our hearts.
Guide us today and each day in your service,
for you are our way, our truth, our life.

Lord Jesus, we love you:
keep us in your love for ever and ever. *Amen!*

or

Blessed are you, Lord God,
king of all creation:
you have taught us by your word.
Open our hearts to your Spirit,
and lead us on the paths of Christ your Son.

All praise and glory be yours for ever. *Amen!*

or

Lord, open our hearts:
let your Spirit speak to us
as we read your word. *Amen!*

or

Lord Jesus,
to whom shall we go?
You have the words of eternal life.

Speak, Lord,
your servants are listening:
here we are, Lord,
ready to do your will. *Amen!*

Prayers After Reading Scripture

Blessed are you, Lord God,
maker of heaven and earth,
ruler of the universe:
you have sent your Holy Spirit
to teach your truth to your holy people.
We praise you for letting us read your word today.

Grant that we may continue to think and pray
over the words we have read,
and to share your thoughts with others
throughout this day.

Loving God, we praise you
and thank you in Jesus' name. *Amen!*

or

God of all graciousness, we thank you
for speaking to us today
through your holy word. *Amen!*

Time is something we rarely think about. Like the air we breathe, it is always there, and seldom is there reason to stop and give it particular attention. But just like the air we breathe, the quality of our time can be better or worse. Smog-filled, pollution-laden air is a problem that can cause us to sicken and eventually even die if we do not take precautions against its toxic effects. Just so, time can be lived out in meaningless or even destructive ways, or it can be "redeemed" and made quite valuable.

The people of the biblical world knew and reflected upon the ways that time itself can differ, either for weal or woe. In the ancient Greek manuscripts of the Bible, there are two different words used to describe time: the first is *chronos*, which refers simply to the measurement of time, its even flow, without any particular significance being attached to it. The second word is *kairos*, a term used to describe time that is filled with meaning, time in which sacred history unfolds according to the measure and meaning set by God alone. *Kairos* is always a moment of salvation, time in which grace and redemption are offered to humankind. But *kairos* does not move at the same pace as *chronos*: a thousand days in the Lord's sight are but an instant, and in a mere instant one can experience a lifetime of meaning.

The Church has borrowed from this biblical understanding of sacred time in the evolution of what we call the "liturgical cycle." Each year the Church insists that time is sacred and redemptive. And in order to awaken our consciousness to the graced potential of time, the liturgy actually re-names and re-defines time by establishing a regular rhythm of feasts and seasons. There is something boldly counter-cultural in the Church's defiance of mere secular time, a faith-filled proclamation that there is more to the passing of days than meets the eye. We believe, in fact, that all time has been redeemed, that all is grace, and that the offer of salvation is ever present in our midst. The cycle of liturgical seasons is the constant unfolding of this offer of grace for all who are willing to adopt the perspective of faith as they look upon the reality of a world transformed in Christ.

The Christian's version of "New Year's Day" is the First Sunday of Advent, when we begin again the entire cycle of the year. Even as the secular culture around us blares its songs of reindeer and tinsel, as if Christmas were already here, the Christian calendar sets aside four weeks of quiet preparation. We are invited to contemplate the coming of the Lord: first his final coming at the end of time; and, then, his coming in human history in the womb of the Virgin Mary; finally (and, ultimately), his coming now—in the eternal "now" of God's *kairos* into which we enter at each and every liturgy. As the secular culture is already packing away the Christmas decorations and moving on to other distractions, the Christian calendar remains fixed upon the mystery of the Incarnation, prolonging the celebration of Christmas throughout a season that lasts for several weeks. The scriptural commentaries and material for reflection and discussion in this book invite you to be part of God's *kairos* each and every week, to enter the liturgical cycle with a specifically Christian perspective and discover there "the time of your life," a year of grace where God is present in every moment if only we live each day with faith.

December 1, 2002

FIRST SUNDAY OF ADVENT

Today's Focus: Come Back!

Especially during the holidays we may look around at our world or our own lives and wonder whether God has abandoned us to our own sinful devices. Yet today's Advent Scriptures assure us that God has not abandoned the world. Christ has come to save and strengthen us and he will come back again.

FIRST READING
Isaiah 63: 16b–17, 19b; 64:2b–7

You, LORD, are our father,
     our redeemer you are named forever.
Why do you let us wander, O LORD, from your ways,
     and harden our hearts so that we fear you not?
Return for the sake of your servants,
     the tribes of your heritage.
Oh, that you would rend the heavens and come down,
     with the mountains quaking before you,
while you wrought awesome deeds we could not hope for,
     such as they had not heard of from of old.
No ear has ever heard, no eye ever seen, any God but you
     doing such deeds for those who wait for him.
Would that you might meet us doing right,
     that we were mindful of you in our ways!
Behold, you are angry, and we are sinful;
     all of us have become like unclean people,
     all our good deeds are like polluted rags;
we have all withered like leaves,
     and our guilt carries us away like the wind.
There is none who calls upon your name,
     who rouses himself to cling to you;
for you have hidden your face from us
     and have delivered us up to our guilt.
Yet, O LORD, you are our father;
     we are the clay and you the potter:
     we are all the work of your hands.

PSALM RESPONSE
Psalm 80:4

Lord, make us turn to you; let us see your face and we shall be saved.

SECOND READING
1 Corinthians 1: 3–9

Brothers and sisters: Grace to you and peace from God our Father and the Lord Jesus Christ.

I give thanks to my God always on your account for the grace of God bestowed on you in Christ Jesus, that in him you were enriched in every way, with all discourse and all knowledge, as the testimony to Christ was confirmed among you, so that you are not lacking in any spiritual gift as you wait for the revelation of our

Lord Jesus Christ. He will keep you firm to the end, irreproachable on the day of our Lord Jesus Christ. God is faithful, and by him you were called to fellowship with his Son, Jesus Christ our Lord.

GOSPEL
Mark 13:33–37

Jesus said to his disciples: "Be watchful! Be alert! You do not know when the time will come. It is like a man traveling abroad. He leaves home and places his servants in charge, each with his own work, and orders the gatekeeper to be on the watch. Watch, therefore; you do not know when the lord of the house is coming, whether in the evening, or at midnight, or at cockcrow, or in the morning. May he not come suddenly and find you sleeping. What I say to you, I say to all: 'Watch!'"

Understanding the Word

As always, the readings for the First Sunday of Advent draw our attention to the coming of the Lord on the Last Day rather than the birth of the Messiah in human flesh. Today's reading from Isaiah captures well the ambivalence that accompanies our expectation of that Day of Judgment. On the one hand, there is a longing, an ache of anticipation that expresses the hope of a people whose wait for deliverance has been prolonged and seems interminable. On the other hand, however, there is a sense of dread on the part of a people whose awareness also includes consciousness of their guilt.

The author of this portion of the Book of Isaiah (called Trito-Isaiah, since chapters 56–66 seem to form a third distinctive part of the overall collection) delivered this message to a disillusioned band of refugees who only a short time earlier had returned triumphantly from exile in Babylon. The reality of the ruined city of Jerusalem and the enormity of the task of rebuilding their nation had begun to sink in, and the people felt keenly the absence of God from their communal life. The prophet gives voice to the conflicting feelings of the people in this lament for their sins, coupled with an impassioned plea for divine intervention.

Scholars have noted the universal appeal of the poetic imagery that characterizes this moving passage: rend the heavens and come down ... good deeds like polluted rags ... withered like leaves ... we are the clay and you are the potter. Such language is as engaging today as it was thousands of years ago, just as the emotions of guilt and desperate hope for deliverance are as familiar in the consciousness of today's believers as they were in the refugees of post-exilic Jerusalem. Isaiah continues to call us to mindfulness, to remember our need for a Savior, One who will deliver us from our sins precisely in his act of righteous judgment. With our Jewish ancestors in faith we cry out, "Return for the sake of your servants."

Perhaps nothing strikes a deeper chord in us than the voice of an abandoned child crying, "Come back!" We now know that such a child is likely to blame herself for her parents' absence and never completely give up hope that they will return. It is a feeling we can resonate with at this time of the year when we are especially sensitive to our own human weakness and the plight of those who seem abandoned by society and by God. We wish Christ would come back and help us!

The words of Paul to the Corinthians make us mindful that we have not been abandoned at all. Christ has come and is here today to deliver the world from all evil. Through Baptism "the grace of God" was bestowed on us and through the Eucharist we "are not lacking in any spiritual gift" as we "wait for the revelation of our Lord Jesus Christ." Every Sunday we are nourished and strengthened to make Christ really present in our world.

CONSIDER/ DISCUSS:
- When have you felt that God had abandoned you?
- What spiritual gifts have you received at Mass?
- How do you feel about Christ coming back at the end of time?

Responding to the Word

In today's Gospel Jesus says that we who have received the gift of Christ's saving and intimate presence in our lives have work to do. That abandoned child, that suffering and desperate world, need us to show them that God has not abandoned them—before it is too late.

- During communion on Sunday consciously open your heart for Christ's saving love to come in.
- Find a small way to foster God's saving presence in the world this Advent.

December 8, 2002

SECOND SUNDAY OF ADVENT

Today's Focus: Hark! The Herald!

The Advent Scriptures for this week are filled with heralds of good news. Isaiah, Jerusalem, the psalmist, Peter, Mark, and John joyfully proclaim that God's promises will be fulfilled. Do we really believe what we hear? Will we have any "good news" of our own to proclaim this Christmas?

FIRST READING
Isaiah 40:1–5, 9–11

Comfort, give comfort to my people,
    says your God.
Speak tenderly to Jerusalem, and proclaim to her
    that her service is at an end,
    her guilt is expiated;
indeed, she has received from the hand of the LORD
    double for all her sins.

A voice cries out:
In the desert prepare the way of the LORD!
    Make straight in the wasteland a highway for our God!
Every valley shall be filled in,
    every mountain and hill shall be made low;
the rugged land shall be made a plain,
    the rough country, a broad valley.
Then the glory of the LORD shall be revealed,
    and all people shall see it together;
    for the mouth of the LORD has spoken.

Go up onto a high mountain,
    Zion, herald of glad tidings;
cry out at the top of your voice,
    Jerusalem, herald of good news!
Fear not to cry out
    and say to the cities of Judah:
    Here is your God!
Here comes with power
    the LORD God,
    who rules by his strong arm;
here is his reward with him,
    his recompense before him.
Like a shepherd he feeds his flock;
    in his arms he gathers the lambs,
carrying them in his bosom,
    and leading the ewes with care.

PSALM RESPONSE
Psalm 85:8
Lord, let us see your kindness, and grant us your salvation.

SECOND READING
2 Peter 3:8–14
Do not ignore this one fact, beloved, that with the Lord one day is like a thousand years and a thousand years like one day. The Lord does not delay his promise, as some regard "delay," but he is patient with you, not wishing that any should perish but that all should come to repentance. But the day of the Lord will come like a thief, and then the heavens will pass away with a mighty roar and the elements will be dissolved by fire, and the earth and everything done on it will be found out.

Since everything is to be dissolved in this way, what sort of persons ought you to be, conducting yourselves in holiness and devotion, waiting for and hastening the coming of the day of God, because of which the heavens will be dissolved in flames and the elements melted by fire. But according to his promise we await new heavens and a new earth in which righteousness dwells. Therefore, beloved, since you await these things, be eager to be found without spot or blemish before him, at peace.

GOSPEL
Mark 1:1–8
The beginning of the gospel of Jesus Christ the Son of God.

As it is written in Isaiah the prophet:
> Behold, I am sending my messenger ahead of you;
> he will prepare your way.
> A voice of one crying out in the desert:
> "Prepare the way of the Lord,
> make straight his paths."

John the Baptist appeared in the desert proclaiming a baptism of repentance for the forgiveness of sins. People of the whole Judean countryside and all the inhabitants of Jerusalem were going out to him and were being baptized by him in the Jordan River as they acknowledged their sins. John was clothed in camel's hair, with a leather belt around his waist. He fed on locusts and wild honey. And this is what he proclaimed: "One mightier than I is coming after me. I am not worthy to stoop and loosen the thongs of his sandals. I have baptized you with water; he will baptize you with the Holy Spirit."

Understanding the Word

Only with difficulty can we appreciate how completely demoralized and discouraged the Jewish people must have been during the period of exile in Babylon. From the perspective of history, we can look upon that time now as a relatively brief interlude in which the fortunes of the Jews reached a low point. But in the midst of that calamitous experience, it must have seemed as if a final blow had been dealt to their hopes of a land of their own. Their evil ways and their infidelity to the covenant with the Lord God had brought them a deserved punishment. There was no reason, humanly speaking, for them to expect that their situation would ever be reversed. The awesome might of Babylon, their captor, seemed impossible to break.

In the midst of this pervasive spirit of hopelessness, the author of the second section of the Book of Isaiah (chapters 40–55, known as Deutero-Isaiah) began to speak words of consolation and promise. Using imagery associated with the Exodus from Egypt centuries earlier, the author reminds the Jewish people that the power of the Lord God is absolute. Unlike the desert wanderings of forty years' duration in the first exodus, their return home this time will be on a superhighway, a straight road through the wilderness, a level roadway made smooth by mountains being cut down and valleys filled in. The prophet's words in this passage rise in a crescendo of encouragement, calling the people out of their despair, reminding them of the tender mercies of their God, and promising deliverance and full restoration of their fortunes.

The final image combines the reassurance that the Lord God's might is supreme ("rules by his strong arm") with the tenderness of a shepherd who cares gently for his scattered sheep ("in his arms he gathers the lambs, carrying them in his bosom"). One can only imagine how these words of the prophet, authenticated with a claim of divine origin, must have brought incredible joy and immense hope to the desperate exiles in Babylon. In the same way, they are meant today to raise the spirits of all who are dispirited by the immediacy of fortunes that seem bleak and hopeless.

Reflecting on the Word

How many towns do you suppose have a newspaper called *The Herald*? It's a good name for a newspaper because it refers to one who proclaims significant news. It also can refer to a person who comes before to announce what will follow, a forerunner like John. The angels who heralded the good news of Jesus' birth fit into a long line of heralds who proclaimed that God's promises would at last be fulfilled.

This week everyone seems to be announcing good news. Isaiah and the psalmist herald and describe others heralding glad tidings. Mark proclaims "the gospel (or 'good news') of Jesus Christ." He also depicts John as a herald in the tradition of Isaiah. And Peter speaks eloquently of God's promise and patience. Can we bring ourselves to hearken to their words and believe them? Do we have any good news of our own to proclaim?

CONSIDER/ DISCUSS:
- Which message of good news in today's Scriptures do you relish most? Which is most difficult to believe?
- From your own experience, what good news can you proclaim about God?
- How can your faith community better proclaim the good news?

Unlike those who were baptized by John, we were baptized "with the Holy Spirit." If that is so, then "what sort of persons ought" we to be? Like Isaiah, John, and Peter, we ought to be both heralding and "hastening the coming of the day of God."

- In prayer recognize the Spirit of holiness dwelling in you.
- Forgive and ask for forgiveness from someone this week.
- Encourage or comfort others by listening or speaking, by your touch or your smile.

December 9, 2002

THE IMMACULATE CONCEPTION OF
THE BLESSED VIRGIN MARY

Today's Focus: The Perfect Choice

As Christmas nears many of us are trying to choose the perfect gift for each person on our Christmas lists. Some of us know one special person for whom we particularly hope to make the perfect choice. The feast of the Immaculate Conception celebrates two perfect choices: God's perfect choice of Mary and Mary's lifetime of perfect choices.

FIRST READING
Genesis 3: 9–15, 20

After the man, Adam, had eaten of the tree, the LORD God called to the man and asked him, "Where are you?" He answered, "I heard you in the garden; but I was afraid, because I was naked, so I hid myself." Then he asked, "Who told you that you were naked? You have eaten, then, from the tree of which I had forbidden you to eat!" The man replied, "The woman whom you put here with me — she gave me fruit from the tree, and so I ate it." The LORD God then asked the woman, "Why did you do such a thing?" The woman answered, "The serpent tricked me into it, so I ate it."

Then the LORD God said to the serpent:
  "Because you have done this, you shall be banned
    from all the animals
    and from all the wild creatures;
  on your belly shall you crawl,
    and dirt shall you eat
    all the days of your life.
  I will put enmity between you and the woman,
    and between your offspring and hers;
  he will strike at your head,
    while you strike at his heel."

The man called his wife Eve, because she became the mother of all the living.

PSALM RESPONSE
Psalm 98:1a

Sing to the Lord a new song, for he has done marvelous deeds.

SECOND READING
Ephesians 1: 3–6, 11–12

Brothers and sisters: Blessed be the God and Father of our Lord Jesus Christ, who has blessed us in Christ with every spiritual blessing in the heavens, as he chose us in him, before the foundation of the world, to be holy and without blemish before him. In love he destined us for adoption to himself through Jesus Christ, in accord with the favor of his will, for the praise of the glory of his grace that he granted us in the beloved.

In him we were also chosen, destined in accord with the purpose of the One who accomplishes all things according to the intention of his will, so that we might exist for the praise of his glory, we who first hoped in Christ.

GOSPEL
Luke 1:26–38

The angel Gabriel was sent from God to a town of Galilee called Nazareth, to a virgin betrothed to a man named Joseph, of the house of David, and the virgin's name was Mary. And coming to her, he said, "Hail, full of grace! The Lord is with you." But she was greatly troubled at what was said and pondered what sort of greeting this might be. Then the angel said to her, "Do not be afraid, Mary, for you have found favor with God. Behold, you will conceive in your womb and bear a son, and you shall name him Jesus. He will be great and will be called Son of the Most High, and the Lord God will give him the throne of David his father, and he will rule over the house of Jacob forever, and of his kingdom there will be no end." But Mary said to the angel, "How can this be, since I have no relations with a man?" And the angel said to her in reply, "The Holy Spirit will come upon you, and the power of the Most High will overshadow you. Therefore the child to be born will be called holy, the Son of God. And behold, Elizabeth, your relative, has also conceived a son in her old age, and this is the sixth month for her who was called barren; for nothing will be impossible for God." Mary said, "Behold, I am the handmaid of the Lord. May it be done to me according to your word." Then the angel departed from her.

Understanding the Word

Some Catholics, when asked what Mary's Immaculate Conception is about, answer that it refers to the scene in today's Gospel where she conceives Jesus in her womb. The error is understandable, perhaps, given the choice of Gospel passages on this feast day. However, it is important to understand both the reference of today's feast (i.e., Mary's conception without sin) and how it is that the story of the Annunciation might fittingly be chosen as today's Gospel reading.

Today's example of how a liturgical feast and the Lectionary readings are related offers us the opportunity to reflect on the nature of the Bible as well as how it is used in the liturgy. The Scripture passage chosen for a particular feast day is not always intended to be a mere historical record of the event commemorated on that day. More often than not, it is the meaning of the event, not just its historical anniversary, that is the reason for the scriptural selections that are made for the day's liturgy. Our liturgical celebrations are much, much more interested in meanings than in historical records or even precise historical accuracy.

In the same way, the authors of sacred Scripture are much more interested in the meanings of the events they narrate than in historical details. Today's Gospel, for example, is part of a larger unit of material classified by Scripture scholars as an "infancy narrative." A common literary device in the secular writings of the ancient world, the infancy narratives we are most familiar with are those found in the Gospels of Matthew and Luke. The intent of the author of an infancy narrative is not to record with scientific accuracy the historical details surrounding the birth of a special person. Rather, it is to create an engaging story that reveals just how special that person was! By describing the extraordinary events surrounding a birth, an infancy narrative evokes the deeper meaning of the individual's life and person. Mary's Immaculate Conception was a unique privilege that was totally dependent on the identity of the child she was to bear. Hence, today's Gospel focuses our attention on the special nature of Jesus and his birth in order to help us understand the privilege that was Mary's. For more background on this Gospel text, look at the comments made on the Fourth Sunday of Advent (December 22).

 ## Reflecting on the Word

So many choices, so little time! As we rush to choose the perfect gift for each person on our Christmas list it is good to recall that the perfect gift has already been given—Jesus Christ. Mary's perfect choice to say "Yes" to God made possible this whole season of gift giving.

We believe that Mary is the one person who always chose perfectly to be the person God wanted her to be—from her conception to her passing into eternal life. She did what Adam and Eve and you and I could not. We look to Mary for inspiration when we have difficulty choosing the perfect gift that God wants from us. We also look at Mary in hope, rejoicing that God has chosen us to share perfection with her in eternal life.

CONSIDER/ DISCUSS:
- How do you imagine or relate to Mary?
- To whom would you most like to give the perfect Christmas gift? Why?
- What perfect gift does God want from you today?

"Before the foundation of the world," God chose Eve to be "the mother of all the living"—even Jesus. God chose Mary to nurture her perfect ovum in her perfect womb. God chose Jesus to "strike at" Satan's head, and God "chose us ... to be holy" and to "praise the glory of his grace." How will we respond to God's perfect choices?

- Ask God what each person on your list wants most from you this Christmas.

- Choose to give God the gift of praise every chance you get this week.

December 15, 2002

THIRD SUNDAY OF ADVENT

Today's Focus: High Expectations

'Tis the season to have high expectations! Children expect to receive that one special gift. Adults expect too much of themselves and one another. Everyone looks forward to the coming of Christmas. Today's Scriptures encourage us to have high expectations for what is to come because the Messiah is in our midst.

FIRST READING
Isaiah 61:1–2a, 10–11

The spirit of the Lord GOD is upon me,
    because the LORD has anointed me;
he has sent me to bring glad tidings to the poor,
    to heal the brokenhearted,
to proclaim liberty to the captives
    and release to the prisoners,
to announce a year of favor from the LORD
    and a day of vindication by our God.

I rejoice heartily in the LORD,
    in my God is the joy of my soul;
for he has clothed me with a robe of salvation
    and wrapped me in a mantle of justice,
like a bridegroom adorned with a diadem,
    like a bride bedecked with her jewels.
As the earth brings forth its plants,
    and a garden makes its growth spring up,
so will the Lord GOD make justice and praise
    spring up before all the nations.

PSALM RESPONSE
Isaiah 61:10b

My soul rejoices in my God.

SECOND READING
1 Thessalonians 5: 16–24

Brothers and sisters: Rejoice always. Pray without ceasing. In all circumstances give thanks, for this is the will of God for you in Christ Jesus. Do not quench the Spirit. Do not despise prophetic utterances. Test everything; retain what is good. Refrain from every kind of evil.

May the God of peace make you perfectly holy and may you entirely, spirit, soul, and body, be preserved blameless for the coming of our Lord Jesus Christ. The one who calls you is faithful, and he will also accomplish it.

GOSPEL
John 1:6–8,
19–28
A man named John was sent from God. He came for testimony, to testify to the light, so that all might believe through him. He was not the light, but came to testify to the light.

And this is the testimony of John. When the Jews from Jerusalem sent priests and Levites to him to ask him, "Who are you?" he admitted and did not deny it, but admitted, "I am not the Christ."

So they asked him, "What are you then? Are you Elijah?" And he said, "I am not." "Are you the Prophet?" He answered, "No." So they said to him, "Who are you, so we can give an answer to those who sent us? What do you have to say for yourself?" He said:

"I am *the voice of one crying out in the desert,*
make straight the way of the Lord,
as Isaiah the prophet said."

Some Pharisees were also sent. They asked him, "Why then do you baptize if you are not the Christ or Elijah or the Prophet?" John answered them, "I baptize with water; but there is one among you whom you do not recognize, the one who is coming after me, whose sandal strap I am not worthy to untie." This happened in Bethany across the Jordan, where John was baptizing.

Understanding the Word

The readings of the Third Sunday of Advent mark a shift of focus from the final coming of the Lord on the Last Day to the first coming of the Messiah in human flesh. The figure and preaching of John the Baptist bridge the two comings and personify this shift. John's message is an eschatological one, an announcement that the days of fulfillment are at hand; but that proclamation takes the form of a very specific announcement about "the one who comes after."

The messianic focus of the day's texts is even more obvious in the passage from the Book of Isaiah that is proclaimed as today's first reading. Our familiarity with this text stems from its use by Jesus himself in his inaugural address at the synagogue in Nazareth (see Luke 4:16–21). By the time of Jesus, the text was regarded as a messianic prophecy, and his assertion that it was fulfilled in his person is effectively a claim to messianic status. Originally, however, this passage from the third section of the Book of Isaiah (chapters 56–66—called Trito-Isaiah by Scripture scholars) referred to a very different context.

The prophetic author of these words preached during the period after the return from exile in Babylon. His hearers were discouraged at the enormity of the task that faced them in the rebuilding of the Temple and the Holy City Jerusalem. The prophet offers words of reassurance by asserting that he has been commissioned by God ("the Lord has anointed me") to rally the people and accomplish the work of restoration. Using familiar words from the Jewish tradition, the prophet points to the custom of a Jubilee Year, in which all lies fallow for a time as a prelude to the rebirth and renewal of a "new creation" at

God's hand. The exuberant imagery would have stood in stark contrast to the gloom that had settled over Jerusalem and its inhabitants, and the prophet deliberately calls the people to trust that in his mission they would see the promises of the Lord fulfilled.

Reflecting on the Word

Robert's heart ached for what he couldn't give his son this Christmas. "Don't get your hopes up, Charlie." "Why, Daddy?" "I'm just not sure Santa's going to make it to our house this year, Sweetie, and I don't want you to be disappointed." Across town, alone in his luxury apartment, Greg thought of his ex-wife and children with whom he would never share Christmas again. He poured himself another drink to quench the violent images he had just seen on the evening news. "To peace on earth," he toasted to no one.

For many of us Christmas means just one more disappointment, one more shattered dream, the gloomy realization that the world is no better place to live than it was last year. But today's Scriptures proclaim that the Messiah has already come into the world to bring healing, liberty, justice, and peace. They encourage us to raise our expectations for God to act here and now, and to raise our voices in rejoicing.

CONSIDER/ DISCUSS:
- Is it better to have high or low expectations? Explain.
- What can discourage you at this time of the year?
- What is "the Spirit of the Lord" anointing you to do about it?

Responding to the Word

There is a challenge for everyone in today's Scriptures. Isaiah calls those who are happy and comfortable this Christmas to participate in shaping the "new creation" he describes. Paul calls those who are troubled to rejoice, to pray and give thanks. And John encourages all of us to have high expectations that the Messiah is indeed among us.

- Expect good things to happen in your life this week.
- Help your faith community in its efforts to serve those in need.

December 22, 2002

FOURTH SUNDAY OF ADVENT

Today's Focus: People, Look East

Are you adding final touches to your Christmas decorations? With today's Scriptures, the Advent carol "People, Look East" invites us to get our houses ready for the dawning of divine Love and to sing of the faithfulness of our God. "People, look east, and sing today: Love the Guest is on the way."

FIRST READING
2 Samuel 7: 1–5, 8b–12, 14a, 16

When King David was settled in his palace, and the LORD had given him rest from his enemies on every side, he said to Nathan the prophet, "Here I am living in a house of cedar, while the ark of God dwells in a tent!" Nathan answered the king, "Go, do whatever you have in mind, for the LORD is with you." But that night the LORD spoke to Nathan and said: "Go, tell my servant David, 'Thus says the LORD: Should you build me a house to dwell in?

"'It was I who took you from the pasture and from the care of the flock to be commander of my people Israel. I have been with you wherever you went, and I have destroyed all your enemies before you. And I will make you famous like the great ones of the earth. I will fix a place for my people Israel; I will plant them so that they may dwell in their place without further disturbance. Neither shall the wicked continue to afflict them as they did of old, since the time I first appointed judges over my people Israel. I will give you rest from all your enemies. The LORD also reveals to you that he will establish a house for you. And when your time comes and you rest with your ancestors, I will raise up your heir after you, sprung from your loins, and I will make his kingdom firm. I will be a father to him, and he shall be a son to me. Your house and your kingdom shall endure forever before me; your throne shall stand firm forever.'"

PSALM RESPONSE
Psalm 89:2a

For ever I will sing the goodness of the Lord.

SECOND READING
Romans 16: 25–27

Brothers and sisters: To him who can strengthen you, according to my gospel and the proclamation of Jesus Christ, according to the revelation of the mystery kept secret for long ages but now manifested through the prophetic writings and, according to the command of the eternal God, made known to all nations to bring about the obedience of faith, to the only wise God, through Jesus Christ be glory forever and ever. Amen.

The angel Gabriel was sent from God to a town of Galilee called Nazareth, to a virgin betrothed to a man named Joseph, of the house of David, and the virgin's name was Mary. And coming to her, he said, "Hail, full of grace! The Lord is with you." But she was greatly troubled at what was said and pondered what sort of greeting this might be. Then the angel said to her, "Do not be afraid, Mary, for you have found favor with God.

"Behold, you will conceive in your womb and bear a son, and you shall name him Jesus. He will be great and will be called Son of the Most High, and the Lord God will give him the throne of David his father, and he will rule over the house of Jacob forever, and of his kingdom there will be no end." But Mary said to the angel, "How can this be, since I have no relations with a man?" And the angel said to her in reply, "The Holy Spirit will come upon you, and the power of the Most High will overshadow you. Therefore the child to be born will be called holy, the Son of God. And behold, Elizabeth, your relative, has also conceived a son in her old age, and this is the sixth month for her who was called barren; for nothing will be impossible for God." Mary said, "Behold, I am the handmaid of the Lord. May it be done to me according to your word." Then the angel departed from her.

Understanding the Word

On the last Sunday of Advent, the focus of the readings is squarely on the impending messianic birth. In the first reading and the Gospel we have a wonderful match of two prophecies: one from Nathan that foretells the glories of the Davidic dynasty, and the other from the angel Gabriel, who in foretelling the birth of the Messiah also announces the ultimate fulfillment of the ancient proclamation of Nathan.

Scripture scholars have helped us to understand how, in his description of the scene at the Annunciation, Luke is doing much more than providing a factual historical record of events. Rather, he has taken a familiar rhetorical device from the ancient world (i.e., a birth announcement) and raised it to its highest expression, both in terms of creative literary style and in terms of its actual content. By skillfully weaving into the narrative references to Jewish messianic hopes, Luke points to Jesus as the long-awaited Messiah. Even more striking, however, are the subtle clues that Luke gives that attribute to this child-Messiah about to be born a divine birth, not an ordinary human conception.

The angel's greeting to Mary is a proclamation that the long-awaited messianic era has finally dawned. His invocation of the Davidic titles is a reference to ancient prophecies that God would act in the midst of the people through the line of David's descendants. But Luke's emphasis on the work of the Holy Spirit is the real key here, signaling to the reader the depth of God's action in this miraculous birth. Echoes of Genesis, in which the divine breath/spirit hovers over the waters of creation, suggest that the child's conception marks a new creation wrought at God's hands. Similarly, the Jewish tradition of the Lord's glory filling the tabernacle is evoked in the angel's promise that the Holy Spirit will "overshadow" Mary, resulting in the child being called "holy, the Son of God."

Reflecting on the Word

In these last few days before Christmas most of us will "make our house fair as we are able, trim the hearth and set the table," making sure everything is ready for Christmas. We even trim the outside of our homes. On the evening news we see houses and yards covered with Christmas lights. And then there are the houses simply lit with a single white candle in every window.

What is all this decorating about? Today's Scriptures remind us that we truly have something to celebrate and some One to welcome. God faithfully fulfilled the promises made long ago in Jesus' conception and birth. In Jesus the Spirit of God took up residence not just once in a young girl's womb, but in human history for all time. Divine Love dawned for all humanity, never to set again.

CONSIDER/ DISCUSS:
- What do Christmas decorations mean to you?
- How do you experience God's faithful love?
- How might you make your "house" ready for "Love the Guest?"

Responding to the Word

"People, look east and sing today!" sings the Advent carol. We are to welcome the dawning of the Messiah's reign by giving God "glory forever and ever." It is not enough to make ready our houses, or even our hearts. We must make our world "fair as we are able," a place that reveals the mystery of God's faithful love for all humanity.

- Welcome a guest into your home this week.
- Sing with real gratitude and joy at Mass or with friends.
- Give joyfully to a charity of your choice.

People Look East, text by Eleanor Farjeon.
Excerpt used by permission of Harold Ober Associates.

December 25, 2002

THE NATIVITY OF THE LORD
CHRISTMAS MASS DURING THE DAY

Today's Focus: Gift Wrap

"Open it! What is it?" "See what I got?" Around the world today children's eyes glow with wonder as they unwrap gifts and reach deep into stockings to find what is hidden within. Our Scriptures, too, unwrap the hidden mystery of God's Word now revealed in Jesus for all to see.

FIRST READING
Isaiah 52:7–10

How beautiful upon the mountains
    are the feet of him who brings glad tidings,
announcing peace, bearing good news,
    announcing salvation, and saying to Zion,
    "Your God is King!"

Hark! Your sentinels raise a cry,
    together they shout for joy,
for they see directly, before their eyes,
    the LORD restoring Zion.
Break out together in song,
    O ruins of Jerusalem!
For the LORD comforts his people,
    he redeems Jerusalem.
The LORD has bared his holy arm
    in the sight of all the nations;
all the ends of the earth will behold
    the salvation of our God.

PSALM RESPONSE
Psalm 98:3c

All the ends of the earth have seen the saving power of God.

SECOND READING
Hebrews 1:1–6

Brothers and sisters: In times past, God spoke in partial and various ways to our ancestors through the prophets; in these last days, he has spoken to us through the Son, whom he made heir of all things and through whom he created the universe,
    who is the refulgence of his glory,
        the very imprint of his being,
    and who sustains all things by his mighty word.
    When he had accomplished purification from sins,
    he took his seat at the right hand of the Majesty on high,
    as far superior to the angels
    as the name he has inherited is more excellent than theirs.

For to which of the angels did God ever say:
You are my son; this day I have begotten you?

25

Or again:
I will be a father to him, and he shall be a son to me?
And again, when he leads the firstborn into the world, he says:
Let all the angels of God worship him.

GOSPEL
*John 1:1–18
or 1–5, 9–14*

In the shorter form of the reading, the passages in brackets are omitted.

In the beginning was the Word,
   and the Word was with God,
   and the Word was God.
He was in the beginning with God.
All things came to be through him,
   and without him nothing came to be.
What came to be through him was life,
   and this life was the light of the human race;
the light shines in the darkness,
   and the darkness has not overcome it.

[A man named John was sent from God. He came for testimony, to testify to the light, so that all might believe through him. He was not the light, but came to testify to the light.] The true light, which enlightens everyone, was coming into the world.

He was in the world,
   and the world came to be through him,
   but the world did not know him.
He came to what was his own,
   but his own people did not accept him.

But to those who did accept him he gave power to become children of God, to those who believe in his name, who were born not by natural generation nor by human choice nor by a man's decision but of God.

And the Word became flesh
   and made his dwelling among us,
   and we saw his glory,
   the glory as of the Father's only Son,
   full of grace and truth.

[John testified to him and cried out, saying, "This was he of whom I said, 'The one who is coming after me ranks ahead of me because he existed before me.'" From his fullness we have all received, grace in place of grace, because while the law was given through Moses, grace and truth came through Jesus Christ. No one has ever seen God. The only Son, God, who is at the Father's side, has revealed him.]

The Gospel selection today is taken from what is called the "Prologue" of John's Gospel. Scripture scholars have pointed out that most likely this section of John's Gospel was borrowed from another source and inserted here as a kind of overall introduction to the rest of the Gospel. The Lectionary offers the option of reading a shorter or longer version of this text. The shorter version, verses 1–5 and 9–14, corresponds to what scholars believe was originally a poetic hymn that existed independently of the Gospel and has been incorporated here as the introductory Prologue. Verses 6–9 and 15–18, which complete today's longer form of the reading, are a prose commentary that the Evangelist has written and woven into the original hymn for the purposes of his Gospel narrative.

The origins of that ancient hymn are mysterious. As a result, scholars have disagreed as to whether it is a Greek composition reflecting the mindset of Hellenistic philosophy or a Semitic creation whose understandings are more rich with biblical overtones. The key expression that scholars focus upon is the term we translate in English as "Word." The Greek original, *logos*, was used in philosophical reflection to describe an intermediary between God and the created world. The *logos* was a principle of order and intelligibility, a way for the human mind to access the divine being. A more Semitic background would refer to the term *dabar*, a notion rich with a sense of God's very presence in the spoken utterance itself. One thinks, for example, of the opening of the Book of Genesis (clearly referred to in the first lines of John's Prologue), in which it is God's creative word that brings about the whole of creation.

Of course, one need not choose one side or the other in this scholarly debate in order to be moved by today's Gospel reading. Most likely, the author of the Gospel was familiar with both Hellenistic and Jewish thought, and his creative genius lay precisely in his ability to blend subtle overtures of both traditions into this text. Little wonder, then, that for us English speakers, the Prologue's description of the "Word" is layered with many levels of meaning and is a fittingly rich commentary on the mystery of the Incarnation that we celebrate today.

Reflecting on the Word

The meticulously wrapped gift labeled "To Claire with Love from Grandmother" had been under the tree for days and days. Little Claire had gazed at the golden paper and stroked the velvet ribbon. She had shaken it, listened to it, smelled it, and even tried to lift a corner of the wrapping to discover what it was. Since she believed that her grandmother loved her very much she really expected to find something wonderful inside. Now it was Christmas Day and Grandmother herself was here. Claire opened the gift with abandon and found costumes—a ballerina, a leopard, a cowgirl. She ran into her grandmother's arms. "Oh Grandmother, now I see how much you love me!"

Today "the Word became flesh and made his dwelling among us, and we saw his glory." Like Claire, we may search nature, our lives, human history, and wise writings for evidence of what we believe—that God loves us. We need search no more. In the human body and blood of Jesus of Nazareth we see clearly just how deeply God has loved humanity from the moment creation began.

**CONSIDER/
DISCUSS:**
- Do you unwrap gifts slowly or quickly? Why?
- What do you see in Jesus?
- How is God's love revealed to you here and now?

Responding to the Word

Little did Claire know that when she used her costumes throughout the coming years she herself would create wonderful stories and friendships and memories. As we unwrap and use the gift of Jesus throughout the year and throughout our lives, what will the Word Made Flesh create in and through us?

- After communion let your imagination see the face of Jesus.
- Create something wonderful out of the love God has given you.

December 29, 2002

THE HOLY FAMILY OF JESUS, MARY, AND JOSEPH

Today's Focus: Family Traditions

"We've always done it this way." From generation to generation family traditions are handed on. Especially at Christmas time, we relish the traditional customs that our grandparents passed on to us. In this feast we see the Holy Family continuing a long and holy "family" tradition.

FIRST READING
Genesis 15:1–6; 21:1–3

The word of the LORD came to Abram in a vision, saying:

"Fear not, Abram!
    I am your shield;
    I will make your reward very great."

But Abram said, "O Lord GOD, what good will your gifts be, if I keep on being childless and have as my heir the steward of my house, Eliezer?" Abram continued, "See, you have given me no offspring, and so one of my servants will be my heir." Then the word of the LORD came to him: "No, that one shall not be your heir; your own issue shall be your heir." The Lord took Abram outside and said, "Look up at the sky and count the stars, if you can. Just so," he added, "shall your descendants be." Abram put his faith in the LORD, who credited it to him as an act of righteousness.

The LORD took note of Sarah as he had said he would; he did for her as he had promised. Sarah became pregnant and bore Abraham a son in his old age, at the set time that God had stated. Abraham gave the name Isaac to this son of his whom Sarah bore him.

PSALM RESPONSE
Psalm 105: 7a, 8a

The Lord remembers his covenant forever.

SECOND READING
Hebrews 11:8, 11–12, 17–19

Brothers and sisters: By faith Abraham obeyed when he was called to go out to a place that he was to receive as an inheritance; he went out, not knowing where he was to go. By faith he received power to generate, even though he was past the normal age — and Sarah herself was sterile — for he thought that the one who had made the promise was trustworthy. So it was that there came forth from one man, himself as good as dead, descendants as numerous as the stars in the sky and as countless as the sands on the seashore.

By faith Abraham, when put to the test, offered up Isaac, and he who had received the promises was ready to offer his only son, of whom it was said, "Through Isaac descendants shall bear your name." He reasoned that God was able to raise even from the dead, and he received Isaac back as a symbol.

GOSPEL
Luke 2:22–40
or 22, 39–40

In the shorter form of the reading, the passage in brackets is omitted.

When the days were completed for their purification according to the law of Moses, they took him up to Jerusalem to present him to the Lord, [just as it is written in the law of the Lord,

Every male that opens the womb shall be consecrated to the Lord,
and to offer the sacrifice of
a pair of turtledoves or two young pigeons,
in accordance with the dictate in the law of the Lord.

Now there was a man in Jerusalem whose name was Simeon. This man was righteous and devout, awaiting the consolation of Israel, and the Holy Spirit was upon him. It had been revealed to him by the Holy Spirit that he should not see death before he had seen the Christ of the Lord. He came in the Spirit into the temple; and when the parents brought in the child Jesus to perform the custom of the law in regard to him, he took him into his arms and blessed God, saying:

"Now, Master, you may let your servant go
    in peace, according to your word,
for my eyes have seen your salvation,
    which you prepared in sight of all the peoples,
a light for revelation to the Gentiles,
    and glory for your people Israel."

The child's father and mother were amazed at what was said about him; and Simeon blessed them and said to Mary his mother, "Behold, this child is destined for the fall and rise of many in Israel, and to be a sign that will be contradicted — and you yourself a sword will pierce — so that the thoughts of many hearts may be revealed." There was also a prophetess, Anna, the daughter of Phanuel, of the tribe of Asher. She was advanced in years, having lived seven years with her husband after her marriage, and then as a widow until she was eighty-four. She never left the temple, but worshiped night and day with fasting and prayer. And coming forward at that very time, she gave thanks to God and spoke about the child to all who were awaiting the redemption of Jerusalem.]

When they had fulfilled all the prescriptions of the law of the Lord, they returned to Galilee, to their own town of Nazareth. The child grew and became strong, filled with wisdom; and the favor of God was upon him.

Scripture scholars have helped us to understand how the infancy narratives fit into the overall plan of the Gospels. Unlike the materials that describe the words and deeds of Jesus during the period of his public ministry, the infancy narratives are more original compositions that support the Christian claim about Jesus' identity by means of scenes and dialogues largely constructed by the Evangelist himself. In today's reading we have an excellent example of how St. Luke has combed the Jewish Scriptures for messianic references, and then woven a narrative that skillfully alludes to precisely those passages of the Jewish Scriptures in which the coming of the Messiah is foretold.

Luke's mention of Gabriel in the annunciation scene (1:26) in the previous chapter hearkens back to a messianic text in the Book of Daniel (9:21–24), in which Gabriel prophesies about a period of seventy weeks of years after which the guilt of the holy city is finally expiated and "a most holy one will be anointed." The opening words of Luke's presentation scene ("When the days were completed ...") are a special expression in the vocabulary of the Jewish Scriptures associated with the arrival of the messianic age. He uses this term several times in the infancy narrative (2:22, 57; 2:6, 21), and here it is clear that he has in mind in particular the messianic prophecy of Malachi 3:1, "... and the Lord whom you seek will suddenly come to his temple." In the way he describes the presentation of Jesus in the Temple, Luke reminds his readers of another messianic figure, Samuel, who was also presented and consecrated to the Lord as a child (1 Samuel 1:11, 22–28), and who remained in the Lord's service throughout his life. Luke uses the figures of Simeon and Anna to allude to material from the Book of Isaiah (Isaiah 40:1; 49:13; 51:12; 61:2) concerning the messianic hope of those who awaited Israel's consolation. In their canticles each proclaims, in effect, the fulfillment of that hope in Jesus.

Reflecting on the Word

What are your dearest family Christmas traditions? For one family it is decorating the tree with the ornaments that each child has received from St. Nicholas, year after year. For another it is the Christmas crèche that came over with their ancestors from Bulgaria. For another it is the aunts and uncles and cousins who gather to celebrate. For all of us there are the cherished stories, rituals, and family values that let us know once again who we are.

In today's feast we see Joseph, Mary, and their child walking in the tradition and in the company of an old and extended holy family. The first reading and the psalm express the core values that were handed on to them from generations of faithful Jews. In the Gospel we see them performing the age-old ritual of presenting their firstborn to the Lord. There the holy elders, Simeon and Anna, encourage them, saying that the promises handed on from generation to generation will be fulfilled in Jesus.

• What story, ritual, or value does your family hold dear?

• How might Joseph and Mary have felt in this Gospel story?

• How do your family traditions or extended family support you?

 Responding to the Word

How are we to become holy? The responsibility for our holiness doesn't rest entirely on each of us, or on our nuclear families. Holiness is a family tradition that is fostered in us the more we connect with our Christian family stories, rituals, and "brothers and sisters" in faith. By doing so we pass on the family tradition of holiness to our children, as Joseph and Mary did.

• Connect with people in your parish "family" after church this week.

• Pass on to someone of the next generation a tradition that has helped you become more holy.

January 1, 2003

THE BLESSED VIRGIN MARY, THE MOTHER OF GOD

Today's Focus: Three Wishes

If you could have three wishes for this year, what would they be? Today's Scriptures present us with three wishes, the last of which is a wish for peace, or "shalom." As we begin our year we pray with Mary, the Mother of God, that the Lord will bless all the earth with "shalom."

FIRST READING
Numbers 6: 22–27

The LORD said to Moses: "Speak to Aaron and his sons and tell them: This is how you shall bless the Israelites. Say to them:

The LORD bless you and keep you!
The LORD let his face shine upon you, and be gracious to you!
The LORD look upon you kindly and give you peace!

So shall they invoke my name upon the Israelites, and I will bless them."

PSALM RESPONSE
Psalm 67:2a

May God bless us in his mercy.

SECOND READING
Galatians 4:4–7

Brothers and sisters: When the fullness of time had come, God sent his Son, born of a woman, born under the law, to ransom those under the law, so that we might receive adoption as sons. As proof that you are sons, God sent the Spirit of his Son into our hearts, crying out, "Abba, Father!" So you are no longer a slave but a son, and if a son then also an heir, through God.

GOSPEL
Luke 2:16–21

The shepherds went in haste to Bethlehem and found Mary and Joseph, and the infant lying in the manger. When they saw this, they made known the message that had been told them about this child. All who heard it were amazed by what had been told them by the shepherds. And Mary kept all these things, reflecting on them in her heart. Then the shepherds returned, glorifying and praising God for all they had heard and seen, just as it had been told to them. When eight days were completed for his circumcision, he was named Jesus, the name given him by the angel before he was conceived in the womb.

The Book of Numbers is not read very often—only here, on the Twenty-sixth Sunday in Year B, and in six passages found in the weekday Lectionary. Since it is one of the first five books of the Bible—called the Torah by our Jewish sisters and brothers—it commands special respect and attention. Jewish tradition ascribed authorship of the entire Torah to Moses, but modern scriptural scholarship has helped us to understand the much more complex origins of the book. Numbers is a loosely edited collection of diverse materials—legal codes, liturgical prescriptions, local religious history, etc.—that developed over many centuries and was eventually put together under the "authorship" of Moses.

The ancient practice of ascribing authorship to a revered figure was understood to reflect the stature of that figure and his influence on all subsequent writing, as well as to claim that a subsequent text was faithful to the vision of the one under whose name it was published. Lacking our contemporary concerns about copyrighted material, the people of Israel were very comfortable with this looser definition of authorship.

Scholars believe that the blessing prayer read today could well be among the oldest material in the Book of Numbers. The three-fold form of the blessing prayer reflects the Hebrew love of parallelism as a way to achieve emphasis. The absence in biblical Hebrew of a superlative resulted in such repetition being used as a way of making a point more emphatically. The three-fold form is basically a repetition of a single idea, but there is a sense of building importance as well. Hence, the final invocation today that prays for peace (*shalom*) captures the sum of all good things that might be wished for the people. The notion of *shalom* in the Bible is far richer and more expansive than our contemporary understanding of peace as an absence of conflict. Rather, it is a word that captures all of the blessings of prosperity and harmony that one might imagine possible as a result of a world at peace.

Reflecting on the Word

If you could have three wishes this year for the people you love, what would they be? Chances are your wishes would include health, wealth, and happiness. We want our loved ones to enjoy the blessings of God here on earth. It is good to remember that there are some people who would answer that question very differently. They might wish that their loved ones might enjoy a place to sleep out of the rain, a meal every day, or freedom from the fear of being beaten.

Today's first reading raises another wish—the wish for peace. All of us want peace on earth; but how will it ever come about? Pope Paul VI said, "If you want peace, work for justice." As we begin the new year we pray that we might extend material blessing and economic justice to all people. Then, and only then, will God bless all the earth with *shalom*.

• What do you most want this year for those you love? What might Mary have wanted for her son?

• What world injustice weighs most heavily on your heart today?

• How does, or might, your faith community "work for justice?"

Responding to the Word

When we ask Mary, the Mother of God, to "pray for us sinners," it must be a prayer for all humanity. We pray for security and happiness for those we love. We pray for an end to hunger and violence against human beings everywhere. And we pray for an end to our own sinful ways that ignore or oppress the poor of our community and around the world.

• Pray at least one decade of the rosary for peace on earth.

• Learn about or work with the poor in your local area.

January 5, 2003

THE EPIPHANY OF THE LORD

Today's Focus: Major Attraction

Many areas have major attractions that bring tourists from far and wide. On the Feast of the Epiphany we recall that Jesus was a major attraction even as a poor and powerless infant. He attracted people to God and we, the Church of Jesus Christ, are called to do the same.

FIRST READING
Isaiah 60:1–6

Rise up in splendor, Jerusalem! Your light has come,
    the glory of the Lord shines upon you.
See, darkness covers the earth,
    and thick clouds cover the peoples;
but upon you the Lord shines,
    and over you appears his glory.
Nations shall walk by your light,
    and kings by your shining radiance.
Raise your eyes and look about;
    they all gather and come to you:
your sons come from afar,
    and your daughters in the arms of their nurses.

Then you shall be radiant at what you see,
    your heart shall throb and overflow,
for the riches of the sea shall be emptied out before you,
    the wealth of nations shall be brought to you.
Caravans of camels shall fill you,
    dromedaries from Midian and Ephah;
all from Sheba shall come
    bearing gold and frankincense,
    and proclaiming the praises of the Lord.

PSALM RESPONSE
Psalm 72:11

Lord, every nation on earth will adore you.

SECOND READING
Ephesians 3: 2–3a, 5–6

Brothers and sisters: You have heard of the stewardship of God's grace that was given to me for your benefit, namely, that the mystery was made known to me by revelation. It was not made known to people in other generations as it has now been revealed to his holy apostles and prophets by the Spirit: that the Gentiles are coheirs, members of the same body, and copartners in the promise in Christ Jesus through the gospel.

GOSPEL
Mathew 2:1–12

When Jesus was born in Bethlehem of Judea, in the days of King Herod, behold, magi from the east arrived in Jerusalem, saying, "Where is the newborn king of the Jews? We saw his star at its rising and have come to do him homage." When King Herod heard this, he was greatly troubled, and all Jerusalem with him. Assembling all the chief priests and the scribes of the people, he inquired of them where the Christ was to be born. They said to him, "In Bethlehem of Judea, for thus it has been written through the prophet:

And you, Bethlehem, land of Judah,
are by no means least among the rulers of Judah;
since from you shall come a ruler,
who is to shepherd my people Israel."

Then Herod called the magi secretly and ascertained from them the time of the star's appearance. He sent them to Bethlehem and said, "Go and search diligently for the child. When you have found him, bring me word, that I too may go and do him homage." After their audience with the king they set out. And behold, the star that they had seen at its rising preceded them, until it came and stopped over the place where the child was. They were overjoyed at seeing the star, and on entering the house they saw the child with Mary his mother. They prostrated themselves and did him homage. Then they opened their treasures and offered him gifts of gold, frankincense, and myrrh. And having been warned in a dream not to return to Herod, they departed for their country by another way.

Understanding the Word

The section of the Book of Isaiah that is read today comes from the third part of the collection, sometimes referred to as Trito-Isaiah. The unknown author of this section lived at the time of the Jewish people's return from exile in Babylon. The major challenge facing them was the reconstruction of Jerusalem—its Temple, buildings, and the social/religious fabric of the people of the Covenant who lived there.

The overwhelming nature of the task led many to the brink of despair. Thus, the prophet's special concern was to lift the hope of the people, to encourage them to continue the work of rebuilding, and to trust that God would help them in their task. We see in today's reading how the prophet uses his poetic gifts to evoke a hope-filled vision for the people. Perhaps inspired by something as simple as a sunrise and the awakening city with its traders arriving, the prophet eloquently foresees a day when the renewed city of Jerusalem will be a hub of commerce and trade, and when prosperity will make Jerusalem the envy of all.

Scripture scholars point out that one of the distinctive features of the theology of Trito-Isaiah is his universalist perspective. By this they mean his conviction that all people, not just the dispersed tribes of Israel, will find in Jerusalem the glory and splendor of the messianic era. The notion that even pagans would someday bask in the glory of the Lord would have been anathema to a previous generation. But perhaps the role played by Cyrus, the pagan king responsible for Israel's return from exile, had begun to change the people's perception of how God's love and mercy might reach out to all people. For the refugees recently returned to the ruined city, such words of hope must have buoyed their spirits in a wonderful way.

Reflecting on the Word

What are the major attractions in your area? Are they natural wonders, spectacular buildings, engaging activities, powerful people, works of art? We expect people to stream to see rock stars and queens, the Eiffel Tower and the Grand Canyon. In today's Scriptures, however, we see "tourists" attracted to two very lowly and humble "sights."

Jerusalem was a sorry sight when the Scripture from Isaiah was written. The prophet's vision must have seemed impossible to those who heard this message. And yet, today Jerusalem is a major tourist attraction. We also know that through the Jews many other people—Christians and Muslims—have been attracted to the one Lord.

Jesus himself must have seemed very weak and insignificant in comparison to the rich and powerful King Herod, and later on compared to the priests and Pharisees. Yet, even from his birth, people streamed to him. Like the "tourists" in today's Gospel, people saw something in him that led them to worship and serve the Lord. And through him they came to understand what God intended for their life journeys.

CONSIDER/
DISCUSS:
- What attracts you to Jesus?
- What or who attracts you to God? Explain.
- What do you think attracts people to (or repels them from) the Church?

We understand the Church to be the new Israel, called to "rise up in splendor" and attract all people to the Lord. We might sometimes experience our Church as a dilapidated stable; yet we must be "the place where the child" is found today. God's glory can certainly shine through the Church and, despite our many flaws, we are called to become the "place" where everyone can find the Lord and "do him homage."

- Ask people how your faith community can better attract people to Christ.
- Be conscious of attracting people to God this week.

January 12, 2003

THE BAPTISM OF THE LORD

Today's Focus: Third Time's a Charm

Three seems to be an almost magical number. How many times have you found success on the third try after telling yourself, "The third time's a charm"? Today's Scriptures are full of triplets that tell of Jesus—the life-giving Word, the Messiah, the Son of God.

FIRST READING
Isaiah 55:1–11

Thus says the LORD:
All you who are thirsty,
    come to the water!
You who have no money,
    come, receive grain and eat;
come, without paying and without cost,
    drink wine and milk!
Why spend your money for what is not bread,
    your wages for what fails to satisfy?
Heed me, and you shall eat well,
    you shall delight in rich fare.
Come to me heedfully,
    listen, that you may have life.
I will renew with you the everlasting covenant,
    the benefits assured to David.
As I made him a witness to the peoples,
    a leader and commander of nations,
so shall you summon a nation you knew not,
    and nations that knew you not shall run to you,
because of the LORD, your God,
    the Holy One of Israel, who has glorified you.
Seek the LORD while he may be found,
    call him while he is near.
Let the scoundrel forsake his way,
    and the wicked man his thoughts;
let him turn to the LORD for mercy;
    to our God, who is generous in forgiving.
For my thoughts are not your thoughts,
    nor are your ways my ways, says the LORD.
As high as the heavens are above the earth
    so high are my ways above your ways
    and my thoughts above your thoughts.
For just as from the heavens
    the rain and snow come down
and do not return there
    till they have watered the earth,
    making it fertile and fruitful,

giving seed to the one who sows
  and bread to the one who eats,
so shall my word be
  that goes forth from my mouth;
my word shall not return to me void,
  but shall do my will,
    achieving the end for which I sent it.

PSALM
RESPONSE
Isaiah 12:3
You will draw water joyfully from the springs of salvation.

SECOND
READING
1 John 5:1–9
Beloved: Everyone who believes that Jesus is the Christ is begotten by God, and everyone who loves the Father loves also the one begotten by him. In this way we know that we love the children of God when we love God and obey his commandments. For the love of God is this, that we keep his commandments. And his commandments are not burdensome, for whoever is begotten by God conquers the world. And the victory that conquers the world is our faith. Who indeed is the victor over the world but the one who believes that Jesus is the Son of God? This is the one who came through water and blood, Jesus Christ, not by water alone, but by water and blood. The Spirit is the one who testifies, and the Spirit is truth. So there are three that testify, the Spirit, the water, and the blood, and the three are of one accord. If we accept human testimony, the testimony of God is surely greater. Now the testimony of God is this, that he has testified on behalf of his Son.

GOSPEL
Mark 1:7–11
This is what John the Baptist proclaimed: "One mightier than I is coming after me. I am not worthy to stoop and loosen the thongs of his sandals. I have baptized you with water; he will baptize you with the Holy Spirit."

It happened in those days that Jesus came from Nazareth of Galilee and was baptized in the Jordan by John. On coming up out of the water he saw the heavens being torn open and the Spirit, like a dove, descending upon him. And a voice came from the heavens, "You are my beloved Son; with you I am well pleased."

 ## Understanding the Word

Today's Gospel narrative describes the preaching of John the Baptist and then John's baptism of Jesus in the Jordan River. These five verses of Mark's text that are read today seem straightforward, and one could easily take them as a simple reporting of factual, historical material. Thanks to the insights of Scripture scholars, however, a more careful reading of the text reveals the complexity and the sophistication of the narrative that Mark has woven.

As if to give the perceptive reader of his Gospel a preview of what is to come, Mark puts forth several clues that reveal the true identity of Jesus as the Messiah and Son of God. Mark provides three "witnesses" who offer testimony regarding Jesus: the Baptist, the dove, and the voice from heaven. The Baptist's testimony was important because in Mark's day there were apparently followers of the Baptist who still asserted his superiority over Jesus, some even suggesting that it was John, not Jesus, who was the long-awaited Messiah. Thus, John's explicit acknowledgment that Jesus was "mightier" is placed right at the beginning of Mark's narrative.

The "heavens being torn open" is a phrase Mark borrows from Isaiah 64:1, a prayer for God's intervention in the last days when all would be set aright for the Chosen People. The suggestion, of course, is that in the person and ministry of Jesus that ancient prayer of Isaiah is finally being answered. Mark reinforces the messianic overtones in the scene by his reference to the descent of the Spirit, a phenomenon clearly associated in the Jewish mind with an eschatological context (see Joel 3:1 and Isaiah 44:3). Mark's choice of the image of a dove to suggest the Spirit's descent appears to be connected with certain biblical traditions in which Israel was symbolized by a dove (Hosea 11:11, Psalms 68:13, 74:19, 56:1). Mark is here implying that Jesus is the new Israel, that is, in him is summed up the entire destiny of the Jewish people. The final testimony, that Jesus is Son of God, is offered by the (divine) voice from heaven, who echoes Isaiah's Servant Songs, and who reveals that God's "beloved," the chosen Servant, is God's very own Son.

Reflecting on the Word

If the third time's a charm, then today's feast ought to succeed in convincing us to "believe that Jesus is the Christ … the Son of God." For the third time in six Sundays we hear John the Baptist say he is "not worthy" even to untie Jesus' sandals. Three witnesses in Mark's Gospel attest to Jesus' identity. The first letter of John also cites "three that testify" that Jesus is the Son of God—"the Spirit, the water, and the blood." And Isaiah describes the life-giving word of God as "water," "rain," and "snow."

The feast of the Baptism of the Lord also joins three baptisms. Jesus' baptism by John in water looks back on Jesus' "baptism" in the water and blood of human birth and looks forward to his "baptism" in the water and blood of human death. Through his incarnation, baptism, and resurrection we recognize that Jesus is the Son of God, the life-giving Word that came down from heaven and returned, having achieved the end for which he was sent.

- Which of Jesus' three "baptisms" most helps you to believe in him? Explain.

- What do you remember about your own or someone else's baptism?

- When have you felt yourself to be "begotten by God" or "victor over the world?"

Responding to the Word

Every Christian is baptized not just with water, but with the Spirit of God that filled Jesus—thus making us children of God. That Spirit immerses us in the family of believers who, week by week, drink in the life-giving word and "eat well" the "rich fare" of the Eucharist. How might that life-giving word be "fruitful" in you?

- Read the Isaiah Scripture aloud three times this week, letting the words water the dry, thirsty places in you.

- Sow the word of God's generous mercy in a thirsty heart this week.

Notes

In the liturgical cycle each year there is a period of weeks between the end of the Christmas season and the beginning of Lent that is called "Ordinary Time." The length of this period varies depending on the date of Easter, and then following Pentecost Ordinary Time once again resumes until the end of the cycle. This year's first segment of Ordinary Time starts this week and continues until March 3; the second segment resumes in June and continues through November.

Normally a particular Gospel is read on a semi-continuous basis during the Sundays of Ordinary Time unless a particular feast day with its own special readings is celebrated. Since we are currently in Year B of the three-year cycle, the Gospel of Mark will be read this year. However, the shorter length of Mark's Gospel allows for a five-week interlude in late summer when the Gospel reading is taken from chapter six of John's Gospel.

The principle of selection for the other readings is a bit different. Generally the first reading is chosen because it contains thematic material that matches a major emphasis of the day's Gospel text. The Psalm that follows in some way usually relates either to the first reading, the Gospel, or both, but that connection is often quite vague and difficult to discern with precision. The reading from the New Testament operates on an independent cycle and offers continuous readings from a number of books of the Christian Scriptures. In Year B we begin with Pauline readings from First and Second Corinthians, followed by Ephesians, the Letter of James, and finally Hebrews. This arrangement reflects decisions taken after the Second Vatican Council's *Constitution on the Sacred Liturgy* mandated (numbers 24, 25, 35, 51) that the Lectionary should be revised to offer the faithful a richer scriptural fare during the Sunday Eucharist's Liturgy of the Word.

Each week the scriptural commentaries and pastoral reflections that follow in this book must choose from among an "embarrassment of riches" and focus on only a small portion of the many themes available. The particular choices that are made do not mean to imply that one theme is more important than another on any given week. Most often we choose a theme common to the first reading and Gospel, but occasionally those texts are ignored in favor of a theme in one of the other readings. Our more limited focus is simply a practical matter dictated by limitations of space. But readers are encouraged in their prayers and meditations to follow other themes as the Spirit dictates.

In this first segment of Ordinary Time, the readings every year begin with an emphasis on call narratives and other themes associated with beginnings. Then, after several weeks, the ministry of Jesus unfolds as the stories of his preaching, his miracles, and his conflicts with demons and other adversaries begin to reveal his identity and his ultimate destiny.

January 19, 2003

SECOND SUNDAY IN ORDINARY TIME

Today's Focus: Call Waiting

Many telephone lines now let you know when you have a call waiting. When you're on the phone and another call comes through, how do you decide which call to answer and which to keep waiting? In today's Scriptures Samuel, Andrew, and Simon Peter decide to answer the call of the Lord.

FIRST READING
1 Samuel 3: 3b–10, 19

Samuel was sleeping in the temple of the Lord where the ark of God was. The Lord called to Samuel, who answered, "Here I am." Samuel ran to Eli and said, "Here I am. You called me." "I did not call you," Eli said. "Go back to sleep." So he went back to sleep. Again the Lord called Samuel, who rose and went to Eli. "Here I am," he said. "You called me." But Eli answered, "I did not call you, my son. Go back to sleep."

At that time Samuel was not familiar with the Lord, because the Lord had not revealed anything to him as yet. The Lord called Samuel again, for the third time. Getting up and going to Eli, he said, "Here I am. You called me." Then Eli understood that the Lord was calling the youth. So he said to Samuel, "Go to sleep, and if you are called, reply, Speak, Lord, for your servant is listening." When Samuel went to sleep in his place, the Lord came and revealed his presence, calling out as before, "Samuel, Samuel!" Samuel answered, "Speak, for your servant is listening."

Samuel grew up, and the Lord was with him, not permitting any word of his to be without effect.

PSALM RESPONSE
Psalm 40:8a, 9a

Here am I, Lord; I come to do your will.

SECOND READING
1 Corinthians 6: 13c–15a, 17–20

Brothers and sisters: The body is not for immorality, but for the Lord, and the Lord is for the body; God raised the Lord and will also raise us by his power.

Do you not know that your bodies are members of Christ? But whoever is joined to the Lord becomes one Spirit with him. Avoid immorality. Every other sin a person commits is outside the body, but the immoral person sins against his own body. Do you not know that your body is a temple of the Holy Spirit within you, whom you have from God, and that you are not your own? For you have been purchased at a price. Therefore glorify God in your body.

GOSPEL

John 1:35–42

John was standing with two of his disciples, and as he watched Jesus walk by, he said, "Behold, the Lamb of God." The two disciples heard what he said and followed Jesus. Jesus turned and saw them following him and said to them, "What are you looking for?" They said to him, "Rabbi" — which translated means Teacher —, "where are you staying?" He said to them, "Come, and you will see." So they went and saw where Jesus was staying, and they stayed with him that day. It was about four in the afternoon. Andrew, the brother of Simon Peter, was one of the two who heard John and followed Jesus. He first found his own brother Simon and told him, "We have found the Messiah" — which is translated Christ. Then he brought him to Jesus. Jesus looked at him and said, "You are Simon the son of John; you will be called Cephas" — which is translated Peter.

Understanding the Word

On the Sunday immediately following the Baptism of the Lord, we are presented in the first reading and the Gospel with narratives that relate how those whose service God desires are called by the Lord. The Gospel story describes a rather straightforward scene in which Jesus encounters several of his (future) disciples. The narrative is tantalizingly sparse, and we yearn for more details of the human interaction that surely must have accompanied this encounter. But the lapidary style of the Johannine description is perhaps deliberate, serving to highlight the essential elements of the call.

The first reading from the First Book of Samuel provides us with a story that is rich in detail, and it contains what were to become classic features of Old Testament prophetic call narratives. There is an element of dramatic tension introduced by the description of Samuel's initial failure to recognize the source of the voice that was summoning him. Since such stories were deliberately symbolic in nature, it is not too much of a stretch to imagine that this initial confusion is included in the story as a way of reminding us of our own, often confused, struggle to discern God's call from the many voices that appeal to us. In the story Samuel is helped by Eli the priest to recognize the divine origin of the call, again providing a detail that may be meant to remind us of the role of the community in our own recognition of God's call.

Samuel's ready response to the Lord ("Speak, for your servant is listening") is really no surprise, given the fact that he has prepared and disposed himself to hear what God might ask of him. He is, after all, already sleeping in the Temple (assigned to guard the sacred flame, or to protect the ark?) when God calls. Some Scripture scholars even suggest that his sleep may have been a trance-like state deliberately induced in the belief that any resulting dreams would contain divine visions and communications.

"Hello." "Hello, Michael?" "Mom! Hold on for a minute while I get rid of this other call." As she waits for her son to return to the line Sara smiles to herself, happy to think that she still gets top priority in Michael's life. "Hi, Mom. I'm back. What can I do for you?" Call waiting can be tricky. When your mother is on the line it may be a simple choice, but it's not always that easy to know which caller to respond to right away, which to put on hold, and which to ignore.

The various people, interests, and responsibilities that "call" to us in our lives can present the same dilemma. How do we decide which to answer? How do we know when the Lord is calling us? Today's readings give us a hint. Samuel and Andrew were deliberately seeking to hear and follow God's call, but Peter was not. All three discerned the Lord's call by responding to the voice of people they knew and trusted.

CONSIDER/ DISCUSS:
- Is there someone whom you never keep waiting "on hold?"
- What helps you discern what God is calling you to do?
- When have you had the sense that the Lord was calling you? What did you do?

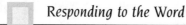

Responding to the Word

CONSIDER/ DISCUSS: Those who have heard the call of the Lord respond in words and in deeds. Both Samuel and Andrew, after hearing and answering the Lord's call, went out and told others about the Lord. Paul's letter to the Corinthians invites us to "glorify God" in our bodies. How are you being called to respond to the Lord this week?

- Go to God or a trusted friend for advice about a decision.
- Offer someone words of wisdom that you have been reluctant to share.

January 26, 2003

THIRD SUNDAY IN ORDINARY TIME

Today's Focus: Journeyman

The next step after apprenticeship is to become a journeyman. It means that one has learned the skills basic to one's trade at the side of a master and is now on the way to becoming a master oneself. Today's Scriptures present several "journeymen" who are on their way with the Lord.

FIRST READING
Jonah 3:1–5, 10

The word of the LORD came to Jonah, saying: "Set out for the great city of Nineveh, and announce to it the message that I will tell you." So Jonah made ready and went to Nineveh, according to the LORD's bidding. Now Nineveh was an enormously large city; it took three days to go through it. Jonah began his journey through the city, and had gone but a single day's walk announcing, "Forty days more and Nineveh shall be destroyed," when the people of Nineveh believed God; they proclaimed a fast and all of them, great and small, put on sackcloth.

When God saw by their actions how they turned from their evil way, he repented of the evil that he had threatened to do to them; he did not carry it out.

PSALM RESPONSE
Psalm 25:4a

Teach me your ways, O Lord.

SECOND READING
1 Corinthians 7: 29–31

I tell you, brothers and sisters, the time is running out. From now on, let those having wives act as not having them, those weeping as not weeping, those rejoicing as not rejoicing, those buying as not owning, those using the world as not using it fully. For the world in its present form is passing away.

GOSPEL
Mark 1:14–20

After John had been arrested, Jesus came to Galilee proclaiming the gospel of God: "This is the time of fulfillment. The kingdom of God is at hand. Repent, and believe in the gospel."

As he passed by the Sea of Galilee, he saw Simon and his brother Andrew casting their nets into the sea; they were fishermen. Jesus said to them, "Come after me, and I will make you fishers of men." Then they abandoned their nets and followed him. He walked along a little farther and saw James, the son of Zebedee, and his brother John. They too were in a boat mending their nets. Then he called them. So they left their father Zebedee in the boat along with the hired men and followed him.

Last Sunday's readings contained two stories of divine calls: the boy Samuel in the Temple, and Andrew and Peter. Today the Gospel narrates another version of the call of the two brothers Andrew and Peter, as well as James and John, also brothers. Each of these narratives displays the familiar elements of call, recognition, and response.

In all three years of its three-year cycle, the Lectionary places at the start of the season of Ordinary Time stories of beginnings. Prominently featured today are the early preaching of Jesus and his gathering of disciples. In the reading from Mark, both of these themes are included, but the focus today seems to be more on Jesus' preaching than on his call of the disciples. This emphasis is achieved by the choice of a first reading that also focuses on the preaching of repentance. The Book of Jonah describes the preaching of repentance by Jonah to the Ninevites and their immediate response to his call. Like Jonah (and, in fact, virtually all of the prophets before him), Jesus' message is also one of repentance. However, unlike his prophetic predecessors who warned of a future day of judgment, Jesus announces that the Reign of God is now at hand. "This is the time of fulfillment," he proclaims, no longer warning of an impending event, but pointing to his own proclamation of the Good News as the evidence that God's Reign has already arrived in their midst.

Scripture scholars point out that here, early on in his Gospel, Mark summarizes the entire ministry of Jesus. The Lord demands not only repentance, but belief as well. And the juxtaposition of the call of the disciples, which follows immediately, serves to underline the consequences of repentance and belief: discipleship. Thus, Mark merges several themes into a single vision—one that includes preaching repentance, belief in the Good News, the call to abandon everything and follow Jesus, and an immediate response to that call—as the ideal image of discipleship.

Reflecting on the Word

First apprentice, then journeyman, and finally master. That's the way someone "travels" when learning a trade. But before "setting out" one must find a trustworthy master who will accept him to study with her. Then he must commit himself to the "journey" of learning the trade. By watching and listening to the master, by imitating her example and following her advice, the disciple gradually learns her "ways."

The Scriptures this week present a journeyman, Jonah, and a master, Jesus. Why did people trust and follow them? People responded to Jonah because he was traveling the way of the Lord himself; he had repented and set out on the journey of discipleship. They responded to Jesus because he was a master worthy of their trust and because he invited them to be his disciples, to walk at his side and to study his ways. People followed them not because of their words, but because they knew the way.

- What have you learned by watching, practicing, doing?
- Whom do you trust even when they tell you to change what you are doing? Why?
- What about Jesus makes you want to be his disciple? What holds you back?

 Responding to the Word

There is one problem with Christian discipleship. No one will ever become a master. The most we can strive for is to be journeymen, like Jonah and Jesus' disciples. We can only show others the way if we commit ourselves to the journey and walk at the Master's side, trusting and listening and following the ways of the Lord.

- Name five skills you are learning as a disciple of Jesus.
- Give up something that is keeping you from following the Lord.

February 2, 2003

THE PRESENTATION OF THE LORD

Today's Focus: Candlemas

This Sunday has sometimes been called "Candlemas" because in many churches candles are lit, blessed, and carried in procession. Forty days after Christmas we recognize that the Light of the World was to be consumed, like the wax of the candles we bless, to produce such radiant brightness.

FIRST
READING
Malachi 3:1–4

Thus says the Lord God:
Lo, I am sending my messenger
    to prepare the way before me;
and suddenly there will come to the temple
    the LORD whom you seek,
and the messenger of the covenant whom you desire.
    Yes, he is coming, says the LORD of hosts.
But who will endure the day of his coming?
    And who can stand when he appears?
For he is like the refiner's fire,
    or like the fuller's lye.
He will sit refining and purifying silver,
    and he will purify the sons of Levi,
refining them like gold or like silver
    that they may offer due sacrifice to the LORD.
Then the sacrifice of Judah and Jerusalem
    will please the LORD,
        as in the days of old, as in years gone by.

PSALM
RESPONSE
Psalm 24:8

Who is this king of glory? It is the Lord!

SECOND
READING
Hebrews 2:
14–18

Since the children share in blood and flesh, Jesus likewise shared in them, that through death he might destroy the one who has the power of death, that is, the devil, and free those who through fear of death had been subject to slavery all their life. Surely he did not help angels but rather the descendants of Abraham; therefore, he had to become like his brothers and sisters in every way, that he might be a merciful and faithful high priest before God to expiate the sins of the people. Because he himself was tested through what he suffered, he is able to help those who are being tested.

GOSPEL
Luke 2:22–40
or 22–32

In the shorter version of the reading, the passage in brackets is omitted.

When the days were completed for their purification according to the law of Moses, Mary and Joseph took Jesus up to Jerusalem to present him to the Lord, just as it is written in the law of the Lord,

Every male that opens the womb shall be consecrated to the Lord,
and to offer the sacrifice of
a pair of turtledoves or two young pigeons,
in accordance with the dictate in the law of the Lord.

Now there was a man in Jerusalem whose name was Simeon. This man was righteous and devout, awaiting the consolation of Israel, and the Holy Spirit was upon him. It had been revealed to him by the Holy Spirit that he should not see death before he had seen the Christ of the Lord. He came in the Spirit into the temple; and when the parents brought in the child Jesus to perform the custom of the law in regard to him, he took him into his arms and blessed God, saying:

"Now, Master, you may let your servant go
in peace, according to your word,
for my eyes have seen your salvation,
which you prepared in sight of all the peoples,
a light for revelation to the Gentiles,
and glory for your people Israel."

[The child's father and mother were amazed at what was said about him; and Simeon blessed them and said to Mary his mother, "Behold, this child is destined to be the fall and rise of many in Israel, and to be a sign that will be contradicted — and you yourself a sword will pierce — so that the thoughts of many hearts may be revealed." There was also a prophetess, Anna, the daughter of Phanuel, of the tribe of Asher. She was advanced in years, having lived seven years with her husband after her marriage, and then as a widow until she was eighty-four. She never left the temple, but worshiped night and day with fasting and prayer. And coming forward at that very time, she gave thanks to God and spoke about the child to all who were awaiting the redemption of Jerusalem.

When they had fulfilled all the prescriptions of the law of the Lord, they returned to Galilee, to their own town of Nazareth. The child grew and became strong, filled with wisdom; and the favor of God was upon him.]

53

It is helpful to understand something of the Jewish background to the scene described in today's Gospel. In the time of Jesus, Jewish women were required by the Torah to undergo a ritual purification following the birth of a child. Forty days after the birth of a son (and eighty after the birth of a daughter), the woman was to make a sacrificial offering in the form of a holocaust (burnt offering) of a lamb and a pigeon (or dove). For those unable to afford a lamb (as, evidently, was the case with Mary), a second dove could be substituted. Luke is describing the fulfillment of this ritual obligation in today's Gospel.

However, Luke uses this familiar scene as a literary device to show his Christian readers how Jesus fulfilled the messianic hopes of ancient Israel. The eschatological prophecy of Malachi, proclaimed as today's first reading, was certainly in the background of Luke's narrative. Malachi's vision of the Lord coming to the Temple in the final age is suggested by Luke's description of the presentation of the infant Jesus by Mary and Joseph. The figures of Simeon and Anna also serve as symbols of how Israel's longing for the Messiah was finally to be fulfilled in the person of Jesus. Simeon's pronouncement, in particular, evokes the many prophecies of Isaiah in which the Messiah is described as a light to the Gentiles (Isaiah 52:9–10, 49:6, 46:13, 42:6, 40:5). The prophetess Anna and her prayer of thanksgiving further underline the fact that the time of fulfillment was at hand.

Although Scripture scholars love to speculate about such things, the specific reference of Simeon's words to Mary is more difficult to ascertain. His prophecy about the "rise and fall of many," the "sign that will be contradicted," and the "sword" all point to the ominous destiny of the child who will bring redemption through his death. But it is not possible to be more specific as to what Luke/Simeon had in mind in this utterance.

Reflecting on the Word

Have you ever noticed how church candles burn? Unlike your candles at home, they leave no wax behind. They slowly get shorter and shorter until they have been completely consumed by the flame. That is because they are made of pure beeswax, which burns hot and bright with all of the wax becoming fuel for the fire.

Today's candle ritual, like the Service of Light at the Easter Vigil, reminds us of the Light of the World that dawned at Christmas. Simeon rightly recognized that Jesus himself would have to become like pure wax. His sacrificial death would fuel the flame that burns brightly as a light of revelation to the Gentiles and glory for Israel.

CONSIDER/ DISCUSS:
- Which is more beautiful to you: a candle that has been partially burned or one that has never been lit? Why?

- How does it feel to watch a favorite candle burn?

- When have you felt that you were being used up, like the wax of a candle, to "give light" to others?

The pure, hot light that emanates from Christ both reveals and purifies. Like the flames that refine ore into pure gold, Christ's light burns away all that is impure or worthless in those who come close to the flame. The process may be painful and frightening. It may require sacrifice, but we are not alone. Jesus "is able to help those who are being tested" because he has walked through fire before us, and lived.

- Identify a part of you that is being burned away by the Light of Christ.
- Make a sacrifice for someone you love this week.

February 9, 2003

FIFTH SUNDAY IN ORDINARY TIME

Today's Focus: Sick at Heart

As St. Valentine's Day approaches you may be writing valentines and remembering someone over whom you suffered a broken heart. Perhaps you look back and wonder what you did wrong to deserve such suffering. Today's Scriptures invite us to look forward and believe in the Lord, who heals the brokenhearted.

FIRST READING
Job 7:1–4, 6–7

Job spoke, saying:
Is not man's life on earth a drudgery?
    Are not his days those of hirelings?
He is a slave who longs for the shade,
    a hireling who waits for his wages.
So I have been assigned months of misery,
    and troubled nights have been allotted to me.
If in bed I say, "When shall I arise?"
    then the night drags on;
    I am filled with restlessness until the dawn.
My days are swifter than a weaver's shuttle;
    they come to an end without hope.
Remember that my life is like the wind;
    I shall not see happiness again.

PSALM RESPONSE
Psalm 147:3a

Praise the Lord, who heals the brokenhearted.

SECOND READING
1 Corinthians 9: 16–19, 22–23

Brothers and sisters: If I preach the gospel, this is no reason for me to boast, for an obligation has been imposed on me, and woe to me if I do not preach it! If I do so willingly, I have a recompense, but if unwillingly, then I have been entrusted with a stewardship. What then is my recompense? That, when I preach, I offer the gospel free of charge so as not to make full use of my right in the gospel.

Although I am free in regard to all, I have made myself a slave to all so as to win over as many as possible. To the weak I became weak, to win over the weak. I have become all things to all, to save at least some. All this I do for the sake of the gospel, so that I too may have a share in it.

GOSPEL
Mark 1:29–39

On leaving the synagogue Jesus entered the house of Simon and Andrew with James and John. Simon's mother-in-law lay sick with a fever. They immediately told him about her. He approached, grasped her hand, and helped her up. Then the fever left her and she waited on them.

When it was evening, after sunset, they brought to him all who were ill or possessed by demons. The whole town was gathered at the door. He cured many who were sick with various diseases, and he drove out many demons, not permitting them to speak because they knew him.

Rising very early before dawn, he left and went off to a deserted place, where he prayed. Simon and those who were with him pursued him and on finding him said, "Everyone is looking for you." He told them, "Let us go on to the nearby villages that I may preach there also. For this purpose have I come." So he went into their synagogues, preaching and driving out demons throughout the whole of Galilee.

Understanding the Word

The Book of Job contains one of the most searing examinations of innocent suffering found anywhere in recorded literature. Scholars have identified similar stories about the suffering of an innocent man—and attempts to grapple with meaningless suffering—in several other ancient cultures. The Book of Job, however, remains a far superior examination of the "problem of evil" in every respect.

Job is a larger-than-life literary creation, a man in whom every conceivable human misery is played out. The dramatic premise of the story is provided by a scene hidden from Job but known to the reader: a heavenly council in which Satan taunts God and wins permission to torment Job and test his faith, despite the fact of his innocence. Such a literary convention was an essential part of the author's attempt to show how shallow was the viewpoint of his contemporaries that suffering is inevitably the result of sin (one's own or that of one's ancestors).

The author introduces "friends" of Job who try to comfort him, and in the process express all of the traditional explanations for the suffering of the innocent man. The section we read today is part of Job's answer to his friend Eliphaz, and in it Job describes his torment and the utter hopelessness of his situation. Eventually, the Book of Job offers only a partial and rather unsatisfactory resolution to the problem of evil: that God's ways are too mysterious for the human mind to fathom (Job 42:2 ff).

It is only in the notion of innocent suffering as redemptive that the Christian perspective offers a more satisfying answer to this classic human dilemma. In addition, our Christian belief in an existence beyond earthly life (a belief not part of Job's vision) allows for a resolution that includes ultimate vindication and a justice that finally triumphs beyond the suffering of the present. Today's Gospel story of Jesus confronting—and triumphing over—various forms of human suffering points to the answer that we Christians would offer to Job in his misery.

Reflecting on the Word

Valentine's Day has been hard for Joe since Camilla died. He had been convinced that their love would pull her through the cancer that robbed him of his Valentine. What had they done wrong? He blamed himself, the doctors, God; on bad days he even blamed Camilla. No one could convince him that any good would come of this. He was sick at heart and nothing would comfort him.

Whether it is a cold or a lost loved one, cancer or a broken heart, we can't seem to stop blaming ourselves for the suffering and sickness that besiege us. Like Job's friends, we keep looking back and asking, "Why?" Today's Gospel invites us to believe that Christ is at our side, ready to grasp our hands and help us up. It invites us to look for the ways in which the Lord is trying to cure us of our "various diseases."

CONSIDER/ DISCUSS:
- When have you felt like Job? How has God healed your broken heart?
- How might the Lord be trying to cure you now?
- How could you help the Lord heal the brokenhearted this week?

Responding to the Word

How can we who are not doctors help the sick and sick at heart? How did Paul reach out to those who were weak? "To the weak [he] became weak." We are not Jesus; we cannot drive out their demons or cure their illnesses. However, we can resist the impulse to run away or to diagnose the reason for their problems. We can recognize our own weakness, listen to their pain, and be with them in their suffering, confident that the Lord will do what we cannot.

- Be present to someone who is suffering this week.
- Donate an hour of your time to a local service or health care facility.

February 16, 2003

SIXTH SUNDAY IN ORDINARY TIME

Today's Focus: Dirty Laundry

Don't air your dirty laundry in public! By this is meant that anything "unclean" that might embarrass one's family is better left unmentioned and unseen. Today's Scriptures explore the unclean status of lepers in the "family" of Israel. Who are the unclean in our society today?

FIRST READING
Leviticus 13: 1–2, 44–46

The Lord said to Moses and Aaron, "If someone has on his skin a scab or pustule or blotch which appears to be the sore of leprosy, he shall be brought to Aaron, the priest, or to one of the priests among his descendants. If the man is leprous and unclean, the priest shall declare him unclean by reason of the sore on his head.

"The one who bears the sore of leprosy shall keep his garments rent and his head bare, and shall muffle his beard; he shall cry out, 'Unclean, unclean!' As long as the sore is on him he shall declare himself unclean, since he is in fact unclean. He shall dwell apart, making his abode outside the camp."

PSALM RESPONSE
Psalm 32:7

I turn to you, Lord, in time of trouble, and you fill me with the joy of salvation.

SECOND READING
1 Corinthians 10:31 — 11:1

Brothers and sisters, Whether you eat or drink, or whatever you do, do everything for the glory of God. Avoid giving offense, whether to the Jews or Greeks or the church of God, just as I try to please everyone in every way, not seeking my own benefit but that of the many, that they may be saved. Be imitators of me, as I am of Christ.

GOSPEL
Mark 1:40–45

A leper came to Jesus and kneeling down begged him and said, "If you wish, you can make me clean." Moved with pity, he stretched out his hand, touched him, and said to him, "I do will it. Be made clean." The leprosy left him immediately, and he was made clean. Then, warning him sternly, he dismissed him at once.

He said to him, "See that you tell no one anything, but go, show yourself to the priest and offer for your cleansing what Moses prescribed; that will be proof for them."

The man went away and began to publicize the whole matter. He spread the report abroad so that it was impossible for Jesus to enter a town openly. He remained outside in deserted places, and people kept coming to him from everywhere.

The notion of ritual impurity prevalent in biblical times is not something that fits easily with our modern mindset. That one might—through no deliberate fault—incur a status requiring exclusion from the community seems quite unfair. Particularly when the source of one's defilement is a biological condition over which one has no control, the exclusion seems arbitrary and unreasonable. Yet, within the logic of Israel's understanding about how one participated in the holiness of God, such purity laws seemed not only reasonable but even necessary.

Divine perfection was such that nothing blemished was considered worthy to be an offering before the all-holy One. In addition, a prevailing cultural assumption held that illness was in some real way a consequence and a sign of sin. An association between demonic control and illness further intensified a primal fear that evil manifests itself in human existence in a range of destructive ways and must be excluded absolutely from the midst of the covenant community. A highly developed corporate identity meant that all were affected by the condition of any one member. These attitudes coalesced in the figure of the leper who is cured in today's Gospel reading. He was an outcast from the community, required by the Mosaic Law to be excluded not only from the worshipping assembly, but from ordinary social contact as well. His moral condition would have been suspect, and the Gospel's description that the leprosy "left him immediately" contains a hint that his problems may indeed have been due to demonic possession.

As part of his cure, Jesus directs the man to go to the priest to be examined and then make the customary offering. This is a practical matter respecting the requirements of the Mosaic Law that charged the priest with passing judgment on whether or not a skin ailment required exclusion from the community and ritual offerings. Jesus is simply reminding the man that his cure, in order to be complete, must include restoration to the community and compliance with the Law.

Reflecting on the Word

Only recently have we discovered the difficulties that result from burying the family's "dirty laundry" in a closet. Family secrets can hide grave sins that affect the whole family and subsequently "infect" future generations, making them truly ill. We have realized, in fact, that sometimes the healthiest thing to do is to air your dirty laundry, rather than letting its increasing stench permeate the house.

So there is some logic to the ancient connection between sin and illness. The sins of the family can make one family member ill. Individuals can suffer from the sins of a whole society. Today's society has its own lepers whom we would rather not discuss, see, or touch—the crack babies, the homeless, the starving, the teen prostitutes. These are the unclean reminders of the sins of our society, outcasts whom we prefer to bury like dirty laundry. Yet the cure is not banishment, but as Jesus demonstrates, reaching out and embracing those who are cast out due to circumstances largely beyond their control.

• What examples can you name of individuals who suffer from society's sins?

• What ways do we have of separating the "sick" from ourselves?

• What makes it difficult for them to reenter society once they have been "made clean?"

 Responding to the Word

At the beginning of this Gospel story the leper is the one who "must dwell apart." Yet, after stretching out his hand and touching the leper, it is Jesus who couldn't "enter a town openly" and "remained outside in deserted places." Those who join Jesus in the effort to cleanse the unclean and conquer the evil in our society might find that they are excluded from social circles themselves.

• Learn more about the plight of the disadvantaged in your community.

• Stretch out your hand to welcome an outcast into your circle of friends.

February 23, 2003

SEVENTH SUNDAY IN ORDINARY TIME

Today's Focus: High Fidelity

Back in the days of vinyl records, some stereos were called "hi-fi's." That meant that they played music with high fidelity—the sound produced was said to be highly faithful to the sound of the musicians in the studio. Today's Scriptures speak with high fidelity of the high fidelity of our God.

FIRST READING
Isaiah 43: 18–19, 21–22, 24b–25

Thus says the LORD:
Remember not the events of the past,
   the things of long ago consider not;
see, I am doing something new!
   Now it springs forth, do you not perceive it?
In the desert I make a way,
   in the wasteland, rivers.
The people I formed for myself,
   that they might announce my praise.
Yet you did not call upon me, O Jacob,
   for you grew weary of me, O Israel.
You burdened me with your sins,
   and wearied me with your crimes.
It is I, I, who wipe out,
   for my own sake, your offenses;
   your sins I remember no more.

PSALM RESPONSE
Psalm 41:5b

Lord, heal my soul, for I have sinned against you.

SECOND READING
2 Corinthians 1: 18–22

Brothers and sisters: As God is faithful, our word to you is not "yes" and "no." For the Son of God, Jesus Christ, who was proclaimed to you by us, Silvanus and Timothy and me, was not "yes" and "no," but "yes" has been in him. For however many are the promises of God, their Yes is in him; therefore, the Amen from us also goes through him to God for glory. But the one who gives us security with you in Christ and who anointed us is God; he has also put his seal upon us and given the Spirit in our hearts as a first installment.

GOSPEL
Mark 2:1–12

When Jesus returned to Capernaum after some days, it became known that he was at home. Many gathered together so that there was no longer room for them, not even around the door, and he preached the word to them. They came bringing to him a paralytic carried by four men. Unable to get near Jesus because of the crowd, they opened up the roof above him. After they had broken through, they let down the mat on which the paralytic was lying. When Jesus saw their faith, he said to the paralytic, "Child, your sins are forgiven." Now some of the scribes were sitting there asking themselves, "Why does this man speak that way? He is blaspheming. Who but God alone can forgive sins?" Jesus immediately knew in his mind what they were thinking to themselves, so he said, "Why are you thinking such things in your hearts? Which is easier, to say to the paralytic, 'Your sins are forgiven,' or to say, 'Rise, pick up your mat and walk'? But that you may know that the Son of Man has authority to forgive sins on earth" — he said to the paralytic, "I say to you, rise, pick up your mat, and go home." He rose, picked up his mat at once, and went away in the sight of everyone. They were all astounded and glorified God, saying, "We have never seen anything like this."

Understanding the Word

It would be difficult to overstate just how cataclysmic was the exile in Babylon for the Jewish people. To all appearances, their relationship with the Lord had been severed and they had lost all of the blessings promised them in the Covenant: the Promised Land, Jerusalem, even the Temple itself. All had been lost, and many of the exiles had despaired of ever regaining a favored place in the Lord's love.

The second part of the Book of Isaiah (chapters 40–55), sometimes dubbed the "Book of Consolation," records the message of a prophet who worked among the people in exile during the late sixth century before Christ. Central to his message was the insistence that the Lord had not abandoned the people—they had abandoned God. Thus, a return to the Lord would allow them to regain once again God's protection and, eventually, the promises that had been lost. The author emphasizes the need for the people to repent of their past sins, but even more insistently he focuses on the mercy and forgiveness of God ("your sins I remember no more").

In the passage we read today, two fundamental themes of biblical revelation are combined: creation and redemption. The author harks back to two decisive events through which the people had come to know God's unfailing love for them. Genesis portrayed the act of creation as a sign of God's love, and so here the author hints at a "new creation" in love ("see, I am doing something new") that is unfolding. But the dominant image is taken from Israel's premier experience of redemption: the Lord's liberation of the Jews from bondage in Egypt. Here the author borrows familiar language associated with the Exodus, and suggests that a new exodus is about to occur, thanks to God's faithfulness to the chosen people.

Reflecting on the Word

"Hi-fi's" were purported to reproduce faithfully the sound of the musicians in the studio. Nevertheless, the actual quality of the music depended on the speakers, how one set the tone and balance, the quality of the record, and the talent of the musicians themselves. In these Scriptures Jesus can be compared to the perfect hi-fi and God to the perfect original music.

By healing the paralytic, Jesus perfectly reproduced the "sound" of God's loving fidelity to the Jewish people in spite of their sins. The healing forgiveness that God showed in returning them to their homeland from Babylon was "played" with high fidelity on the perfectly tuned "instrument"—Jesus. And those who heard what Jesus said and saw the miraculous results responded in awe, glorifying the "high fidelity" of God.

CONSIDER/ DISCUSS:
- Do you feel that God has been faithful to you? Explain.
- What part of this Gospel story do you like best? Why?
- Where are you in need of God's healing forgiveness today?

Responding to the Word

What is the faithful response to the high fidelity of a God who always says "yes" to us? It is to glorify God, proclaiming "Amen! Yes, God is great indeed!" It is also to act with "regard for the lowly and the poor" as the psalm for today proclaims. We are to go out of our way to help those who are in need, like the people in today's Gospel who broke through both the crowd and the roof to bring the man who was paralyzed to Jesus to be healed.

- Go out of your way to care for those in need.
- Glorify God for something that happens this week.

March 2, 2003

EIGHTH SUNDAY IN ORDINARY TIME

Today's Focus: Honeymoon

Today's Scriptures speak of a new covenant so intimate that it is like a marriage between God and us. Just as a newly married couple might go away by themselves on a honeymoon, we are invited to take time to savor God's love and nurture our relationship with Christ.

FIRST READING
Hosea 2: 16b, 17b, 21–22

Thus says the LORD:
I will lead her into the desert
    and speak to her heart.
She shall respond there as in the days of her youth,
    when she came up from the land of Egypt.
I will espouse you to me forever:
    I will espouse you in right and in justice,
    in love and in mercy;
I will espouse you in fidelity,
    and you shall know the Lord.

PSALM RESPONSE
Psalm 103:8a

The Lord is kind and merciful.

SECOND READING
2 Corinthians 3: 1b–6

Brothers and sisters: Do we need, as some do, letters of recommendation to you or from you? You are our letter, written on our hearts, known and read by all, shown to be a letter of Christ ministered by us, written not in ink but by the Spirit of the living God, not on tablets of stone but on tablets that are hearts of flesh.

Such confidence we have through Christ toward God. Not that of ourselves we are qualified to take credit for anything as coming from us; rather, our qualification comes from God, who has indeed qualified us as ministers of a new covenant, not of letter but of spirit; for the letter brings death, but the Spirit gives life.

GOSPEL
Mark 2:18–22

The disciples of John and of the Pharisees were accustomed to fast. People came to him and objected, "Why do the disciples of John and the disciples of the Pharisees fast, but your disciples do not fast?" Jesus answered them, "Can the wedding guests fast while the bridegroom is with them? As long as they have the bridegroom with them they cannot fast. But the days will come when the bridegroom is taken away from them, and then they will fast on that day. No one sews a piece of unshrunken cloth on an old cloak. If he does, its fullness pulls away, the new from the old, and the tear gets worse. Likewise, no one pours new wine into old wineskins. Otherwise, the wine will burst the skins, and both the wine and the skins are ruined. Rather, new wine is poured into fresh wineskins."

Understanding the Word

Understanding the true meaning of our words is not simply a matter of examining their content. The context within which those words are written and spoken is always crucial for a proper understanding of their full meaning. To say "I love you" as a casual good-bye to one's spouse on the way to work is one thing; to utter those same words from the cross to one's executioners means something considerably different.

In the same way, understanding the true meaning of the words proclaimed in the Sunday Lectionary requires of us a grasp of their fuller context. This means we must look not only at their context in the biblical book from which a reading is taken; we must also situate a particular text in the context of the day's other readings, as well as the liturgical season or feast in which it occurs. Today, for example, both the Gospel and the first reading contain a similar theme (marriage) that apparently links them together in some way. Interpreting today's Scripture proclamation properly, then, requires us to understand the context that is provided by the juxtaposition of these two texts.

In the larger context of the liturgical cycle, we have followed a series of Gospel texts in recent weeks that deal with the notion of discipleship—what it means and what it costs to be a disciple of Jesus. The original context of today's reading from Hosea was his use of the image of marriage as a symbol of God's covenant relationship with Israel. The prophet reminded his audience of the intimacy the Lord established with the chosen people—an intimacy as deep and lasting as that established in marriage—and therefore deserving of the same fidelity and permanence. Having read this text of Hosea in the liturgical assembly today, the Markan Gospel reading in which Jesus uses a parable about a wedding suddenly takes on new meaning. We are led to understand that discipleship with Jesus is about a relationship as intimate and faithful as marriage, equally demanding, and requiring a life-long commitment and fidelity.

Reflecting on the Word

Oftentimes a newly married couple will go away on a honeymoon. Tickets are bought, bags are packed, and off they go to somewhere far away from friends, family, and work. They leave everything else behind in order to focus entirely on each other. As they savor one another's love, they are nurturing an intimacy that will sustain them as they live out their commitment to the covenant of marriage "in sickness and in health, in good times and in bad."

A similar image is presented in today's reading from Hosea. God takes Israel out into the desert. There their intimate relationship blossoms once more and the covenant between God and Israel is renewed. In the Gospel Jesus speaks of feasting while the bridegroom is present. Here he seems to beckon us to drink in the new wine of God's faithful love that is eternally fresh and active in our lives. Such "honeymooning" with God can give us the nourishment and strength to live out our commitment to Christ even in times of testing.

**CONSIDER/
DISCUSS:**
- Do you feel more like a "fresh wineskin" or an "old cloak" today? Explain.
- What has God written on your heart or in your life lately?
- How might you drink in God's love more fully this week?

 ### Responding to the Word

Believe it or not, Lent begins this Wednesday and today's Scriptures can help us decide what we should fast from this year. Jesus' disciples may not have fasted from food but, like honeymooners, they left many things behind so that they could devote their lives entirely to Christ. Is there something that keeps us from being intimate with or faithful to Christ? If so, perhaps fasting from it will enable us to feast more fully on the love of God this Lent.

- Decide what you will fast from during Lent.
- Each day this week find a way to savor God's love for you.
- Share the gift of food or intimacy with someone this week.

Just as the words we say have many shades of meaning depending on the context in which they are spoken, so the scriptural passages read at Mass take on new meanings depending on the context in which they are placed. The key to the interpretive context of the readings chosen for the Lenten season lies in an understanding that Lent is, above all, a season of preparation for baptism—the initial baptism of those in the catechumenate, and the renewal of our baptism for the rest of us who are already fully initiated.

Although the readings of Year A hold a privileged place as catechetical documents during the Period of Purification and Enlightenment, the readings of each of the three years are profoundly baptismal in nature. Thus, an overview of the texts we will read in Year B reveals a very rich network of themes that have to do with baptism. The passages selected from the Jewish Scriptures focus attention on the theme of covenant, the special relationship of mutual commitment that bonded the Chosen People to the Lord as their God. Baptism, of course, has always been understood as the ritual that establishes the new covenant in the blood of Jesus. The ancient stories of covenant that we read this year are each, in their own way, foreshadowing some dimension of the new covenant in grace that we enter into through baptism.

The New Testament readings are a more varied lot, with themes that initially may seem quite diverse. However, a closer examination once again reveals that baptism is the key to understanding what they have in common. Each of the readings focuses on Christ, into whom we have been plunged and to whom we have been configured through the waters of baptism. Our Christian understanding of baptism is that we have been mystically joined to Christ through the ritual bath of water. Thus, we are offered a series of readings that speak about our identity in Christ, about Christ's obedience and humility, and his saving death that has made him a stumbling block to the foolish, but wisdom to the enlightened.

The Gospels this year are taken from both Mark and John. On the first Sunday of Lent we hear as usual the story of the temptation in the desert; thereafter the emphasis seems to be on the destiny that awaits Jesus—his death that will bring salvation to the world. For those preparing for baptism, as well as for us who plan on renewing our baptismal promises at Easter, these texts are a sobering reminder that baptism is a dying with Jesus, in order that we might also know the salvation of rising with him through the waters of baptism.

March 9, 2003

FIRST SUNDAY OF LENT

Today's Focus: Safe Passage

When a spring flood engulfs a community the safest place to be may be in a boat. As we begin our passage through Lent, we remember the safe passage the ark provided to Noah's family in the flood and the safe passage that Christ offers to all who brave the waters of baptism.

FIRST READING
Genesis 9:8–15

God said to Noah and to his sons with him: "See, I am now establishing my covenant with you and your descendants after you and with every living creature that was with you: all the birds, and the various tame and wild animals that were with you and came out of the ark. I will establish my covenant with you, that never again shall all bodily creatures be destroyed by the waters of a flood; there shall not be another flood to devastate the earth." God added: "This is the sign that I am giving for all ages to come, of the covenant between me and you and every living creature with you: I set my bow in the clouds to serve as a sign of the covenant between me and the earth. When I bring clouds over the earth, and the bow appears in the clouds, I will recall the covenant I have made between me and you and all living beings, so that the waters shall never again become a flood to destroy all mortal beings."

PSALM RESPONSE
Psalm 25:10

Your ways, O Lord, are love and truth to those who keep your covenant.

SECOND READING
1 Peter 3:18–22

Beloved: Christ suffered for sins once, the righteous for the sake of the unrighteous, that he might lead you to God. Put to death in the flesh, he was brought to life in the Spirit. In it he also went to preach to the spirits in prison, who had once been disobedient while God patiently waited in the days of Noah during the building of the ark, in which a few persons, eight in all, were saved through water. This prefigured baptism, which saves you now. It is not a removal of dirt from the body but an appeal to God for a clear conscience, through the resurrection of Jesus Christ, who has gone into heaven and is at the right hand of God, with angels, authorities, and powers subject to him.

GOSPEL
Mark 1:12–15.

The Spirit drove Jesus out into the desert, and he remained in the desert for forty days, tempted by Satan. He was among wild beasts, and the angels ministered to him.

After John had been arrested, Jesus came to Galilee proclaiming the gospel of God: "This is the time of fulfillment. The kingdom of God is at hand. Repent, and believe in the gospel."

Understanding the Word

The prominence of the theme of covenant in the Lenten readings this year makes it fitting that we focus today on the first reading, the story of God's covenant with all of creation following the great flood. The fact that this covenant, unlike other stories of covenant in the Jewish Scriptures, was with all of creation rather than just with the Jewish people, is significant. In the narrative of the great flood, the biblical author is actually suggesting that God has brought about a new creation. The first creation involved God's bringing order out of the primordial chaos (in Hebrew, *tehom*). Here, the same word, *tehom*, is used to name the flood-waters that covered the earth in the days of Noah. By promising never again to destroy creation with *tehom*, God is offering a fresh start to the entire created world.

Scripture scholars suggest that the rainbow in the story has its roots in ancient myths that told of warrior gods who inflicted harm on mortals as well as subdued the chaos by the might of the bow. In this story, the bow becomes a reminder both to God and to the people that never again would divine might be unleashed with such destructive force against the world. What was once a symbol of terror becomes instead a sign of reassurance. God's benevolence comes to the fore in this ancient tale that foreshadows the subsequent covenants that the Lord would forge in partnership with the Chosen People.

Covenants in the biblical context are always initiated by God, freely and out of gratuitous love. The human partner in the covenant is always an unequal, and always undeserving of the protection that God offers. Furthermore, the covenant is always offered to successive generations, to an entire people (in today's case to all humankind!), as a sign and reminder that God is ever-faithful and that the divine mercy endures forever. Finally, in some form or other, each and every biblical covenant is an experience of deliverance, of salvation, that God alone can offer.

Reflecting on the Word

It isn't too early in some parts of the country for a spring flood to swell rivers and engulf whole communities. Drowning becomes a real possibility for those who find themselves at the mercy of raging water that can pick up cars and break apart houses. Who hasn't seen news stories of people saved from the roofs of their homes by rescue boats? Once inside the boat victims may feel safe, but they still have turbulent waters to pass through before finding themselves on dry ground.

71

Their situation is not so different from that of Noah and his family. Although the ark kept them safe from the deluge, they still had a long and difficult passage to make before finding land. In today's Gospel, too, immediately following Jesus' baptism by John, the Spirit drives him out into the desert to struggle with the forces of evil. Jesus shows us that the salvation offered in baptism does not save us from turbulence and trial, but it does offer us safe passage through our struggles if we rest in the "hold" of God's faithful mercy.

CONSIDER/ DISCUSS:
- Describe a time when you were really afraid. How did you feel when you were safe?
- How does your faith in Christ "save" you in difficult times?
- What does the season of Lent mean to you?

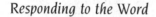

Responding to the Word

On this first Sunday of the Lenten season Jesus bids us to "repent," or reorient ourselves to the good news that God's kingdom is all around us. In baptism and by faith Christ is available to save and lead believers through every desert and every deluge, throughout the forty days of Lent and beyond. What reorientation might prepare you to make or renew your baptismal promises this Easter?

- In prayer give your deepest fears to God and believe in God's ability to save you.
- Provide "safe passage" to someone going through troubled waters by offering your money, your service, or your listening ear.

March 16, 2003

SECOND SUNDAY OF LENT

Today's Focus: The Power and the Glory

In the account of the Transfiguration Jesus is seen in his powerful and glorified state. Yet today's Scriptures don't affirm people who focus on gaining power or glory. Those who will be glorified by God are those who make themselves utterly powerless, like Abraham and Isaac and Jesus.

FIRST READING
Genesis 22:1–2, 9a, 10–13, 15–18

God put Abraham to the test. He called to him, "Abraham!" "Here I am!" he replied. Then God said: "Take your son Isaac, your only one, whom you love, and go to the land of Moriah. There you shall offer him up as a holocaust on a height that I will point out to you."

When they came to the place of which God had told him, Abraham built an altar there and arranged the wood on it. Then he reached out and took the knife to slaughter his son. But the LORD's messenger called to him from heaven, "Abraham, Abraham!" "Here I am!" he answered. "Do not lay your hand on the boy," said the messenger. "Do not do the least thing to him. I know now how devoted you are to God, since you did not withhold from me your own beloved son." As Abraham looked about, he spied a ram caught by its horns in the thicket. So he went and took the ram and offered it up as a holocaust in place of his son.

Again the LORD's messenger called to Abraham from heaven and said: "I swear by myself, declares the LORD, that because you acted as you did in not withholding from me your beloved son, I will bless you abundantly and make your descendants as countless as the stars of the sky and the sands of the seashore; your descendants shall take possession of the gates of their enemies, and in your descendants all the nations of the earth shall find blessing — all this because you obeyed my command."

PSALM RESPONSE
Psalm 116:9

I will walk before the Lord, in the land of the living.

SECOND READING
Romans 8: 31b–34

Brothers and sisters: If God is for us, who can be against us? He who did not spare his own Son but handed him over for us all, how will he not also give us everything else along with him? Who will bring a charge against God's chosen ones? It is God who acquits us. Who will condemn? Christ Jesus it is who died — or, rather, was raised — who also is at the right hand of God, who indeed intercedes for us.

GOSPEL

Mark 9:2–10
Jesus took Peter, James, and John and led them up a high mountain apart by themselves. And he was transfigured before them, and his clothes became dazzling white, such as no fuller on earth could bleach them. Then Elijah appeared to them along with Moses, and they were conversing with Jesus. Then Peter said to Jesus in reply, "Rabbi, it is good that we are here! Let us make three tents: one for you, one for Moses, and one for Elijah." He hardly knew what to say, they were so terrified. Then a cloud came, casting a shadow over them; from the cloud came a voice, "This is my beloved Son. Listen to him." Suddenly, looking around, they no longer saw anyone but Jesus alone with them.

As they were coming down from the mountain, he charged them not to relate what they had seen to anyone, except when the Son of Man had risen from the dead. So they kept the matter to themselves, questioning what rising from the dead meant.

Understanding the Word

Just as the Gospel of the First Sunday of Lent is always about the temptation of Jesus in the desert, so the Gospel of the Second Sunday of Lent is the story of Jesus' transfiguration in all three years of the Lectionary. The remarkable character of the event is obvious even on a superficial level. However, there are a sufficient number of implicit allusions woven into the narrative to make it clear that the Evangelist wishes the reader to recognize that this remarkable event is also a highly symbolic one, pregnant with meaning.

In Mark's Gospel the phrase "apart by themselves" always signals that a special revelatory event is about to be described (see 4:34, 6:31–32, 7:33, 9:2, 9:28, 13:3). The setting on a mountaintop is also suggestive of other decisive moments of revelation on other mountaintops (for example Sinai and Horeb, in Exodus 24 and 1 Kings 19). Peter's suggestion that they remain and set up three tents is surely an allusion to the Jewish Feast of Tabernacles (i.e., tents or booths), a harvest festival commemorating the Jewish people's sojourn in the desert. In the time of Jesus it was popularly believed that the Messiah would appear during this feast to establish his reign. Thus, Peter's suggestion is actually an affirmation that now is the time of the Messiah. The voice out of the cloud identifies Jesus with the Servant of Isaiah, another messianic reference that links this scene with Mark's earlier description of the voice at Jesus' baptism when he was also called God's "beloved" (1:11).

Mark's Gospel often has Jesus admonishing people not to reveal who he is, a literary technique that has come to be called the "Messianic Secret." Here we see a good example of how Mark uses the technique to further his story line, emphasizing the linkage between Jesus' identity and the centrality of his suffering and death as the fulfillment of his messianic destiny. For Mark, the ultimate revelation of Jesus' identity as Messiah will only happen in his death and resurrection. To learn that truth is to have finally grasped the meaning of discipleship (or, in our Lenten context, the meaning of baptism).

Reflecting on the Word

Patrice was on top of the world. She had made it into law school. She knew exactly how long it would take to finish, when she would get her loans paid off, what she would have to do to become a partner in a firm. Then she would have her children. She had her life perfectly planned—until the pregnancy test came back positive. What would happen to her hopes of practicing law? Could God possibly want her to have this child?

Perhaps Abraham and Jesus felt similar doubts. God had led Abraham to believe that through Isaac he would have descendants as numerous as the stars. Could God now really want Isaac to die? What would happen to the covenant? In today's Gospel Jesus' identity is affirmed as God's "Beloved Son," the Messiah chosen to establish God's reign on earth. What could he possibly accomplish by dying in the prime of life? Wouldn't it mean the end of everything? Both men chose the path of powerless obedience, a choice that allowed God's power and glory to shine through them.

**CONSIDER/
DISCUSS:**
- In the Genesis story what might Isaac and Sarah have been feeling?

- Have you been confronted with a situation that seemed to shatter all your dreams? What happened?

- How is God urging you to embrace powerlessness in your life?

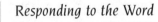

Responding to the Word

For those who give up seeking their own power and glory, accomplishments are transfigured into blessings to be shared and pride is transfigured into gratitude. With Abraham and Jesus we are called to rely entirely on God, who alone has power and deserves glory. With the psalmist we might be "greatly afflicted" yet God has "loosed" our "bonds" through Jesus' death and resurrection. For this we join the psalmist and Abraham in offering our "sacrifice of thanksgiving," the Eucharist.

- Fast from anxiety over money or success this week.

- During the Eucharist thank God for your blessings and entrust your future to the Lord.

- Share your material blessings with those in your community who are powerless or afflicted.

March 23, 2003

THIRD SUNDAY OF LENT, YEAR B

Today's Focus: Sign Value

The Scriptures for this Sunday refer to three signs of the covenant—the Ten Commandments, the temple in Jerusalem, and the death and resurrection of Jesus Christ. Like most signs of deeper realities, all three have tremendous value—but only for those who commit themselves totally to the covenant they represent.

> *For pastoral reasons, the readings given for Year A may be used in place of these readings. See page 80.*

In the shorter form of the reading, the passages in brackets are omitted.

FIRST READING
Exodus 20: 1–17 or 20:1–3, 7–8, 12–17

In those days, God delivered all these commandments:

"I, the LORD, am your God, who brought you out of the land of Egypt, that place of slavery. You shall not have other gods besides me. [You shall not carve idols for yourselves in the shape of anything in the sky above or on the earth below or in the waters beneath the earth; you shall not bow down before them or worship them. For I, the LORD, your God, am a jealous God, inflicting punishment for their fathers' wickedness on the children of those who hate me, down to the third and fourth generation; but bestowing mercy down to the thousandth generation on the children of those who love me and keep my commandments.]

"You shall not take the name of the LORD, your God, in vain. For the LORD will not leave unpunished the one who takes his name in vain.

"Remember to keep holy the sabbath day. [Six days you may labor and do all your work, but the seventh day is the sabbath of the LORD, your God. No work may be done then either by you, or your son or daughter, or your male or female slave, or your beast, or by the alien who lives with you. In six days the LORD made the heavens and the earth, the sea and all that is in them; but on the seventh day he rested. That is why the LORD has blessed the sabbath day and made it holy.]

"Honor your father and your mother, that you may have a long life in the land which the LORD, your God, is giving you.

You shall not kill.
You shall not commit adultery.
You shall not steal.
You shall not bear false witness against your neighbor.
You shall not covet your neighbor's house.
You shall not covet your neighbor's wife,
   nor his male or female slave, nor his ox or ass,
   nor anything else that belongs to him."

PSALM RESPONSE
John 6:68c

Lord, you have the words of everlasting life.

SECOND READING
1 Corinthians 1: 22–25

Brothers and sisters: Jews demand signs and Greeks look for wisdom, but we proclaim Christ crucified, a stumbling block to Jews and foolishness to Gentiles, but to those who are called, Jews and Greeks alike, Christ the power of God and the wisdom of God. For the foolishness of God is wiser than human wisdom, and the weakness of God is stronger than human strength.

GOSPEL
John 2:13–25

Since the Passover of the Jews was near, Jesus went up to Jerusalem. He found in the temple area those who sold oxen, sheep, and doves, as well as the money changers seated there. He made a whip out of cords and drove them all out of the temple area, with the sheep and oxen, and spilled the coins of the money changers and overturned their tables, and to those who sold doves he said, "Take these out of here, and stop making my Father's house a marketplace." His disciples recalled the words of Scripture,

Zeal for your house will consume me.

At this the Jews answered and said to him, "What sign can you show us for doing this?" Jesus answered and said to them, "Destroy this temple and in three days I will raise it up." The Jews said, "This temple has been under construction for forty-six years, and you will raise it up in three days?" But he was speaking about the temple of his body. Therefore, when he was raised from the dead, his disciples remembered that he had said this, and they came to believe the Scripture and the word Jesus had spoken.

While he was in Jerusalem for the feast of Passover, many began to believe in his name when they saw the signs he was doing. But Jesus would not trust himself to them because he knew them all, and did not need anyone to testify about human nature. He himself understood it well.

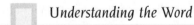

Understanding the Word

The Ten Commandments stand at the heart of the Jewish tradition and remain an essential dimension of our Christian experience as well. In previous weeks we have seen how the theme of covenant—as a preparation for the baptismal covenant celebrated at Easter—occupies an important place in our cycle of Lenten readings. The notion of covenant as a relationship between two parties carries with it an expectation of mutual accountability and fidelity to the terms of the covenant. When God forged the covenant with the Jewish people on Mt. Sinai, it was with the pledge to be their protector-God who would forever permit them familiar access as the Chosen People. For their part, the Jewish people were to observe the dictates of the Law, summarized most succinctly here in the form of the Ten Commandments.

The research of Scripture scholars has helped us understand how the Decalogue, as it is called, was both like and unlike other treaties that were a commonplace feature of the ancient culture of which Israel was a part. Remarkable similarities exist between the commandments of the Law and the terms of a Hittite suzerainty treaty. One thing that is distinctive about Israel's Law, however, is the absolute nature of its injunctions. In place of a Hittite treaty's conditional language, "If you do thus and such ... then such and such will ...," the Jewish law is unconditional: "You shall not ... you shall ..."—a clear indication of how the Israelites recognized the divine origin of the commandments. In addition, even the commandments (4–10) that regulate affairs between humans are regarded as integral to Israel's relationship with the Lord, their God. To violate these commandments is not just a crime against another person, it is a crime against God. The first three commandments, even more, reflect the absolute, monotheistic claim that God made upon the Jewish people: To be in a covenant relationship with the Lord requires an exclusive relationship, just as discipleship with Jesus—ritualized in baptism—demands a total allegiance to him and none other.

 Reflecting on the Word

In the Sixties there was a pop song about a diamond ring that had lost its meaning and luster for the singer. The covenant of love that it had represented was broken. His sweetheart had given her love to someone else. Once a sign of their exclusive commitment to each other, the ring no longer held any sign value for the singer.

Both the tablets on which the Ten Commandments were written and the temple in Jerusalem provided signs to the Israelites of their covenant with God. But, like a diamond ring, the stones and walls themselves meant nothing. Their true sign value rested in the commitment of the people to give their total allegiance to the Lord. Similarly Jesus' suffering, death, and resurrection can seem meaningless to non-Christians. His Passion only has real value as a sign of God's love to those who commit themselves to loving as Jesus loved—with their whole lives.

**CONSIDER/
DISCUSS:**
- What possession, place, or event has had real sign value for you?
- When you look at the entire first reading, what do you find most meaningful?
- Why do you think Jesus was so angry with the people conducting business in the temple area?

For "those who are called" baptism should be a sign of our covenant with God. Lent is a good time to ask ourselves whether our baptism has any sign value in our daily lives. Does the ritual we will renew, or undergo, at Easter represent a deeper reality—our total allegiance to "Christ crucified?" Does it mean that we are willing to die with Christ, confident that he will lead us to everlasting life?

- Use the commandments as a guide in discerning how you have been unfaithful to your baptismal covenant with God.

- Make amends with someone you have hurt.

- Before Easter attend a communal penitential service or receive the sacrament of penance.

March 23, 2003

THIRD SUNDAY OF LENT, YEAR A

Today's Focus: Thirsty for Love

If left unquenched, physical thirst can result in a horrible death. Spiritual thirst can lead to spiritual death if we try to satisfy it with the wrong things. Today's Scriptures show us that Christ is the only one who can truly satisfy our spirits when we are thirsty for love.

FIRST READING
Exodus 17: 3–7

In those days, in their thirst for water, the people grumbled against Moses, saying, "Why did you ever make us leave Egypt? Was it just to have us die here of thirst with our children and our livestock?" So Moses cried out to the LORD, "What shall I do with this people? A little more and they will stone me!" The LORD answered Moses, "Go over there in front of the people, along with some of the elders of Israel, holding in your hand, as you go, the staff with which you struck the river. I will be standing there in front of you on the rock in Horeb. Strike the rock, and the water will flow from it for the people to drink." This Moses did, in the presence of the elders of Israel. The place was called Massah and Meribah, because the Israelites quarreled there and tested the LORD, saying, "Is the LORD in our midst or not?"

PSALM RESPONSE
Psalm 95:8

If today you hear his voice, harden not your hearts.

SECOND READING
Romans 5: 1–2, 5–8

Brothers and sisters: Since we have been justified by faith, we have peace with God through our Lord Jesus Christ, through whom we have gained access by faith to this grace in which we stand, and we boast in hope of the glory of God.

And hope does not disappoint, because the love of God has been poured out into our hearts through the Holy Spirit who has been given to us. For Christ, while we were still helpless, died at the appointed time for the ungodly. Indeed, only with difficulty does one die for a just person, though perhaps for a good person one might even find courage to die. But God proves his love for us in that while we were still sinners Christ died for us.

In the shorter version of the reading, the three passages in brackets are omitted.

GOSPEL
John 4:5–42 or 4:5–15, 19b–26, 39a, 40–42

Jesus came to a town of Samaria called Sychar, near the plot of land that Jacob had given to his son Joseph. Jacob's well was there. Jesus, tired from his journey, sat down there at the well. It was about noon.

A woman of Samaria came to draw water. Jesus said to her, "Give me a drink." His disciples had gone into the town to buy food. The Samaritan woman said to him, "How can you, a Jew, ask me, a Samaritan woman, for a drink?" — For Jews use nothing in common with Samaritans. — Jesus answered and said to her, "If you knew the gift of God and who is saying to you, 'Give me a drink,' you would have asked him and he would have given you living water." The woman said to him, "Sir, you do not even have a bucket and the cistern is deep; where then can you get this living water? Are you greater than our father Jacob, who gave us this cistern and drank from it himself with his children and his flocks?" Jesus answered and said to her, "Everyone who drinks this water will be thirsty again; but whoever drinks the water I shall give will never thirst; the water I shall give will become in him a spring of water welling up to eternal life." The woman said to him, "Sir, give me this water, so that I may not be thirsty or have to keep coming here to draw water."

[Jesus said to her, "Go call your husband and come back." The woman answered and said to him, "I do not have a husband." Jesus answered her, "You are right in saying, 'I do not have a husband.' For you have had five husbands, and the one you have now is not your husband. What you have said is true." The woman said to him, "Sir,] I can see that you are a prophet. Our ancestors worshiped on this mountain; but you people say that the place to worship is in Jerusalem." Jesus said to her, "Believe me, woman, the hour is coming when you will worship the Father neither on this mountain nor in Jerusalem. You people worship what you do not understand; we worship what we understand, because salvation is from the Jews. But the hour is coming, and is now here, when true worshipers will worship the Father in Spirit and truth; and indeed the Father seeks such people to worship him. God is Spirit, and those who worship him must worship in Spirit and truth."

The woman said to him, "I know that the Messiah is coming, the one called the Christ; when he comes, he will tell us everything." Jesus said to her, "I am he, the one speaking with you."

[At that moment his disciples returned, and were amazed that he was talking with a woman, but still no one said, "What are you looking for?" or "Why are you talking with her?" The woman left her water jar and went into the town and said to the people, "Come see a man who told me everything I have done. Could he possibly be the Christ?" They went out of the town and came to him. Meanwhile, the disciples urged him, "Rabbi, eat." But he said to them, "I have food to eat of which you do not know." So the disciples said to one another, "Could someone have brought him something to eat?" Jesus said to them, "My food is to do the will of the one who sent me and to finish his work. Do you not say, 'In four months the harvest will be here'? I tell you, look up and see the fields ripe for the harvest. The reaper is already receiving payment and gathering crops for eternal life, so that the sower and reaper can rejoice together. For here the saying is verified that 'One sows and another reaps.' I sent you to reap what you have not worked for; others have done the work, and you are sharing the fruits of their work." |

Many of the Samaritans of that town began to believe in him | because of the word of the woman who testified, "He told me everything I have done." | When the Samaritans came to him, they invited him to stay with them; and he stayed there two days. Many more began to believe in him because of his word, and they said to the woman, "We no longer believe because of your word; for we have heard for ourselves, and we know that this is truly the savior of the world."

Understanding the Word

We have noted that the key to interpreting the Lenten readings, regardless of which year of the liturgical cycle one is observing, is to recognize their baptismal character. However, it is clear that the Lectionary has made the readings of Year A the preferred texts for communities preparing candidates for Easter baptism. To this end, in Years B and C the Lectionary allows communities to substitute the readings from Year A if they so choose on the Third, Fourth, and Fifth Sundays of Lent. One surmises that the principal reason for this permission is to reinforce the imagery contained in the scrutinies that are celebrated on those three Sundays with the Elect who are being prepared for Easter baptism. Recognizing that many communities will exercise this option, this week and the next two weeks we provide commentaries and reflections for the readings from Year A as well as Year B.

The image of living or flowing water is an important focus in today's readings. The arid climate of the Holy Land made water a charged symbol of life and renewal. But the people also knew from their personal experience of the Dead Sea what happens to a body of water when the water cannot flow on. The salty waters of that vast catch basin could not support life in any way. Thus, when Jesus promises to give flowing water, he presents himself as a source of life for all who thirst.

The motif of thirst is an important counterpoint to the water images in today's readings. For, just as some kinds of water may be salty and unfit to drink, so our thirst has a dangerous side to it, as the figures of both the Israelites in the first reading and the Samaritan woman in the Gospel clearly reveal. One's thirst, if not properly quenched, can easily lead one astray. The Israelites in the desert grumbled against Moses (and God) in their thirst; the Samaritan woman sought to quench her desires in relationships that were not satisfying. Only in baptism, where the love of God is "poured out into our hearts" (Romans, second reading), and where we are put into a relationship with Christ, do we experience the fulfillment of all our thirsty desires.

82

Reflecting on the Word

Frank wasn't surprised to see Daniel peering at him from behind the banister post this time. His brother had already gotten up for a drink of water twice that evening. "Hey, Danny, why aren't you in bed?" "I'm firsty, Frankie." "Thirsty? Come here, my man." Daniel ran into his open arms. "I know what you're thirsty for." Frank scooped him up and nestled into the rocking chair with him. "You're thirsty for love."

How often do we feel thirsty or hungry for something, but not recognize what we're thirsting for? Spiritual thirst can be so severe that we feel we'll die if it isn't satisfied with money or possessions or any number of easy alternatives. It isn't until God's love quenches our thirst that we realize what we had been missing all along. The Gospel story of Jesus and the Samaritan woman leaves no question about where we can go to quench our thirst for love.

CONSIDER/ DISCUSS:
- How have you tried unsuccessfully to quench your thirst for love?
- What keeps people from turning to Christ to satisfy their thirsts?
- What thirst in you does Christ long to quench today?

Responding to the Word

The Samaritan woman could have turned and walked away angry when Jesus said to her, "You have had five husbands and the one you have now is not your husband." But she stayed. Like the baptismal candidates who are celebrating the scrutiny this Sunday, she opened her ears and softened her heart to "hear God's voice" even when the words Jesus spoke made her face her human weakness. Can all of us do the same?

- Deliberately open your ears and soften your heart before hearing God's word this Sunday.
- Listen for God's truth about yourself. Celebrate the sacrament of penance before Easter.
- Respond to someone's unspoken thirst for love.

March 30, 2003

FOURTH SUNDAY OF LENT, YEAR B

Today's Focus: Come Home

During Lent we have seen that baptism is like being saved from a flood, and that it invites us to place our faith and our allegiance entirely in Christ. Today we see that through the grace of baptism we can also leave the exile of darkness behind and come home to live in the light of Christ.

For pastoral reasons, the readings given for Year A may be used in place of these readings. See page 87.

FIRST READING
2 Chronicles 36:14–16, 19–23

In those days, all the princes of Judah, the priests, and the people added infidelity to infidelity, practicing all the abominations of the nations and polluting the LORD's temple which he had consecrated in Jerusalem.

Early and often did the LORD, the God of their fathers, send his messengers to them, for he had compassion on his people and his dwelling place. But they mocked the messengers of God, despised his warnings, and scoffed at his prophets, until the anger of the LORD against his people was so inflamed that there was no remedy. Their enemies burnt the house of God, tore down the walls of Jerusalem, set all its palaces afire, and destroyed all its precious objects. Those who escaped the sword were carried captive to Babylon, where they became servants of the king of the Chaldeans and his sons until the kingdom of the Persians came to power. All this was to fulfill the word of the LORD spoken by Jeremiah: "Until the land has retrieved its lost sabbaths, during all the time it lies waste it shall have rest while seventy years are fulfilled."

In the first year of Cyrus, king of Persia, in order to fulfill the word of the LORD spoken by Jeremiah, the LORD inspired King Cyrus of Persia to issue this proclamation throughout his kingdom, both by word of mouth and in writing: "Thus says Cyrus, king of Persia: All the kingdoms of the earth the LORD, the God of heaven, has given to me, and he has also charged me to build him a house in Jerusalem, which is in Judah. Whoever, therefore, among you belongs to any part of his people, let him go up, and may his God be with him!"

PSALM RESPONSE
Psalm 137:6ab

Let my tongue be silenced, if I ever forget you!

SECOND READING
Ephesians 2: 4–10

Brothers and sisters: God, who is rich in mercy, because of the great love he had for us, even when we were dead in our transgressions, brought us to life with Christ — by grace you have been saved —, raised us up with him, and seated us with him in the heavens in Christ Jesus, that in the ages to come he might show the immeasurable riches of his grace in his kindness to us in Christ Jesus. For by grace you have been saved through faith, and this is not from you; it is the gift of God; it is not from works, so no one may boast. For we are his handiwork, created in Christ Jesus for the good works that God has prepared in advance, that we should live in them.

GOSPEL
John 3:14–21

Jesus said to Nicodemus: "Just as Moses lifted up the serpent in the desert, so must the Son of Man be lifted up, so that everyone who believes in him may have eternal life."

For God so loved the world that he gave his only Son, so that everyone who believes in him might not perish but might have eternal life. For God did not send his Son into the world to condemn the world, but that the world might be saved through him. Whoever believes in him will not be condemned, but whoever does not believe has already been condemned, because he has not believed in the name of the only Son of God. And this is the verdict, that the light came into the world, but people preferred darkness to light, because their works were evil. For everyone who does wicked things hates the light and does not come toward the light, so that his works might not be exposed. But whoever lives the truth comes to the light, so that his works may be clearly seen as done in God.

Understanding the Word

In the Church's catechesis of those preparing for baptism at Easter (or for those of us who are preparing to renew our baptism), one of the most important teachings to be grasped is the mystery of divine love that is revealed to us in Christ and through our baptism into the Christ-event. Indeed, this is perhaps the core teaching of our entire Christian experience, that ours is a "God, who is rich in mercy, because of the great love he had for us." (Ephesians 2:4)

This teaching about a God who is slow to anger and rich in mercy is not unique to the Christian experience: it is a recurring theme throughout the Jewish Scriptures. Today's reading from the Book of Chronicles contains a sort of "mini-history" of Israel that highlights God's mercies in choosing Cyrus the Persian to be an instrument of deliverance when the people were in captivity in Babylon. Despite their sinfulness and the deserved punishment they were undergoing, God's mercy was lavished on the people in the form of a miraculous act of liberation.

The letter to the Ephesians, in much more theological terms, gives a similar account of a God "who brought us to life with Christ—by grace you have been saved." The author stresses that it was when we were "dead in our transgressions" that God saved us, an act of pure grace. He emphasizes that it is not our own efforts that freed us from sin ("this is not from you"); rather, "it is the gift of God." This, of course, is the heart of the entire Pauline corpus, that salvation comes to us by faith in God's mercy, revealed in the death of Jesus. The Gospel today contains virtually the same message. It is from chapter three of John, the dialogue between Nicodemus and Jesus. Some scholars even speculate that this dialogue was written to assist in the task of preparing candidates for baptism. Its themes of light-darkness, water, rebirth, and certainly its core message (3:16) make such a possibility seem quite likely.

Reflecting on the Word

Andrea had done everything her parents had warned her against and had lied to cover it up. But it's impossible to keep a secret in a small town, so she stopped talking to them. When they continued "nagging" her she moved out "forever," telling her parents she "didn't have a family" anymore. Eight months later, broke and lonely, she chanced to see her father on the street. Certain he would condemn her, she turned way—too late. "Hello, Andrea. How have you been?" Andrea could not contain her tears when she heard the words, "Sweetheart, your mom and I would love for you to come home."

What must it have been like for the Israelites to learn that they were free to go home from their exile? No questions asked. All debts forgiven. A new beginning. If we can imagine their joy and gratitude perhaps we can understand more deeply the tremendous gift we have been given in baptism—God's mercy gives us the courage to leave our self-imposed exiles and come home.

CONSIDER/ DISCUSS:
- What story do you know of someone coming home?
- How does God help you to "come home?"
- What does it mean to you to "believe in" the Son of God?

Responding to the Word

Jesus' words to Nicodemus can help us understand why we don't always "come toward the light." Sometimes we prefer the darkness even though it exiles us from those we love. More often we might fear being condemned if our deeds are brought to light or we may simply be unable to find our way in the dark. That's when we need the light of Christ to help us believe once more in God's merciful love.

- In John 3:16 replace "the world" with your own name. Say that verse aloud to yourself slowly three times.
- Remember God's mercy for you and forget someone's debt to you.
- Invite a non-practicing Catholic to come to church with you this week.

March 30, 2003

FOURTH SUNDAY OF LENT, YEAR A

Today's Focus: Twenty/Twenty

In today's Gospel Jesus gives a blind person the ability to see what he could never see before. What about us? Often our view of the world is blurred by our own limited vision. How would we perceive things differently if we were given the ability to see with God's twenty/twenty vision?

FIRST READING
1 Samuel 16: 1b, 6–7, 10–13a

The LORD said to Samuel: "Fill your horn with oil, and be on your way. I am sending you to Jesse of Bethlehem, for I have chosen my king from among his sons."

As Jesse and his sons came to the sacrifice, Samuel looked at Eliab and thought, "Surely the Lord's anointed is here before him." But the LORD said to Samuel: "Do not judge from his appearance or from his lofty stature, because I have rejected him. Not as man sees does God see, because man sees the appearance but the LORD looks into the heart." In the same way Jesse presented seven sons before Samuel, but Samuel said to Jesse, "The LORD has not chosen any one of these." Then Samuel asked Jesse, "Are these all the sons you have?" Jesse replied, "There is still the youngest, who is tending the sheep." Samuel said to Jesse, "Send for him; we will not begin the sacrificial banquet until he arrives here." Jesse sent and had the young man brought to them. He was ruddy, a youth handsome to behold and making a splendid appearance. The LORD said, "There — anoint him, for this is the one!" Then Samuel, with the horn of oil in hand, anointed David in the presence of his brothers; and from that day on, the spirit of the LORD rushed upon David.

PSALM RESPONSE
Psalm 23:1

The Lord is my shepherd; there is nothing I shall want.

SECOND READING
Ephesians 5: 8–14

Brothers and sisters: You were once darkness, but now you are light in the Lord. Live as children of light, for light produces every kind of goodness and righteousness and truth. Try to learn what is pleasing to the Lord. Take no part in the fruitless works of darkness; rather expose them, for it is shameful even to mention the things done by them in secret; but everything exposed by the light becomes visible, for everything that becomes visible is light. Therefore, it says:

"Awake, O sleeper,
and arise from the dead,
and Christ will give you light."

GOSPEL
John 9:1–41 or
9:1, 6–9,
13–17, 34–38

As Jesus passed by he saw a man blind from birth. [His disciples asked him, "Rabbi, who sinned, this man or his parents, that he was born blind?" Jesus answered,

"Neither he nor his parents sinned;
it is so that the works of God might be made visible through him.

We have to do the works of the one who sent me while it is day. Night is coming when no one can work. While I am in the world, I am the light of the world." When he had said this,] he spat on the ground and made clay with the saliva, and smeared the clay on his eyes, and said to him, "Go wash in the Pool of Siloam" — which means Sent —. So he went and washed, and came back able to see.

His neighbors and those who had seen him earlier as a beggar said, "Isn't this the one who used to sit and beg?" Some said, "It is, " but others said, "No, he just looks like him." He said, "I am." [So they said to him, "How were your eyes opened?" He replied, "The man called Jesus made clay and anointed my eyes and told me, 'Go to Siloam and wash.' So I went there and washed and was able to see." And they said to him, "Where is he?" He said, "I don't know."]

They brought the one who was once blind to the Pharisees. Now Jesus had made clay and opened his eyes on a sabbath. So then the Pharisees also asked him how he was able to see. He said to them, "He put clay on my eyes, and I washed, and now I can see." So some of the Pharisees said, "This man is not from God, because he does not keep the sabbath." But others said, "How can a sinful man do such signs?" And there was a division among them. So they said to the blind man again, "What do you have to say about him, since he opened your eyes?" He said, "He is a prophet."

[Now the Jews did not believe that he had been blind and gained his sight until they summoned the parents of the one who had gained his sight. They asked them, "Is this your son, who you say was born blind? How does he now see?" His parents answered and said, "We know that this is our son and that he was born blind. We do not know how he sees now, nor do we know who opened his eyes. Ask him, he is of age; he can speak for himself." His parents said this because they were afraid of the Jews, for the Jews had already agreed that if anyone acknowledged him as the Christ, he would be expelled from the synagogue. For this reason his parents said, "He is of age; question him."

So a second time they called the man who had been blind and said to him, "Give God the praise! We know that this man is a sinner." He replied, "If he is a sinner, I do not know. One thing I do know is that I was blind and now I see." So they said to him, "What did he do to you? How did he open your eyes?" He answered them, "I told you already and you did not listen. Why do you want to hear it again? Do you want to become his disciples, too?" They ridiculed him and said, "You are that man's disciple; we are disciples of Moses! We know that God spoke to Moses, but we do not know where this one is from." The man answered and said to them, "This is what is so amazing, that you do not know where he is from, yet he opened my eyes. We know that God does not listen to sinners, but if one is devout and does his will, he listens to him. It is unheard of that anyone ever opened the eyes of a person born blind. If this man were not from God, he would not be able to do anything." | They answered and said to him, "You were born totally in sin, and are you trying to teach us?" Then they threw him out.

When Jesus heard that they had thrown him out, he found him and said, "Do you believe in the Son of Man?" He answered and said, "Who is he, sir, that I may believe in him?" Jesus said to him, "You have seen him, the one speaking with you is he." He said, "I do believe, Lord," and he worshiped him. | Then Jesus said, "I came into this world for judgment, so that those who do not see might see, and those who do see might become blind."

Some of the Pharisees who were with him heard this and said to him, "Surely we are not also blind, are we?" Jesus said to them,

"If you were blind, you would have no sin;
but now you are saying, 'We see,' so your sin remains." |

Understanding the Word

In the early Church one of the names that was given to the ritual we now call baptism was "enlightenment." To be fully initiated into the Christian mystery was to be enlightened, to have one's eyes opened, to see with the light of faith rather than to remain in the darkness of unbelief. It is important to know this historical background to the sacrament of baptism in order to understand why the Lectionary has chosen to include today's readings during the Lenten season. The Gospel text from John about the man born blind clearly was written to be read on more than one level. Much more than a miracle story of a cure, it is a story about the search for faith, about recognizing Jesus for who he truly is, about the cost of discipleship and the courage to declare oneself. It is also a story of blindness that operates on a spiritual level—about how individuals and groups can remain "in the dark," despite what should be obvious to all. That this passage was used extensively in the instruction of candidates for baptism in the early centuries is well attested. Some scholars even go so far as to speculate that perhaps the story was created in its present form to meet the needs of those under instruction for baptism. In any event, we read this story today as a wonderful reminder of what is ultimately at stake in baptism (our own, or those to be baptized at Easter): The ritual of baptism "opens our eyes" to see clearly that Jesus is the Messiah, the Son of God, and with this knowledge we are able to enter into a deeply personal relationship with him in faith. That relationship allows us—as St. Paul says in today's second reading—to "live as children of light."

The first reading from the Book of Samuel is a wonderful preparation for today's Gospel text. It tells the story of Samuel's anointing of David as king of Israel. Only Samuel, guided and directed by the Lord, is able to see who is God's chosen one, for "the Lord looks into the heart."

Reflecting on the Word

Barb enjoys telling the story of when her daughter, then eight years old, received her first pair of glasses, giving her twenty/twenty vision. It was in the middle of the summer. As soon as they walked out of the optometrist's office the little girl pointed up in wonder, "Look at the trees, Mommy! They have leaves on them!"

In today's Old Testament reading we encounter Samuel having just such a sudden recognition of something he had not seen before—that David, the shepherd, was also to be the Lord's anointed king. Just so, the second reading describes the sudden ability to see that comes when we wake from sleep. Christ opens our eyes and gives us immediate, twenty/twenty vision. In the Gospel Jesus first gives the blind man physical sight and later opens his eyes to see Jesus for who he really is.

CONSIDER/ DISCUSS:

- What experience have you had with blindness? What kind of "vision" might a person who is blind have?
- Who and what did the blind man "see" differently after Jesus opened his eyes?
- How does seeing with God's twenty/twenty vision change or sharpen your view of the world around you?

Responding to the Word

The man in the Gospel who is given twenty/twenty eyesight can see Jesus for who he really is—his Lord and Savior, his shepherd who supplies his every need. When we renew or make our baptismal promises on Easter we will claim the same vision of Jesus. And that vision should affect our view of—and our response to—everything and everyone around us.

- Pray for the ability to see Jesus more clearly for who he really is.
- Before you act or speak today try to "put on" God's twenty/twenty vision.
- Respond to one of the needs that you think God sees in our world.

April 6, 2003

FIFTH SUNDAY OF LENT, YEAR B

Today's Focus: Heart to Heart

This week we see yet another facet of baptism. To be baptized is to know in our hearts the heart of Jesus Christ who, like a grain of wheat, fell to the ground and died so that we might reap the harvest of eternal forgiveness. Such heart-to-heart knowledge empowers us to follow in his path.

For pastoral reasons, the readings given for Year A may be used in place of these readings. See page 94.

FIRST READING
Jeremiah 31: 31–34

The days are coming, says the LORD, when I will make a new covenant with the house of Israel and the house of Judah. It will not be like the covenant I made with their fathers the day I took them by the hand to lead them forth from the land of Egypt; for they broke my covenant, and I had to show myself their master, says the LORD. But this is the covenant that I will make with the house of Israel after those days, says the LORD. I will place my law within them and write it upon their hearts; I will be their God, and they shall be my people. No longer will they have need to teach their friends and relatives how to know the LORD. All, from least to greatest, shall know me, says the LORD, for I will forgive their evildoing and remember their sin no more.

PSALM RESPONSE
Psalm 51:12a

Create a clean heart in me, O God.

SECOND READING
Hebrews 5:7–9

In the days when Christ Jesus was in the flesh, he offered prayers and supplications with loud cries and tears to the one who was able to save him from death, and he was heard because of his reverence. Son though he was, he learned obedience from what he suffered; and when he was made perfect, he became the source of eternal salvation for all who obey him.

GOSPEL
John 12:20–33

Some Greeks who had come to worship at the Passover Feast came to Philip, who was from Bethsaida in Galilee, and asked him, "Sir, we would like to see Jesus." Philip went and told Andrew; then Andrew and Philip went and told Jesus. Jesus answered them, "The hour has come for the Son of Man to be glorified. Amen, amen, I say to you, unless a grain of wheat falls to the ground and dies, it remains just a grain of wheat; but if it dies, it produces much fruit. Whoever loves his life loses it, and whoever hates his life in this world will preserve it for eternal life. Whoever serves me must follow me, and where I am, there also will my servant be. The Father will honor whoever serves me.

"I am troubled now. Yet what should I say? 'Father, save me from this hour'? But it was for this purpose that I came to this hour. Father, glorify your name." Then a voice came from heaven, "I have glorified it and will glorify it again." The crowd there heard it and said it was thunder; but others said, "An angel has spoken to him." Jesus answered and said, "This voice did not come for my sake but for yours. Now is the time of judgment on this world; now the ruler of this world will be driven out. And when I am lifted up from the earth, I will draw everyone to myself." He said this indicating the kind of death he would die.

Understanding the Word

The prophet Jeremiah spoke God's Word to the Jewish people during one of the most difficult periods of their history. Initially, he warned them that unless they returned to God by being faithful to the covenant, disaster would befall them. In subsequent years, after having seen how the people ignored his warnings, Jeremiah was also witness to the downfall of the nation, just as he had predicted. He interpreted those catastrophic events as divine judgment, a deserved punishment for the people's infidelity to the covenant.

Yet, in spite of all that he had witnessed, and still without evidence of the people's repentance for their sins, Jeremiah is able to utter words of profound hope that God would once again forgive the Chosen People. Today's first reading is an enormously important passage, not only in the history of the Jewish people, but also for us as disciples of Jesus who see in it a foreshadowing of the Christian dispensation. The prophet announces that God has chosen to forgive the people, and that as a sign of divine forgiveness a new covenant will be established. Contrasting the new covenant with the one made with Moses on Mt. Sinai, Jeremiah says that the new covenant will be written on the people's hearts rather than on tablets of stone. No longer will the community's tradition be the sole bearer of the covenant; henceforth, God will speak directly and personally to each individual, forgiving sin and calling for a return to God in faithfulness. No longer will mere outward compliance with the dictates of the Law suffice; henceforth, God asks for an obedience that springs from the depths of one's heart.

Precisely that kind of obedience is highlighted in today's second reading, where the author of the Letter to the Hebrews describes Jesus as the mediator of the new covenant whose obedience has made him the source of salvation for all who, in turn, obey him. It is not difficult to see again this week the familiar Lenten theme of baptism as entrance into the new covenant, the covenant foretold by Jeremiah and now accomplished in the blood of Jesus.

Reflecting on the Word

Do you ever have heart-to-heart talks with other people? Such talks often entail sharing intimate knowledge about yourselves that you have not shared before. You may reveal how much you care about each other. You might exchange counsel or encouragement in a tough situation. You might even name the pain that you have suffered because of the other person and find healing of both your hearts.

In this Sunday's New Testament readings we encounter Jesus having intimate conversations with his Father-God—what we might call heart-to-heart talks. In these interchanges they share the pain and pride, the fears and forgiveness that are deep within their hearts. The first reading describes God not speaking but writing on the hearts of human beings in a way that allows them to know the Lord's heart deeply and intimately. The more they (we) know the heart of the Lord, the more their (our) own hearts will be changed to respond as Jesus did to God's forgiving, loving heart.

CONSIDER/ DISCUSS:
- Do you and God have heart-to-heart talks? Explain.
- What has your heart learned from suffering?
- When is it most difficult for you to respond with obedience as Jesus did?

Responding to the Word

It is not quick or easy for God to "create a clean heart" in us. Since the time of Jeremiah and even before that God has been trying. Baptism isn't a magic wand that instantly transforms our hearts. Yet "now is the time," says Jesus, for him to "draw everyone" to himself. Perhaps the more often we have heart-to-heart talks with God, the easier it will be for us to follow Jesus' way of obedience.

- Have a heart-to-heart talk with God. Listen to God's heart.
- Write what is in your heart in a letter to someone this week.
- Practice obedience by doing what someone asks you to do.

April 6, 2003

FIFTH SUNDAY OF LENT, YEAR A

Today's Focus: Quality of Life

The story of the raising of Lazarus explores the deepest significance of baptism—that it is a sharing in God's own life. While this divine life includes life everlasting after we die, it also changes our lives on earth. Through baptism God offers us a divine quality of life here and now.

FIRST READING
Ezekiel 37:12–14

Thus says the LORD GOD: O my people, I will open your graves and have you rise from them, and bring you back to the land of Israel. Then you shall know that I am the LORD, when I open your graves and have you rise from them, O my people! I will put my spirit in you that you may live, and I will settle you upon your land; thus you shall know that I am the LORD. I have promised, and I will do it, says the LORD.

PSALM RESPONSE
Psalm 130:7

With the Lord there is mercy and fullness of redemption.

SECOND READING
Romans 8:8–11

Brothers and sisters: Those who are in the flesh cannot please God. But you are not in the flesh; on the contrary, you are in the spirit, if only the Spirit of God dwells in you. Whoever does not have the Spirit of Christ does not belong to him. But if Christ is in you, although the body is dead because of sin, the spirit is alive because of righteousness. If the Spirit of the one who raised Jesus from the dead dwells in you, the one who raised Christ from the dead will give life to your mortal bodies also, through his Spirit dwelling in you.

In the shorter version of the reading, the five passages in brackets are omitted.

GOSPEL
John 11:1–45 or 11:3–7, 17, 20–27, 33b–45

[Now a man was ill, Lazarus from Bethany, the village of Mary and her sister Martha. Mary was the one who had anointed the Lord with perfumed oil and dried his feet with her hair; it was her brother Lazarus who was ill. So] the sisters sent word to him saying, "Master, the one you love is ill." When Jesus heard this he said,

"This illness is not to end in death,
but is for the glory of God,
that the Son of God may be glorified through it."

Now Jesus loved Martha and her sister and Lazarus. So when he heard that he was ill, he remained for two days in the place where he was. Then after this he said to his disciples, "Let us go back to Judea." [The disciples said to him, "Rabbi, the Jews were just trying to stone you, and you want to go back there?" Jesus answered,

"Are there not twelve hours in a day?
If one walks during the day, he does not stumble,
   because he sees the light of this world.
But if one walks at night, he stumbles,
   because the light is not in him."

He said this, and then told them, "Our friend Lazarus is asleep, but I am going to awaken him." So the disciples said to him, "Master, if he is asleep, he will be saved." But Jesus was talking about his death, while they thought that he meant ordinary sleep. So then Jesus said to them clearly, "Lazarus has died. And I am glad for you that I was not there, that you may believe. Let us go to him." So Thomas, called Didymus, said to his fellow disciples, "Let us also go to die with him."]

When Jesus arrived, he found that Lazarus had already been in the tomb for four days. [Now Bethany was near Jerusalem, only about two miles away. And many of the Jews had come to Martha and Mary to comfort them about their brother.] When Martha heard that Jesus was coming, she went to meet him; but Mary sat at home. Martha said to Jesus, "Lord, if you had been here, my brother would not have died. But even now I know that whatever you ask of God, God will give you." Jesus said to her, "Your brother will rise." Martha said to him, "I know he will rise, in the resurrection on the last day." Jesus told her,

   "I am the resurrection and the life;
   whoever believes in me, even if he dies, will live,
   and everyone who lives and believes in me will never die.

Do you believe this?" She said to him, "Yes, Lord. I have come to believe that you are the Christ, the Son of God, the one who is coming into the world."

[When she had said this, she went and called her sister Mary secretly, saying, "The teacher is here and is asking for you." As soon as she heard this, she rose quickly and went to him. For Jesus had not yet come into the village, but was still where Martha had met him. So when the Jews who were with her in the house comforting her saw Mary get up quickly and go out, they followed her, presuming that she was going to the tomb to weep there. When Mary came to where Jesus was and saw him, she fell at his feet and said to him, "Lord, if you had been here, my brother would not have died." When] Jesus [saw her weeping and the Jews who had come with her weeping, he] became perturbed and deeply troubled, and said, "Where have you laid him?" They said to him, "Sir, come and see." And Jesus wept. So the Jews said, "See how he loved him." But some of them said, "Could not the one who opened the eyes of the blind man have done something so that this man would not have died?"

So Jesus, perturbed again, came to the tomb. It was a cave, and a stone lay across it. Jesus said, "Take away the stone." Martha, the dead man's sister, said to him, "Lord, by now there will be a stench; he has been dead for four days." Jesus said to her, "Did I not tell you that if you believe you will see the glory of God?" So they took away the stone. And Jesus raised his eyes and said,

"Father, I thank you for hearing me.
I know that you always hear me;
but because of the crowd here I have said this,
that they may believe that you sent me."

And when he had said this, He cried out in a loud voice, "Lazarus, come out!" The dead man came out, tied hand and foot with burial bands, and his face was wrapped in a cloth. So Jesus said to them, "Untie him and let him go."

Now many of the Jews who had come to Mary and seen what he had done began to believe in him.

Understanding the Word

The scrutiny ritual is celebrated on the Third, Fourth, and Fifth Sundays of Lent with those preparing for Easter baptism. The prayers used for those three scrutinies are intimately related to the three great Johannine Gospel texts that are read on the corresponding Sundays: Jesus' offer of Living Water to the Samaritan woman at the well, Jesus' gift of sight to the man born blind, and Jesus' gift of life to Lazarus. One cannot possibly understand the full meaning of those Gospel texts as they are proclaimed in our Sunday assembly without noting their baptismal undertones. Each Gospel—in fact, the entire set of readings for each Sunday—is an instruction on the full meaning of Christian initiation.

Today's readings about the gift of life serve as a kind of culmination of this three-week series of scriptural instructions on the meaning of our baptism. Ezekiel's prophecy about God opening the graves of the chosen people to bring them back to life was first delivered to the Jewish people when they were in exile in Babylon. The text begins with Ezekiel's vision of a field of dry bones that come to life under the power of God's life-giving spirit (perhaps inspired by his memory of a desert battlefield strewn with the dried-up carcasses of fallen Israelite soldiers). The vision ends with the verses we read today. In this section the prophet shifts the metaphor to speak of graves being opened up and the people rising from them back to life.

Ezekiel's text is a perfect preparation for the Gospel story of Lazarus emerging alive from his grave at the command of Jesus. John's highly theological narrative makes it clear that Jesus is not merely resuscitating Lazarus. Rather, this is a miracle whose deeper meaning is about resurrection with Christ, the source of all life. Paul's Letter to the Romans is the perfect link between Ezekiel and John. He connects the message of both texts to our experience of receiving the Holy Spirit in baptism: "The One who raised Christ from the dead will give life to your mortal bodies also, through his Spirit dwelling in you."

Reflecting on the Word

The quality of life is an important factor in choosing where to live or in making life-and-death decisions. A young biracial family may move to a town with a diverse population and a variety of family-oriented activities. A cancer patient may discontinue treatments that prolong her agony. How long we live is not always as important as the quality of the lives we lead.

The first and second readings today make clear that the new life Christ offers us is of the highest quality. In baptism God's own Spirit dwells in us, giving our lives a divine quality that will live beyond death. This same Spirit dwelling in us can enable us to reject any fatal errors that would diminish the quality of our lives here on earth. The Spirit even empowers us to help others leave their graves behind.

CONSIDER/ DISCUSS:
- How do you measure your quality of life?
- Do you think Lazarus was happy to return to life? Explain.
- How have you experienced the Spirit of God dwelling in a person or in your faith community?

Responding to the Word

There is something rather frightening about eternal life. If our lives after death will last forever we should consider carefully in this life what the quality of our next life will be. Life in hell would be everlasting agony. Yet life together with God would be everlasting joy. It seems that even after death the length of life is not as important as the quality. All the more reason to embrace the divine quality of life now and reject whatever is not of God.

- Write down what rejecting "Satan" will mean to you this Easter.
- At Mass pray that the Spirit of God might dwell more deeply in your faith community.
- Perform a compassionate or life-giving act this week.

April 13, 2003

PALM SUNDAY OF THE LORD'S PASSION

Today's Focus: Lift High the Cross!

Today and throughout this Holy Week we celebrate the suffering and death of Jesus. Why do we celebrate such a terrible course of events? Is it to make us feel sad or horrified or guilty? No, we celebrate the crucifixion in order to rekindle our confident hope in Jesus as Christ and Lord.

FIRST READING
Isaiah 50:4–7

The Lord GOD has given me
    a well-trained tongue,
that I might know how to speak to the weary
    a word that will rouse them.
Morning after morning
    he opens my ear that I may hear;
and I have not rebelled,
    have not turned back.
I gave my back to those who beat me,
    my cheeks to those who plucked my beard;
my face I did not shield
    from buffets and spitting.

The Lord GOD is my help,
    therefore I am not disgraced;
I have set my face like flint,
    knowing that I shall not be put to shame.

PSALM RESPONSE
Psalm 22:2a

My God, my God, why have you abandoned me?

SECOND READING
Philippians 2: 6–11

Christ Jesus, though he was in the form of God,
    did not regard equality with God
    something to be grasped.
Rather, he emptied himself,
    taking the form of a slave,
    coming in human likeness;
    and found human in appearance,
    he humbled himself,
    becoming obedient to the point of death,
    even death on a cross.
Because of this, God greatly exalted him
    and bestowed on him the name
    which is above every name,
    that at the name of Jesus
    every knee should bend,
    of those in heaven and on earth and under the earth,
    and every tongue confess that
    Jesus Christ is Lord,
    to the glory of God the Father.

GOSPEL
Mark 14:
1 — 15:47 or
15:1–39

[The Passover and the Feast of Unleavened Bread were to take place in two days' time. So the chief priests and the scribes were seeking a way to arrest him by treachery and put him to death. They said, "Not during the festival, for fear that there may be a riot among the people."

When he was in Bethany reclining at table in the house of Simon the leper, a woman came with an alabaster jar of perfumed oil, costly genuine spikenard. She broke the alabaster jar and poured it on his head. There were some who were indignant. "Why has there been this waste of perfumed oil? It could have been sold for more than three hundred days' wages and the money given to the poor." They were infuriated with her. Jesus said, "Let her alone. Why do you make trouble for her? She has done a good thing for me. The poor you will always have with you, and whenever you wish you can do good to them, but you will not always have me. She has done what she could. She has anticipated anointing my body for burial. Amen, I say to you, wherever the gospel is proclaimed to the whole world, what she has done will be told in memory of her."

Then Judas Iscariot, one of the Twelve, went off to the chief priests to hand him over to them. When they heard him they were pleased and promised to pay him money. Then he looked for an opportunity to hand him over.

On the first day of the Feast of Unleavened Bread, when they sacrificed the Passover lamb, his disciples said to him, "Where do you want us to go and prepare for you to eat the Passover?" He sent two of his disciples and said to them, "Go into the city and a man will meet you, carrying a jar of water. Follow him. Wherever he enters, say to the master of the house, 'The Teacher says, "Where is my guest room where I may eat the Passover with my disciples?"' Then he will show you a large upper room furnished and ready. Make the preparations for us there." The disciples then went off, entered the city, and found it just as he had told them; and they prepared the Passover.

When it was evening, he came with the Twelve. And as they reclined at table and were eating, Jesus said, "Amen, I say to you, one of you will betray me, one who is eating with me." They began to be distressed and to say to him, one by one, "Surely it is not I?" He said to them, "One of the Twelve, the one who dips with me into the dish. For the Son of Man indeed goes, as it is written of him, but woe to that man by whom the Son of Man is betrayed. It would be better for that man if he had never been born."

While they were eating, he took bread, said the blessing, broke it, and gave it to them, and said, "Take it; this is my body." Then he took a cup, gave thanks, and gave it to them, and they all drank from it. He said to them, "This is my blood of the covenant, which will be shed for many. Amen, I say to you, I shall not drink again the fruit of the vine until the day when I drink it new in the kingdom of God." Then, after singing a hymn, they went out to the Mount of Olives.

Then Jesus said to them, "All of you will have your faith shaken, for it is written:

> I will strike the shepherd,
> and the sheep will be dispersed.

But after I have been raised up, I shall go before you to Galilee." Peter said to him, "Even though all should have their faith shaken, mine will not be." Then Jesus said to him, "Amen, I say to you, this very night before the cock crows twice you will deny me three times." But he vehemently replied, "Even though I should have to die with you, I will not deny you." And they all spoke similarly.

Then they came to a place named Gethsemane, and he said to his disciples, "Sit here while I pray." He took with him Peter, James, and John, and began to be troubled and distressed. Then he said to them, "My soul is sorrowful even to death. Remain here and keep watch." He advanced a little and fell to the ground and prayed that if it were possible the hour might pass by him; he said, "Abba, Father, all things are possible to you. Take this cup away from me, but not what I will but what you will." When he returned he found them asleep. He said to Peter, "Simon, are you asleep? Could you not keep watch for one hour? Watch and pray that you may not undergo the test. The spirit is willing but the flesh is weak." Withdrawing again, he prayed, saying the same thing. Then he returned once more and found them asleep, for they could not keep their eyes open and did not know what to answer him. He returned a third time and said to them, "Are you still sleeping and taking your rest? It is enough. The hour has come. Behold, the Son of Man is to be handed over to sinners. Get up, let us go. See, my betrayer is at hand."

Then, while he was still speaking, Judas, one of the Twelve, arrived, accompanied by a crowd with swords and clubs who had come from the chief priests, the scribes, and the elders. His betrayer had arranged a signal with them, saying, "The man I shall kiss is the one; arrest him and lead him away securely." He came and immediately went over to him and said, "Rabbi." And he kissed him. At this they laid hands on him and arrested him. One of the bystanders drew his sword, struck the high priest's servant, and cut off his ear. Jesus said to them in reply, "Have you come out as against a robber, with swords and clubs, to seize me? Day after day I was with you teaching in the temple area, yet you did not arrest me; but that the Scriptures may be fulfilled." And they all left him and fled. Now a young man followed him wearing nothing but a linen cloth about his body. They seized him, but he left the cloth behind and ran off naked.

They led Jesus away to the high priest, and all the chief priests and the elders and the scribes came together. Peter followed him at a distance into the high priest's courtyard and was seated with the guards, warming himself at the fire. The chief priests and the entire Sanhedrin kept trying to obtain testimony against Jesus in order to put him to death, but they found none. Many gave false witness against him, but their testimony did not agree. Some took the stand and testified falsely against him, alleging, "We heard him say, 'I will destroy this temple made with hands and within three days I will build another not made with hands.'" Even so their testimony did not agree. The high priest rose before the assembly and questioned Jesus, saying, "Have you no answer? What are these men testifying against you?" But he was silent and answered nothing. Again the high priest asked him and said to him, "Are you the Christ, the son of the Blessed One?" Then Jesus answered, "I am;

> and 'you will see the Son of Man
>> seated at the right hand of the Power
>> and coming with the clouds of heaven.'"

At that the high priest tore his garments and said, "What further need have we of witnesses? You have heard the blasphemy. What do you think?" They all condemned him as deserving to die. Some began to spit on him. They blindfolded him and struck him and said to him, "Prophesy!" And the guards greeted him with blows.

While Peter was below in the courtyard, one of the high priest's maids came along. Seeing Peter warming himself, she looked intently at him and said, "You too were with the Nazarene, Jesus." But he denied it saying, "I neither know nor understand what you are talking about." So he went out into the outer court. Then the cock crowed. The maid saw him and began again to say to the bystanders, "This man is one of them." Once again he denied it. A little later the bystanders said to Peter once more, "Surely you are one of them; for you too are a Galilean." He began to curse and to swear, "I do not know this man about whom you are talking." And immediately a cock crowed a second time. Then Peter remembered the word that Jesus had said to him, "Before the cock crows twice you will deny me three times." He broke down and wept.]

As soon as morning came, the chief priests with the elders and the scribes, that is, the whole Sanhedrin, held a council. They bound Jesus, led him away, and handed him over to Pilate. Pilate questioned him, "Are you the king of the Jews?" He said to him in reply, "You say so." The chief priests accused him of many things. Again Pilate questioned him, "Have you no answer? See how many things they accuse you of." Jesus gave him no further answer, so that Pilate was amazed.

Now on the occasion of the feast he used to release to them one prisoner whom they requested. A man called Barabbas was then in prison along with the rebels who had committed murder in a rebellion. The crowd came forward and began to ask him to do for them as he was accustomed. Pilate answered, "Do you want me to release to you the king of the Jews?" For he knew that it was out of envy that the chief priests had handed him over. But the chief priests stirred up the crowd to have him release Barabbas for them instead. Pilate again said to them in reply, "Then what do you want me to do with the man you call the king of the Jews?" They shouted again, "Crucify him." Pilate said to them, "Why? What evil has he done?" They only shouted the louder, "Crucify him." So Pilate, wishing to satisfy the crowd, released Barabbas to them and, after he had Jesus scourged, handed him over to be crucified.

The soldiers led him away inside the palace, that is, the praetorium, and assembled the whole cohort. They clothed him in purple and, weaving a crown of thorns, placed it on him. They began to salute him with, "Hail, King of the Jews!" and kept striking his head with a reed and spitting upon him. They knelt before him in homage. And when they had mocked him, they stripped him of the purple cloak, dressed him in his own clothes, and led him out to crucify him.

They pressed into service a passer-by, Simon, a Cyrenian, who was coming in from the country, the father of Alexander and Rufus, to carry his cross.

They brought him to the place of Golgotha—which is translated Place of the Skull—. They gave him wine drugged with myrrh, but he did not take it. Then they crucified him and divided his garments by casting lots for them to see what each should take. It was nine o'clock in the morning when they crucified him. The inscription of the charge against him read, "The King of the Jews." With him they crucified two revolutionaries, one on his right and one on his left. Those passing by reviled him, shaking their heads and saying, "Aha! You who would destroy the temple and rebuild it in three days, save yourself by coming down from the cross." Likewise the chief priests, with the scribes, mocked him among themselves and said, "He saved others; he cannot save himself. Let the Christ, the King of Israel, come down now from the cross that we may see and believe." Those who were crucified with him also kept abusing him.

At noon darkness came over the whole land until three in the afternoon. And at three o'clock Jesus cried out in a loud voice, "Eloi, Eloi, lema sabachthani?" which is translated, "My God, my God, why have you forsaken me?" Some of the bystanders who heard it said, "Look, he is calling Elijah." One of them ran, soaked a sponge with wine, put it on a reed and gave it to him to drink, saying, "Wait, let us see if Elijah comes to take him down." Jesus gave a loud cry and breathed his last.

The veil of the sanctuary was torn in two from top to bottom. When the centurion who stood facing him saw how he breathed his last he said, "Truly this man was the Son of God!" [There were also women looking on from a distance. Among them were Mary Magdalene, Mary the mother of the younger James and of Joses, and Salome. These women had followed him when he was in Galilee and ministered to him. There were also many other women who had come up with him to Jerusalem.

When it was already evening, since it was the day of preparation, the day before the sabbath, Joseph of Arimathea, a distinguished member of the council, who was himself awaiting the kingdom of God, came and courageously went to Pilate and asked for the body of Jesus. Pilate was amazed that he was already dead. He summoned the centurion and asked him if Jesus had already died. And when he learned of it from the centurion, he gave the body to Joseph. Having bought a linen cloth, he took him down, wrapped him in the linen cloth, and laid him in a tomb that had been hewn out of the rock. Then he rolled a stone against the entrance to the tomb. Mary Magdalene and Mary the mother of Joses watched where he was laid.]

Understanding the Word

On Palm Sunday each year we read from chapter two of the Letter of Paul to the Philippians, which contains what is perhaps one of the most profound reflections on the mystery of the Incarnation found anywhere in Sacred Scripture. The author quotes the text of an early Christian hymn whose poetic structure itself gives expression to the mystery of divine condescension and exaltation that is involved in the Incarnation.

By taking on our human flesh, the Second Person of the Blessed Trinity has "emptied himself" of all divine privilege. That self-emptying was so complete and total that his human existence is presented as the "form of a slave." Moreover, this divine Person has embraced even the ultimate experience of being human by embracing his own mortality. And that embrace of death was not just any death—but the ignominious death of crucifixion. Thus does the hymn describe the complete "descent" of divinity into human flesh.

At this nadir of self-emptying, the poetic movement reverses itself, and God's exaltation of Jesus is jubilantly proclaimed: God greatly exalted him, and the divine name, "Lord," is now rightly his. The ancient Christian profession of faith, "Jesus Christ is Lord," concludes the hymn, reminding us of the core elements of our Christian belief: (1) **Jesus** is the earthly name given to the One who was born into our human existence and shared our history with us in every way. (2) He is indeed the Anointed One, the long-awaited **Christ** promised to the Jewish people. (3) He is also Son of God, a divine Person who in every respect deserves the title "**Lord**," reserved by the Chosen People for God alone.

Since we have noted in previous weeks the baptismal character of the Lenten readings, it seems useful to note here that this hymn is introduced by a phrase that, unfortunately, is not included in the Lectionary selection today. Verse five, just preceding today's reading, says, "Have that mind in you which was in Christ Jesus ..." It is not stretching the author's intent very far to suggest that implicit in this admonition is the further thought: "[Because of your baptism, you do and you must] have that mind ..."

Reflecting on the Word

"Why do we have that horrible crucifix in our house? It gives me the creeps!" Matthew complained while home on spring break. "My Protestant friends don't have statues of dead bodies hanging around. They focus on joy and resurrection. All we ever think about is suffering and death!"

Why do Catholics have crucifixes, as well as bare crosses, in our churches and homes? Why do we listen to the whole Passion narrative twice during Holy Week? One answer lies in the fact that life isn't always joyful. We, our loved ones, and people all around the world endure suffering, cruelty, violence and injustice, untimely and painful deaths. Jesus' willingness to undergo even such a death gives us strength in times of trial. God's powerful act of raising him from the grave gives us confident hope. The Spirit's presence within us gives us courage to aid those in our world who are still on the cross today.

CONSIDER/ DISCUSS:
- What does the crucifix mean to you?
- What character in the Passion narrative came alive for you this year? Explain.
- When have you or someone you know felt abandoned by God?

Responding to the Word

What kind of mindset must Jesus have had in order to accept the death that he endured? Like the psalmist, he had confident hope in the love and power of God even when things looked utterly hopeless. This is the "mind which was in Christ Jesus." It is the mind that the baptized receive again and again when we "confess that Jesus Christ is Lord."

- Remember and praise God for five ways in which you have been rescued.
- Mean what you sing during the "Holy, holy" and memorial acclamation this Sunday.
- Give hope to the hopeless by sharing one hour of your time this week.

Just as the key to interpreting the readings of Lent is recognizing their baptismal character, so the Lectionary's texts during the season of Easter are centered on helping the newly initiated unpack the meaning of the new life that is theirs through baptism. For fifty days, the readings that are chosen in the Lectionary all have to do with the new life of those transformed in baptism. The term "mystagogy" is the technical name for the post-baptismal instruction given to those who were baptized at the Easter Vigil, and the Lectionary readings proclaimed throughout this season are the foundation of all mystagogical catechesis.

The first readings during the Easter season are taken from the Acts of the Apostles rather than from the Hebrew Scriptures. In various ways the readings from Acts offer a glimpse of what a community looks like when it has been transformed by the presence of the Spirit of the Risen One. We hear stories of the remarkable unity that was experienced among the early believers. We are reminded of the way that the risen Christ worked cures and offered forgiveness at the hands of those who were filled with his Spirit. We hear stories of dramatic conversions that changed lives forever.

In similar fashion, the second readings provide a more particular perspective, suggesting how individual Christians' lives are transformed through the power of the Spirit at baptism. A series of semi-continuous texts from the First Letter of John draws our attention time and again to the central command and experience of every Christian: the love of God that is one with our love of neighbor.

Finally, the Gospel texts during this season are centered on the risen Jesus, describing his appearances and his teachings in the post-Resurrection Church. He is revealed in the midst of the disciples, in the breaking of the bread and the proclamation of his word. He is shepherd and vine, source of unity, and giver of the Spirit.

Throughout the Easter season we prolong our celebration of the core belief that makes us Christian: our conviction that Jesus Christ has indeed risen from the dead. The readings help us to celebrate that truth by reminding us of the many ways that believers continue to experience the presence of the Risen One in their midst. We know that he lives still in a community transformed by the power of his Spirit, in the lives of individual Christians transformed by baptism, in the liturgical assembly where he is experienced as present in Word and Sacrament. All of these are ways that Christians continue to know and experience Jesus Christ living in their midst, and the Scripture readings remind us of the continuity of experience that exists between the earliest believers and us.

April 20, 2003

EASTER SUNDAY
THE RESURRECTION OF THE LORD

Today's Focus: Eyewitness Accounts

On Easter morning everything—the Scriptures, the people around us, the liturgy, even nature—seems to bear witness that Jesus Christ is risen today. Like the eyewitness accounts in today's Scriptures, they help us to believe. Can we ourselves give eyewitness accounts that Christ's Spirit is risen and active today?

FIRST READING
Acts 10:34a, 37–43

Peter proceeded to speak and said: "You know what has happened all over Judea, beginning in Galilee after the baptism that John preached, how God anointed Jesus of Nazareth with the Holy Spirit and power. He went about doing good and healing all those oppressed by the devil, for God was with him. We are witnesses of all that he did both in the country of the Jews and in Jerusalem. They put him to death by hanging him on a tree. This man God raised on the third day and granted that he be visible, not to all the people, but to us, the witnesses chosen by God in advance, who ate and drank with him after he rose from the dead. He commissioned us to preach to the people and testify that he is the one appointed by God as judge of the living and the dead. To him all the prophets bear witness, that everyone who believes in him will receive forgiveness of sins through his name.

PSALM RESPONSE
Psalm 118:24

This is the day the Lord has made; let us rejoice and be glad.

SECOND READING
Colossians 3:1–4

Brothers and sisters: If then you were raised with Christ, seek what is above, where Christ is seated at the right hand of God. Think of what is above, not of what is on earth. For you have died, and your life is hidden with Christ in God. When Christ your life appears, then you too will appear with him in glory.

– or –

1 Corinthians 5:6b–8

Brothers and sisters: Do you not know that a little yeast leavens all the dough? Clear out the old yeast, so that you may become a fresh batch of dough, inasmuch as you are unleavened. For our paschal lamb, Christ, has been sacrificed. Therefore, let us celebrate the feast, not with the old yeast, the yeast of malice and wickedness, but with the unleavened bread of sincerity and truth.

On the first day of the week, Mary of Magdala came to the tomb early in the morning, while it was still dark, and saw the stone removed from the tomb. So she ran and went to Simon Peter and to the other disciple whom Jesus loved, and told them, "They have taken the Lord from the tomb, and we don't know where they put him." So Peter and the other disciple went out and came to the tomb. They both ran, but the other disciple ran faster than Peter and arrived at the tomb first; he bent down and saw the burial cloths there, but did not go in. When Simon Peter arrived after him, he went into the tomb and saw the burial cloths there, and the cloth that had covered his head, not with the burial cloths but rolled up in a separate place. Then the other disciple also went in, the one who had arrived at the tomb first, and he saw and believed. For they did not yet understand the Scripture that he had to rise from the dead.

Understanding the Word

When one is speaking of the resurrection of Jesus Christ from the dead, it may seem irreverent to ask, "So what?" Yet, in a way, the Scripture readings that are proclaimed throughout the Easter season are answering exactly that question. Each week—and, in fact, in each reading—we are provided with yet another aspect of the meaning that the Resurrection holds for us and for all people everywhere. The texts that the Lectionary places before us throughout the fifty days of Easter are like a kaleidoscope, turning ever so gradually week by week, revealing each time some new perspective on this mystery so rich in meaning that its significance is inexhaustible.

The first reading today and throughout this season is taken from the Acts of the Apostles. Ostensibly, the Acts is a companion piece to Luke's Gospel, a second volume that traces the history of the early Christian community following the Resurrection. Yet, just as the Gospel was a theological narrative designed to convince the reader of the identity of Jesus as Messiah and Son of God, so the Acts is more a theological essay than history in the sense that we understand it today. Luke's purposes in writing the Acts are in part historical, but his interests are much more than historical. Acts is a document meant to convince—to win over the reader to the conviction that the community of Jesus' disciples truly is the place where he lives on in the power of his Spirit. Luke records miraculous conversions and cures; he tells stories meant to show that the post-Resurrection community carries on the mission and ministry of Jesus with the same powerful Spirit that animated him. In addition, he goes to great lengths—as Peter's sermon in today's reading demonstrates—to show that the message of salvation won by Jesus is meant for all people, not just those of Jewish persuasion. Just as Luke's Gospel recorded the special concern Jesus directed to the outcast and marginalized, so in the Acts, Luke makes it clear that Jesus' disciples have been sent in the power of the Spirit to all people everywhere. That is the significance that Luke wishes us to recognize in Peter's sermon that we hear today in the house of Cornelius, a Gentile convert.

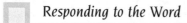

Reflecting on the Word

The conviction and enthusiasm of eyewitness accounts gives them a certain ring of truth. Yet the more eyewitnesses there are the more variance there may be in the details reported. Different witnesses may have seen different things—or seen things differently—but they usually agree on the fundamental truth about what happened.

The Easter Scriptures record the eyewitness accounts of Mary Magdalene, John, and Peter. Their credibility rests not on the precise details, but on the conviction and enthusiasm of the eyewitnesses. It is their belief in the Resurrection that convinces others to believe.

Like these scriptural eyewitnesses, today's believers are also "witnesses chosen by God in advance, who ate and drank with him after he rose from the dead." We are called to "testify that he is the one appointed by God" by giving eyewitness accounts of how the Spirit of the risen Christ is alive today. Our accounts may not agree in every detail, but the core truth will be the same, that Jesus Christ is risen indeed!

CONSIDER/ DISCUSS:
- What do you like, or not like, about today's Gospel?
- Who or what helps you to believe in the Resurrection?
- How have you witnessed Christ's Spirit alive and active lately?

Responding to the Word

"Christ is risen!" was once a common greeting on Easter morning. The expected reply, "Risen indeed!" communicated the conviction of an eyewitness. In other words, the respondent was saying, "I myself have witnessed Christ's Spirit alive and active in the world." Have you been an eyewitness to the Resurrection? Have you given your account so that others might believe?

- Give an account of a time when you experienced Christ's presence during Mass.
- Greet someone on Easter with the good news that "Christ is risen!"
- Celebrate Easter with "sincerity and truth."

April 27, 2003

SECOND SUNDAY OF EASTER

Today's Focus: Born-Again Christians

Many people these days call themselves born-again Christians. Today's Easter Scriptures describe believers who have been "begotten by God" with new life in Christ's name. What does that new life look like? Perhaps the new Catholics in our parishes can show us how to become a "born-again" Christian community.

FIRST READING
Acts 4:32–35

The community of believers was of one heart and mind, and no one claimed that any of his possessions was his own, but they had everything in common. With great power the apostles bore witness to the resurrection of the Lord Jesus, and great favor was accorded them all. There was no needy person among them, for those who owned property or houses would sell them, bring the proceeds of the sale, and put them at the feet of the apostles, and they were distributed to each according to need.

PSALM RESPONSE
Psalm 118:1

Give thanks to the Lord for he is good, his love is everlasting.

SECOND READING
1 John 5:1–6

Beloved: Everyone who believes that Jesus is the Christ is begotten by God, and everyone who loves the Father loves also the one begotten by him. In this way we know that we love the children of God when we love God and obey his commandments. For the love of God is this, that we keep his commandments. And his commandments are not burdensome, for whoever is begotten by God conquers the world. And the victory that conquers the world is our faith. Who indeed is the victor over the world but the one who believes that Jesus is the Son of God?

This is the one who came through water and blood, Jesus Christ, not by water alone, but by water and blood. The Spirit is the one that testifies, and the Spirit is truth.

GOSPEL
John 20:19–31

On the evening of that first day of the week, when the doors were locked, where the disciples were, for fear of the Jews, Jesus came and stood in their midst and said to them, "Peace be with you." When he had said this, he showed them his hands and his side. The disciples rejoiced when they saw the Lord. Jesus said to them again, "Peace be with you. As the Father has sent me, so I send you." And when he had said this, he breathed on them and said to them, "Receive the Holy Spirit. Whose sins you forgive are forgiven them, and whose sins you retain are retained."

Thomas, called Didymus, one of the Twelve, was not with them when Jesus came. So the other disciples said to him, "We have seen the Lord." But he said to them, "Unless I see the mark of the nails in his hands and put my finger into the nailmarks and put my hand into his side, I will not believe."

Now a week later his disciples were again inside and Thomas was with them. Jesus came, although the doors were locked, and stood in their midst and said, "Peace be with you." Then he said to Thomas, "Put your finger here and see my hands, and bring your hand and put it into my side, and do not be unbelieving, but believe." Thomas answered and said to him, "My Lord and my God!" Jesus said to him, "Have you come to believe because you have seen me? Blessed are those who have not seen and have believed."

Now Jesus did many other signs in the presence of his disciples that are not written in this book. But these are written that you may come to believe that Jesus is the Christ, the Son of God, and that through this belief you may have life in his name.

Understanding the Word

It is not often that the author of one of the books of the Bible comes right out and tells us directly why he is writing what he is writing. We have the example of Luke at the beginning of his Gospel, writing to a certain Theophilus, in which he indicates that his reason for composing the Gospel is "so that you may realize the certainty of the teachings you have received." (1:4) And in today's Gospel reading, taken from the conclusion of his Gospel, John makes a similar statement. He has chosen to record certain events—and not others—he says, so "that you may come to believe that Jesus is the Christ, the Son of God, and that through this belief you may have life in his name." (20:31)

This statement of purpose is an extremely important key to understanding how to interpret the narratives in John's Gospel. They are not detached, unbiased historical records, as we would expect to find in a good newspaper. Nor are they fabricated propaganda meant to deceive and manipulate. Rather, they are words of a believer, shaping his narrative as an invitation to others, so that they, too, might share the author's enthusiasm and convictions regarding Jesus of Nazareth, his message, his ministry, and—ultimately—the meaning of his death and resurrection.

In today's story of Jesus appearing to the disciples on Easter Sunday evening and again a week later, John is making an appeal to his readers to place their faith in the truth of the Resurrection based on the testimony of eyewitnesses, without demanding first-hand evidence themselves. John is also making a case for his readers to believe that the risen Lord has given to the disciples his own Spirit, and with that Spirit the same powers with which he himself was invested during his earthly ministry. In today's Gospel John illustrates this transfer of power by the explicit words of Jesus granting to his followers the authority to forgive sins.

Reflecting on the Word

Born again. Conception in the womb. New life begins. The "water and blood" of childbirth. Starting over as a newborn baby, perfectly trusting and pure. Unencumbered by the accumulated wealth, self-importance, and indebtedness of adults. This is how we can describe new Christians. They are "neophytes," or new buds, born again from the tree of the cross. Such new birth may begin when we "believe that Jesus is the Christ, the Son of God," but it doesn't end there.

Our first reading describes the Christian community as a whole society that has been "born again." Unlike ordinary communities, these neophytes are willing to submit to one another's leadership, uninterested in possessions and forgetful of any debts or social stigmas that had previously divided them. In short, they "love the children of God." The Gospel describes a very different community—one imprisoned in old fears and suspicions, even after Christ breathes his new life, his Spirit, into them. Which Scripture reading describes your faith community?

CONSIDER/
DISCUSS:
- Who do you know who acts like someone who has "received the Holy Spirit?"

- What does your faith community do that resembles the community in Acts?

- How might the new members of your parish help your community become "born again?"

Responding to the Word

For Catholics, being born again is a community affair. As the reading from the letter of John indicates, being begotten by God shows itself in loving all the children of God. There is one and only one Spirit that Jesus breathes into believers, a Spirit that brings to life and unites the whole community of Christians in making Christ's love and forgiveness present in the world.

- Get to know someone new at church this weekend.

- Ask a newcomer what ideas he or she might have for your parish.

- Propose a new way of doing a ministry in your parish. Be prepared for resistance!

May 4, 2003

THIRD SUNDAY OF EASTER

Today's Focus: Booster Shot

The calendar and the Scriptures tell us it's still Easter. Yet right about now our enthusiasm may be waning and our old attitudes may have returned. It's impossible for us to live as the ideal Christian community for long. This week's Gospel reminds us that we need our weekly "booster shot" of the Eucharist.

FIRST READING
Acts 3:13–15, 17–19

Peter said to the people: "The God of Abraham, the God of Isaac, and the God of Jacob, the God of our fathers, has glorified his servant Jesus, whom you handed over and denied in Pilate's presence when he had decided to release him. You denied the Holy and Righteous One and asked that a murderer be released to you. The author of life you put to death, but God raised him from the dead; of this we are witnesses. Now I know, brothers, that you acted out of ignorance, just as your leaders did; but God has thus brought to fulfillment what he had announced beforehand through the mouth of all the prophets, that his Christ would suffer. Repent, therefore, and be converted, that your sins may be wiped away."

PSALM RESPONSE
Psalm 4:7a

Lord, let your face shine on us.

SECOND READING
1 John 2:1–5a

My children, I am writing this to you so that you may not commit sin. But if anyone does sin, we have an Advocate with the Father, Jesus Christ the righteous one. He is expiation for our sins, and not for our sins only but for those of the whole world. The way we may be sure that we know him is to keep his commandments. Those who say, "I know him," but do not keep his commandments are liars, and the truth is not in them. But whoever keeps his word, the love of God is truly perfected in him.

GOSPEL
Luke 24:35–48

The two disciples recounted what had taken place on the way, and how Jesus was made known to them in the breaking of bread.

While they were still speaking about this, he stood in their midst and said to them, "Peace be with you." But they were startled and terrified and thought that they were seeing a ghost. Then he said to them, "Why are you troubled? And why do questions arise in your hearts? Look at my hands and my feet, that it is I myself. Touch me and see, because a ghost does not have flesh and bones as you can see I have." And as he said this, he showed them his hands and his feet. While they were still incredulous for joy and were amazed, he asked them, "Have you anything here to eat?" They gave him a piece of baked fish; he took it and ate it in front of them.

He said to them, "These are my words that I spoke to you while I was still with you, that everything written about me in the law of Moses and in the prophets and psalms must be fulfilled." Then he opened their minds to understand the Scriptures. And he said to them, "Thus it is written that the Christ would suffer and rise from the dead on the third day and that repentance, for the forgiveness of sins, would be preached in his name to all the nations, beginning from Jerusalem. You are witnesses of these things."

Understanding the Word

Today's Gospel reading takes place immediately following Luke's account of the appearance of Jesus to the two disciples on the road to Emmaus. Those disciples have hurried back to Jerusalem to report what has happened, and this is where today's narrative picks up the story. Scripture scholars point out the similarities between this narrative and the Emmaus account that has just preceded it. In both stories, Jesus is not immediately recognized; in both cases, Jesus explains the Scriptures that referred to him and helps the disciples to understand the meaning of his death and resurrection; finally, in both narratives the disciples share a meal with Jesus.

One of the things that Luke appears to be doing in repeating this pattern is to drive home to his readers a single point—namely, that whenever they gather together a similar dynamic unfolds. They may not initially remember or acknowledge that the Lord is with them in their assembly. However, the reading of Scripture and its unfolding through explanations (that is, its homiletic interpretation) help those gathered to "recognize" the presence of the Lord. That recognition is then consummated in the fellowship meal, the breaking of the bread, that they share. Clearly, Luke is shaping his stories of the appearances of the risen Lord in a way meant to bring the readers to recognize themselves in the story. Luke hopes to trigger an "aha!" experience—for the members of his own community and for us as well—so that we will be convinced of the reality of the risen Lord's presence in our midst. The liturgical assembly was for Luke—and remains for us—the privileged place where this experience happens. However, as the Gospel's concluding mandate of Jesus to the disciples—to preach and witness in the world—makes clear, Luke also wishes us to realize that in our daily lives we can also experience that same continuing presence of the Lord in our midst.

Some vaccinations only last so long. After a predictable amount of time the immunity wears off and people are susceptible to the same old disease again. That's when it's time for a booster shot. It seems that we also need booster shots for faith. Baptism alone is not enough. The joy and peace that filled our communities two weeks ago are probably starting to flag and our old selves may be starting to re-emerge. We need a weekly dose of Resurrection appearances, in the Eucharist we share.

All three of this week's readings as well as the psalm point out the weakness of our human faith. Yet they emphasize the forgiveness and blessing that are always available to those who turn to "Jesus Christ the righteous one." Can we recognize ourselves in Luke's Gospel today? Do we realize how deeply we depend on our weekly booster shot of the Eucharist to remember and reclaim the saving presence of the risen Lord?

CONSIDER/ DISCUSS:
- Where do you recognize yourself in today's Scriptures? Explain.
- How does this week's Gospel selection compare to last week's Gospel?
- In whose "flesh and bones," "hands and feet," have you seen the risen Lord?

Responding to the Word

The Eucharist is more than a booster shot. Besides immunizing us it is meant to energize us to take Christ's presence out into the world. While it may be easy to see ourselves in today's Scriptures as the weak sinners whose failings are forgiven time and again, we should also envision ourselves in the role of Peter, who preached, and John and Luke, who wrote these Scriptures. In the Eucharist Jesus feeds us and sends us to "preach in his name to all the nations." We are his witnesses.

- List five ways that you have been or think you might be Christ's witness.
- Listen attentively to the whole Eucharistic Prayer at Mass this Sunday.
- Give some of your possessions to those in need this week.

May 11, 2003

FOURTH SUNDAY OF EASTER

Today's Focus: Farm Boy

In some high schools farm kids are scorned and rejected. Yet it's no exaggeration to say that society owes its life to farmers who care for the world's crops and livestock. This week's Scriptures remind us that Jesus was as rejected as a shepherd, a farm boy, yet we owe our very life to him.

FIRST READING
Acts 4:8–12

Peter, filled with the Holy Spirit, said: "Leaders of the people and elders: If we are being examined today about a good deed done to a cripple, namely, by what means he was saved, then all of you and all the people of Israel should know that it was in the name of Jesus Christ the Nazarene whom you crucified, whom God raised from the dead; in his name this man stands before you healed. He is

> the stone rejected by you, the builders, which has become the cornerstone.

There is no salvation through anyone else, nor is there any other name under heaven given to the human race by which we are to be saved."

PSALM RESPONSE
Psalm 118:22

The stone rejected by the builders has become the cornerstone.

SECOND READING
1 John 3:1–2

Beloved: See what love the Father has bestowed on us that we may be called the children of God. Yet so we are. The reason the world does not know us is that it did not know him. Beloved, we are God's children now; what we shall be has not yet been revealed. We do know that when it is revealed we shall be like him, for we shall see him as he is.

GOSPEL
John 10:11–18

Jesus said: "I am the good shepherd. A good shepherd lays down his life for the sheep. A hired man, who is not a shepherd and whose sheep are not his own, sees a wolf coming and leaves the sheep and runs away, and the wolf catches and scatters them. This is because he works for pay and has no concern for the sheep. I am the good shepherd, and I know mine and mine know me, just as the Father knows me and I know the Father; and I will lay down my life for the sheep. I have other sheep that do not belong to this fold. These also I must lead, and they will hear my voice, and there will be one flock, one shepherd. This is why the Father loves me, because I lay down my life in order to take it up again. No one takes it from me, but I lay it down on my own. I have power to lay it down, and power to take it up again. This command I have received from my Father."

115

Understanding the Word

The Fourth Sunday of Easter is known as Good Shepherd Sunday because in all three years of the Lectionary cycle the Gospel reading is taken from chapter 10 of John's Gospel, where Jesus describes himself as the Good Shepherd. One might ask why these readings are read each year during the Easter season. The answer lies in recalling that the Lectionary texts during this time are mystagogical in nature. That is, they are in some way or other meant to unpack the meaning of Christian initiation for those who have been baptized at the Easter Vigil (as well as for those of us who renewed our baptism at Easter).

This text—like next week's Gospel that describes Jesus as the vine and us as the branches—is a fitting commentary on baptism because it explores the relationship between Jesus and those who belong to him. We believe that in baptism we are joined to Christ, that we are made members of his body, that we share his own life through the gift of his Spirit. By proclaiming these texts about Jesus the Good Shepherd who is willing to give his life for the sake of his sheep, we are invited to understand more deeply just how profound is the love that Jesus has for us. His sole concern is for our welfare—for our salvation. It is a concern and a love that Jesus shares with the Father, as John's Gospel makes abundantly clear in many other passages.

Today's second reading also picks up on the same theme, though it calls us "children of God" rather than sheep: "See what love the Father has bestowed on us that we may be called the children of God." For a neophyte (or for a "veteran") contemplating the wonder of baptism, these images of shepherding or being chosen children evoke the mystery of a God whose great love invites us into intimate, lasting relationship, a relationship that actually allows us to share forever in the divine life itself.

Reflecting on the Word

When I was in high school the "city" kids kept their distance from the "bus" kids. We rejected them without even knowing them. We called them "bus" kids because they lived on farms and rode the bus to school. They wore the wrong clothes and had suntan lines in the wrong places on their arms and foreheads. They smelled of manure and sometimes had hay stuck to their boots. They couldn't come to any parties even if they were invited because they had to get up before dawn to do chores. They did things that were repulsive to us—like helping cows give birth, feeding slop to pigs, cleaning horse manure from the barn, and, yes, herding and shearing sheep.

As we ponder the Scriptures for this week it's impossible to miss the references to Jesus as an outcast, one who was rejected by a world that didn't even know him. Yet this "shepherd"—this smelly farm boy who did what no one else would stoop to do (lay down his life for his sheep)—is precisely the one whom we are invited to embrace.

- What is your experience of farmers or shepherds?
- Which verses of this Gospel reading speak to you most deeply?
- How are you keeping your distance from the Good Shepherd?

 Responding to the Word

There is a promise and a warning for us in the letter of John this week. John says that "we shall be like him," meaning Christ. With Christ we will know God's ultimate love and mercy. With Christ we must also prepare to be ridiculed and rejected. And we must be prepared to sacrifice—perhaps even to lay down our lives—for the children of God, Christ's beloved sheep.

- Invite an outsider into your circle of friends.
- Sacrifice some of your time for those in need.
- Risk rejection by offering your assistance to a ministry in your parish.

May 18, 2003

FIFTH SUNDAY OF EASTER

Today's Focus: Fruit of the Vine

This week's Gospel selection describes the Christian community as a vineyard filled with branches from only one vine—Jesus Christ. Judging from today's first reading, the year that Paul's "branch" was joined to the Christian community was a very good year for the fruit of the vine of Christ.

FIRST READING
Acts 9:26–31

When Saul arrived in Jerusalem he tried to join the disciples, but they were all afraid of him, not believing that he was a disciple. Then Barnabas took charge of him and brought him to the apostles, and he reported to them how he had seen the Lord, and that he had spoken to him, and how in Damascus he had spoken out boldly in the name of Jesus. He moved about freely with them in Jerusalem, and spoke out boldly in the name of the Lord. He also spoke and debated with the Hellenists, but they tried to kill him. And when the brothers learned of this, they took him down to Caesarea and sent him on his way to Tarsus.

The church throughout all Judea, Galilee, and Samaria was at peace. It was being built up and walked in the fear of the Lord, and with the consolation of the Holy Spirit it grew in numbers.

PSALM RESPONSE
Psalm 22:26a

I will praise you, Lord, in the assembly of your people.

SECOND READING
1 John 3:18–24

Children, let us love not in word or speech but in deed and truth. Now this is how we shall know that we belong to the truth and reassure our hearts before him in whatever our hearts condemn, for God is greater than our hearts and knows everything. Beloved, if our hearts do not condemn us, we have confidence in God and receive from him whatever we ask, because we keep his commandments and do what pleases him. And his commandment is this: we should believe in the name of his Son, Jesus Christ, and love one another just as he commanded us. Those who keep his commandments remain in him, and he in them, and the way we know that he remains in us is from the Spirit he gave us.

GOSPEL
John 15:1–8

Jesus said to his disciples: "I am the true vine, and my Father is the vine grower. He takes away every branch in me that does not bear fruit, and every one that does he prunes so that it bears more fruit. You are already pruned because of the word that I spoke to you. Remain in me, as I remain in you. Just as a branch cannot bear fruit on its own unless it remains on the vine, so neither can you unless you remain in me. I am the vine, you are the branches. Whoever remains in me and I in him will bear much fruit, because without me you can do nothing. Anyone who does not remain in me will be thrown out like a branch and wither; people will gather them and throw them into a fire and they will be burned. If you remain in me and my words remain in you, ask for whatever you want and it will be done for you. By this is my Father glorified, that you bear much fruit and become my disciples."

Understanding the Word

Today's readings continue the Church's mystagogical instruction on the meaning of baptism. In the Acts of the Apostles, Luke's understanding of the Resurrection is linked to certain characteristics that are evident in the life of the Christian community and in the lives of individual believers. In other words, one of the proofs that Jesus truly is alive is the change that is obvious in those who have received his Spirit. Today's reading from Acts reminds us how dramatic is the conversion of Saul/Paul. Paul is so completely different after he has encountered the risen Lord that the disciples in Jerusalem find it hard to believe at first. However, Paul's fearless witness, even at the risk of his life, is a proof to the disciples (and Luke intends it to be a proof to us as well) that the risen Lord's Spirit truly is at work in him and has indeed profoundly transformed him from within.

The mystagogical message implicit in this text, of course, has to do with our own inner transformation. Baptism is meant to make us fearless believers, bold witnesses to the reality of the Lord's resurrection, no matter what opposition we may encounter. The second reading from the first Letter of John is even more explicit in pointing out another message, not just in words, "but in deed and in truth." For the author of this letter, genuine faith in Jesus is inseparable from active love of neighbor. "And his commandment is this: we should believe ... and love one another ..."

The result of a life of faith and love is that we "remain in him, and he in [us]." This is exactly the theme that is developed in the Gospel, where the notion of shared life takes on its most profound expression in the image of vine and branches. The meaning of baptism, at its deepest level, is found in an experience of sharing God's own life through our becoming a living member of the Body of Christ.

Reflecting on the Word

When we explore the Gospel image of the vine and the branches we usually focus on Christ, the vine. The branches are almost as important if the vineyard is to produce plentiful, succulent grapes. Branches with firm connections to the root system by the main vine will thrive and increase the yield of the vineyard. Branches also require pruning so that they don't put too much energy into their own growth and too little energy into bearing fruit. Finally, one branch alone might break under the weight of heavy clusters of grapes. By intertwining and reaching out their tendrils in mutual support the branches help each other to remain on the vine and live.

Today's first reading begins shortly after Paul's baptism. Like Paul, all the baptized who remain firmly attached to Christ will increase the fruitfulness of the "vineyard" that is the Church. All the baptized need continual "pruning" if we are to remain fruitful. And none of us can go it alone. We must "intertwine" and support one another by our love if we are to "remain in him" and bear the fruit of the vine.

CONSIDER/ DISCUSS:
- How do the characters and events in today's reading from Acts resemble a vineyard?
- What supports you as you try to "remain in" Christ?
- What fruit is Christ ripening and bearing through you?

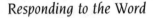 *Responding to the Word*

The "wine" we share in the Eucharist is the fruit of the one true vine, Jesus Christ. We are privileged to receive it thanks to the work of generations of "branches" like Paul, who remained in Christ, bore fruit, and supported new branches as they grew strong in faith. May the premier vintage of the Eucharist fill us with the spiritual life that flows through the vine and the branches of Christ.

- Consciously drink in Christ's life when you share the Blood of Christ.
- Ask Christ to make your words and deeds bear plentiful fruit.
- Witness Christ's love by a word or a deed today.

May 25, 2003

SIXTH SUNDAY OF EASTER

Today's Focus: Love One Another

In Jesus' command today to "love one another" we are met with an extraordinary challenge. Yes, we are to love those in our family, those we work with, those we like. But we are also to love those we never notice, those we purposely avoid, and even those we are tempted to despise.

FIRST READING
Acts 10:25–26, 34–35, 44–48

When Peter entered, Cornelius met him and, falling at his feet, paid him homage. Peter, however, raised him up, saying, "Get up. I myself am also a human being."

Then Peter proceeded to speak and said, "In truth, I see that God shows no partiality. Rather, in every nation whoever fears him and acts uprightly is acceptable to him."

While Peter was still speaking these things, the Holy Spirit fell upon all who were listening to the word. The circumcised believers who had accompanied Peter were astounded that the gift of the Holy Spirit should have been poured out on the Gentiles also, for they could hear them speaking in tongues and glorifying God. Then Peter responded, "Can anyone withhold the water for baptizing these people, who have received the Holy Spirit even as we have?" He ordered them to be baptized in the name of Jesus Christ.

PSALM RESPONSE
Psalm 98:2b

The Lord has revealed to the nations his saving power.

SECOND READING
1 John 4:7–10

Beloved, let us love one another, because love is of God; everyone who loves is begotten by God and knows God. Whoever is without love does not know God, for God is love. In this way the love of God was revealed to us: God sent his only Son into the world so that we might have life through him. In this is love: not that we have loved God, but that he loved us and sent his Son as expiation for our sins.

GOSPEL
John 15:9–17

Jesus said to his disciples: "As the Father loves me, so I also love you. Remain in my love. If you keep my commandments, you will remain in my love, just as I have kept my Father's commandments and remain in his love.

"I have told you this so that my joy may be in you and your joy might be complete. This is my commandment: love one another as I love you. No one has greater love than this, to lay down one's life for one's friends. You are my friends if you do what I command you. I no longer call you slaves, because a slave does not know what his master is doing. I have called you friends, because I have told you everything I have heard from my Father. It was not you who chose me, but I who chose you and appointed you to go and bear fruit that will remain, so that whatever you ask the Father in my name he may give you. This I command you: love one another."

Understanding the Word

The scene described in today's first reading from chapter 10 of the Acts of the Apostles is sometimes referred to as the "Gentile Pentecost," parallel in many ways to the momentous importance of the "Jewish Pentecost" described at the beginnings of Acts. The continuing importance of this event for us today is signaled by the fact that we have already heard a segment of the speech Peter gave on this occasion as the first reading of Easter Sunday, and now we return to another narrative of the events that unfolded in the home of the Gentile Cornelius.

Scripture scholars point out the importance of geography in the two-volume work of Luke-Acts. In his Gospel, Luke narrates the long journey of Jesus to Jerusalem, the symbolic center of his ministry and, of course, the place where the saving events of his death and resurrection fulfill his destiny. Then, as he ascends to heaven at the beginning of Acts (verse 8), Jesus sends his disciples out to preach the Good News, first in Jerusalem (as described in chapters 1–7), then in Judea and Samaria (chapters 8–9), and finally "to the ends of the earth" (chapters 10–28). The events narrated in chapter 10 mark a decisive turning point in the mission of the young Church, as it begins the process of announcing the Good News of Jesus' death and resurrection outside the confines of Judaism.

The conversion of Cornelius is clearly a momentous shift for the apostolic community, and Luke makes certain that the reader understands it as the work of the Holy Spirit. In order to underline its importance, Luke returns to this event in the subsequent chapter of Acts and again in chapter 15, where he recounts the decisions taken at the Council of Jerusalem. What could have remained a small Jewish sect was to become a world religion, offering salvation to every person on earth, thanks to this event that shattered the narrow preconceptions of the first disciples.

122

Today's Scriptures tell us that "God is love" and that "God shows no partiality." Jesus showed us that God's love for humanity extends to all the ends of the earth. No longer can one group of people claim to deserve or receive the love of God more than another. No one is worthy of such great love.

In response to God's love Jesus commands us to "love one another as I have loved you." What might that kind of love look like? Jews give up their age-old disdain for Gentiles. A rural parish goes out of its way to welcome migrant workers into the community. Neighbors join together to repair each other's homes. Tons of food, clothing, and supplies are sent to people in need. A couple adopts orphaned siblings. A mother reconciles with her homosexual son. A father confronts his daughter with her drug addiction. A lawyer takes a cut in pay to defend the poor. A soldier gives his life in battle.

CONSIDER/ DISCUSS:
- What phrases in today's Scriptures best reveal God's love to you? How do you feel when you hear those words?

- What incident can you recall when someone did something difficult out of love?

- Whom are you being challenged to love better today?

Responding to the Word

Last week we heard about branches that remain in God's love and bear fruit. Today's Gospel again challenges the baptized to "bear fruit that will remain," the fruit of love. When we truly love, others know we love them by our attitude and our actions. Like spring flowers, they blossom under the warmth of our love. How do those around you experience your love for them? How is God's love bearing fruit in you?

- Reach out to someone you have been avoiding.

- Let go of a negative assumption about a group of people who are different from you.

- Support or work at a local charity this week.

May 29, 2003

THE ASCENSION
OF THE LORD

Many archdioceses and dioceses celebrate The Ascension on June 1, replacing the Seventh Sunday of Easter

Today's Focus: Mission Statement

Does your parish or corporation have a mission statement? Does it help you to set priorities and focus your activities? Today's Scriptures give us a concise statement of the mission of the Church of Jesus Christ. It can guide and support us as we strive to continue Christ's messianic mission on earth.

FIRST READING
Acts 1:1–11

In the first book, Theophilus, I dealt with all that Jesus did and taught until the day he was taken up, after giving instructions through the Holy Spirit to the apostles whom he had chosen. He presented himself alive to them by many proofs after he had suffered, appearing to them during forty days and speaking about the kingdom of God. While meeting with them, he enjoined them not to depart from Jerusalem, but to wait for "the promise of the Father about which you have heard me speak; for John baptized with water, but in a few days you will be baptized with the Holy Spirit."

When they had gathered together they asked him, "Lord, are you at this time going to restore the kingdom to Israel?" He answered them, "It is not for you to know the times or seasons that the Father has established by his own authority. But you will receive power when the Holy Spirit comes upon you, and you will be my witnesses in Jerusalem, throughout Judea and Samaria, and to the ends of the earth." When he had said this, as they were looking on, he was lifted up, and a cloud took him from their sight. While they were looking intently at the sky as he was going, suddenly two men dressed in white garments stood beside them. They said, "Men of Galilee, why are you standing there looking at the sky? This Jesus who has been taken up from you into heaven will return in the same way as you have seen him going into heaven."

PSALM RESPONSE
Psalm 47:6

God mounts his throne to shouts of joy: a blare of trumpets for the Lord.

SECOND READING
Ephesians 1: 17–23

Brothers and sisters: May the God of our Lord Jesus Christ, the Father of glory, give you a Spirit of wisdom and revelation resulting in knowledge of him. May the eyes of your hearts be enlightened, that you may know what is the hope that belongs to his call, what are the riches of glory in his inheritance among the holy ones, and what is the surpassing greatness of his power for us who believe, in accord with the exercise of his great might, which he worked in Christ, raising him from the dead and seating him at his right hand in the heavens, far above every principality, authority, power, and dominion, and every name that is named not only in this age but also in the one to come. And he put all things beneath his feet and gave him as head over all things to the church, which is his body, the fullness of the one who fills all things in every way.

– or –

In the shorter form of the reading, the passage in brackets is omitted.

SECOND READING
Ephesians 4: 1–13 or 4:1–7, 11–13

Brothers and sisters, I, a prisoner for the Lord, urge you to live in a manner worthy of the call you have received, with all humility and gentleness, with patience, bearing with one another through love, striving to preserve the unity of the spirit through the bond of peace: one body and one Spirit, as you were also called to the one hope of your calling; one Lord, one faith, one baptism; one God and Father of all, who is over all and through all and in all.

But grace was given to each of us according to the measure of Christ's gift. [Therefore, it says:
He *ascended on high and took prisoners captive;*
he gave gifts to men.

What does "he ascended" mean except that he also descended into the lower regions of the earth? The one who descended is also the one who ascended far above all the heavens, that he might fill all things.]

And he gave some as apostles, others as prophets, others as evangelists, others as pastors and teachers, to equip the holy ones for the work of ministry, for building up the body of Christ, until we all attain to the unity of faith and knowledge of the Son of God, to mature manhood, to the extent of the full stature of Christ.

GOSPEL
Mark 16:15–20

Jesus said to his disciples: "Go into the whole world and proclaim the gospel to every creature. Whoever believes and is baptized will be saved; whoever does not believe will be condemned. These signs will accompany those who believe: in my name they will drive out demons, they will speak new languages. They will pick up serpents with their hands, and if they drink any deadly thing, it will not harm them. They will lay hands on the sick, and they will recover."

So then the Lord Jesus, after he spoke to them, was taken up into heaven and took his seat at the right hand of God. But they went forth and preached everywhere, while the Lord worked with them and confirmed the word through accompanying signs.

It may surprise some to know that in the earliest narratives of the events surrounding Jesus' death and resurrection, no distinction is made between his resurrection and his ascension. Their theological unity, or perhaps even the temporal experience of the early community, made it seem that the two were inseparable aspects of a single mystery. It is only in the later writings of Luke and John that further theological reflection has helped the Christian community to distinguish different dimensions of the mystery. Liturgical tradition has followed the forty-day chronology formulated by Luke. We would miss the point, however, if we were to demand a precise historical chronology of events such as the Resurrection-Ascension that are primarily spiritual in nature and that clearly surpass the bounds of time and space as we know them.

What is important for us to grasp is the meaning, the significance, of the Ascension, and Luke's carefully developed narrative structure offers us valuable insights into his own reflections in that regard. Luke's description of the Ascension in today's first reading from Acts is a deliberate parallel to the opening verses of his Gospel. The recurrence of key themes in both volumes of Luke's work is not coincidental. The baptism of Jesus in the Gospel is paralleled by the disciples' baptism with the Spirit at Pentecost. Jesus' forty days in the desert that prepared him for his mission are paralleled by his forty days with the disciples after the Resurrection, in which he prepares them for their mission. At the conclusion of Luke's Gospel, Jesus commands the disciples to witness to all nations; here, the command is repeated in virtually the same words. And the Gospel's description of the final return of Jesus is echoed here in a description of his Ascension with matching imagery.

All of this carefully orchestrated parallelism is used by Luke to drive home the significance of the Ascension. For Luke, it is the decisive turning point that marks the end of Jesus' earthly ministry and the beginning of the disciples' Spirit-led ministry.

Reflecting on the Word

These days most corporations and churches have vision and mission statements. Often they begin with a model vision that the institution strives to live up to. They go on to state what the institution seeks to do—how it puts its vision into practice. A parish vision and mission statement might say: "We are the Body of Christ. Utilizing the gifts of each member, we collaborate to bring more and more people into God's kingdom of freedom, justice, holiness, and love."

On this feast we are given the ultimate vision and mission statement for the Church. It goes something like this: Christ is now working with and for us "at the right hand of God." Through the power of the Holy Spirit we are to be Christ's witnesses "to the ends of the earth." We seek to do so by "proclaiming the gospel to every creature" and "building up the body of Christ until we all attain the unity of faith and knowledge of the Son of God."

- What useful mission statements have you come in contact with?
- How might today's Scriptures help you set priorities or make decisions in your life?
- What part of the above mission statement is hardest for you to buy into? Why?

Responding to the Word

How many CEOs would have the courage to leave their corporation and trust the employees to run things in their absence? That seems to be just what Christ does in today's readings. Considering the two-thousand-year history of the Church, many would question the wisdom of his decision! And yet, Christ knew that the Spirit would always guide the Church in continuing his messianic mission.

- Listen for the Holy Spirit to guide your actions this week.
- Speak good news to someone who needs to hear it.
- Build up your parish by introducing yourself to someone or by offering to share your time or talent.

June 1, 2003

SEVENTH SUNDAY OF EASTER

Today's Focus: Sacred and Secular

It's easy to think of holy people, sacred places and things as set apart from the secular world. Yet we cannot hear today's Scriptures without realizing that God's holy people belong in the midst of the world, where they can reveal the love of God that makes all the world sacred.

FIRST READING
Acts 1:15–17, 20a, 20c–26

Peter stood up in the midst of the brothers — there was a group of about one hundred and twenty persons in the one place —. He said, "My brothers, the Scripture had to be fulfilled which the Holy Spirit spoke beforehand through the mouth of David, concerning Judas, who was the guide for those who arrested Jesus. He was numbered among us and was allotted a share in this ministry.

"For it is written in the Book of Psalms:
May another take his office.

"Therefore, it is necessary that one of the men who accompanied us the whole time the Lord Jesus came and went among us, beginning from the baptism of John until the day on which he was taken up from us, become with us a witness to his resurrection." So they proposed two, Judas called Barsabbas, who was also known as Justus, and Matthias. Then they prayed, "You, Lord, who know the hearts of all, show which one of these two you have chosen to take the place in this apostolic ministry from which Judas turned away to go to his own place." Then they gave lots to them, and the lot fell upon Matthias, and he was counted with the eleven apostles.

PSALM RESPONSE
Psalm 103:19a

The Lord has set his throne in heaven.

SECOND READING
1 John 4:11–16

Beloved, if God so loved us, we also must love one another. No one has ever seen God. Yet, if we love one another, God remains in us, and his love is brought to perfection in us.

This is how we know that we remain in him and he in us, that he has given us of his Spirit. Moreover, we have seen and testify that the Father sent his Son as savior of the world. Whoever acknowledges that Jesus is the Son of God, God remains in him and he in God. We have come to know and to believe in the love God has for us.

God is love, and whoever remains in love remains in God and God in him.

GOSPEL

John 17:11b–19

Lifting up his eyes to heaven, Jesus prayed, saying: "Holy Father, keep them in your name that you have given me, so that they may be one just as we are one. When I was with them I protected them in your name that you gave me, and I guarded them, and none of them was lost except the son of destruction, in order that the Scripture might be fulfilled. But now I am coming to you. I speak this in the world so that they may share my joy completely. I gave them your word, and the world hated them, because they do not belong to the world any more than I belong to the world. I do not ask that you take them out of the world but that you keep them from the evil one. They do not belong to the world any more than I belong to the world. Consecrate them in the truth. Your word is truth. As you sent me into the world, so I sent them into the world. And I consecrate myself for them, so that they also may be consecrated in truth."

Understanding the Word

In the Gospel of John, the Last Supper is the setting for a formal discourse of Jesus that Scripture scholars have referred to as the "high priestly prayer." After speaking to his assembled disciples, Jesus is portrayed as addressing his Father in a long and carefully constructed prayer. Recent scholarship has noted remarkable similarities between the form of this prayer and ancient (as well as contemporary) Eucharistic Prayers used at Mass. In our Eucharistic Prayers, the gifts of bread and wine are consecrated—that is, transformed—so that they become effective instruments communicating God's love to the world. Our liturgical tradition helps us understand how the subjects of the prayer in today's Gospel— the disciples themselves—were similarly "consecrated" in God's service by Jesus so that they might become effective instruments communicating God's love to the world.

Traditional theological language used to say that Jesus established the sacrament of Holy Orders at the Last Supper by ordaining the apostles. That language may have had a certain anachronistic naiveté, but its core truth seems substantiated by today's understanding of the nature of the high priestly prayer of Jesus that John has constructed here. The time between the Ascension and Pentecost focuses on the mission of the disciples, and John's Gospel provides us with yet another example of how that "commissioning" of the disciples was remembered and celebrated in the early community.

The account of the selection of Matthias to replace Judas that is contained in today's first reading from Acts is consistent with this focus. In what is clearly meant to be recognized as a kind of liturgical assembly, the Holy Spirit is invoked to identify and then "mission" Matthias for the apostolic ministry. That ministry is specified by Peter, who says that a successor to Judas is needed to "become with us a witness to [the Lord Jesus'] resurrection."

Ordained bishops and priests. Consecrated brothers and sisters. As children, many of us thought of them as different from us, not even human. Even now, as adults, some of us may tend to think of them as leading their holy lives set apart from the rest of humanity, communing only with God in prayer.

Today's readings should convince us that it isn't an either/or choice. And priests and sisters aren't the only ones who are holy. All Christians are the Elect, God's holy, chosen people. We who "have come to know and to believe in the love God has for us" have indeed had our lives transformed, or consecrated, by this firsthand knowledge. Yet, our special status should not separate us from secular concerns or from human relationships. We are called to live holy lives within the world, consecrating the world by our acts of love. We are sent into the world just as Christ was—to witness the truth of God's love that alone blesses the whole world and makes each human life holy.

CONSIDER/ DISCUSS:
- How might Judas (also known as Barsabbas or Justus) have been feeling in today's first reading?

- Does it help you to pray about your decisions or concerns? Explain.

- How has God's love consecrated or transformed your life?

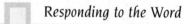

Responding to the Word

While there are many ways in which we could allow God's love to penetrate the world around us, it's often easier simply to keep it between "me and Jesus." Separating religion from politics, Christian values from the competitive world, worship from real life is the easy way out. This week how might you let your experience of the sacred more deeply influence your secular decisions and actions?

- Pray about a decision or a worry that is weighing you down.

- Look for a way to bless a coworker's or friend's life by an act of love this week.

- Call a government representative to express your opinion about a pressing social issue.

June 8, 2003

PENTECOST SUNDAY

Today's Focus: Turning Fifty

Fifty days after Easter Sunday we celebrate the fulfillment of all God's promises in the feast of Pentecost. Like those who celebrate their fiftieth birthday, we can spend today looking back at the past with regret or embracing the fullness of the Spirit's fruits that have matured in us over time.

FIRST READING
Acts 2:1–11

When the time for Pentecost was fulfilled, they were all in one place together. And suddenly there came from the sky a noise like a strong driving wind, and it filled the entire house in which they were. Then there appeared to them tongues as of fire, which parted and came to rest on each one of them. And they were all filled with the Holy Spirit and began to speak in different tongues, as the Spirit enabled them to proclaim.

Now there were devout Jews from every nation under heaven staying in Jerusalem. At this sound, they gathered in a large crowd, but they were confused because each one heard them speaking in his own language. They were astounded, and in amazement they asked, "Are not all these people who are speaking Galileans? Then how does each of us hear them in his native language? We are Parthians, Medes, and Elamites, inhabitants of Mesopotamia, Judea and Cappadocia, Pontus and Asia, Phrygia and Pamphylia, Egypt and the districts of Libya near Cyrene, as well as travelers from Rome, both Jews and converts to Judaism, Cretans and Arabs, yet we hear them speaking in our own tongues of the mighty acts of God."

PSALM RESPONSE
Psalm 104:30

Lord, send out your Spirit, and renew the face of the earth.

SECOND READING
1 Corinthians 12: 3b–7, 12–13

Brothers and sisters: No one can say, "Jesus is Lord," except by the Holy Spirit. There are different kinds of spiritual gifts but the same Spirit; there are different forms of service but the same Lord; there are different workings but the same God who produces all of them in everyone. To each individual the manifestation of the Spirit is given for some benefit.

As a body is one though it has many parts, and all the parts of the body, though many, are one body, so also Christ. For in one Spirit we were all baptized into one body, whether Jews or Greeks, slaves or free persons, and we were all given to drink of one Spirit.

– or –

Galatians 5:
16–25

Brothers and sisters, live by the Spirit and you will certainly not gratify the desire of the flesh. For the flesh has desires against the Spirit, and the Spirit against the flesh; these are opposed to each other, so that you may not do what you want. But if you are guided by the Spirit, you are not under the law. Now the works of the flesh are obvious: immorality, impurity, lust, idolatry, sorcery, hatreds, rivalry, jealousy, outbursts of fury, acts of selfishness, dissensions, factions, occasions of envy, drinking bouts, orgies, and the like. I warn you, as I warned you before, that those who do such things will not inherit the kingdom of God. In contrast, the fruit of the Spirit is love, joy, peace, patience, kindness, generosity, faithfulness, gentleness, self-control. Against such there is no law. Now those who belong to Christ Jesus have crucified their flesh with its passions and desires. If we live in the Spirit, let us also follow the Spirit.

GOSPEL
John 20:19–23

On the evening of that first day of the week, when the doors were locked, where the disciples were, for fear of the Jews, Jesus came and stood in their midst and said to them, "Peace be with you." When he had said this, he showed them his hands and his side. The disciples rejoiced when they saw the Lord. Jesus said to them again, "Peace be with you. As the Father has sent me, so I send you." And when he had said this, he breathed on them and said to them, "Receive the Holy Spirit. Whose sins you forgive are forgiven them, and whose sins you retain are retained."

– or –

John 15:26–27;
16:12–15

Jesus said to his disciples: "When the Advocate comes whom I will send you from the Father, the Spirit of truth that proceeds from the Father, he will testify to me. And you also testify, because you have been with me from the beginning.

"I have much more to tell you, but you cannot bear it now. But when he comes, the Spirit of truth, he will guide you to all truth. He will not speak on his own, but he will speak what he hears, and will declare to you the things that are coming. He will glorify me, because he will take from what is mine and declare it to you. Everything that the Father has is mine; for this reason I told you that he will take from what is mine and declare it to you."

Understanding the Word

Throughout the Easter season we have frequently noted the care with which Luke has constructed what might seem to be nothing more than simple recollections of events. More often than not, however, we have discovered the theological purpose at work in Luke's narratives by examining subtle allusions to other parts of sacred Scripture or even parallels within his own two-volume composition. Today's narrative from Acts is no exception to this pattern.

The readings from the Jewish Scriptures that the Lectionary uses for the Vigil Mass of Pentecost are all present in the background of Luke's story of the first Christian Pentecost. By subtle allusion and the use of familiar imagery and language, Luke evokes the story of the tower of Babel from Genesis 11, the appearance of God to Moses on Mount Sinai from Exodus 19, the gift of the Spirit in the vision of dry bones from Ezekiel 37, and Joel's prophecy of the Spirit being poured out on all flesh. Luke brings all of these themes together by situating the gift of the Holy Spirit to the believers on the Jewish feast of Pentecost.

In Luke's day Jews observed the fiftieth day after Passover as a harvest festival that was long associated with the gift of the Law at Sinai. Jewish tradition spoke of the seven weeks in the desert between the departure from Egypt and the arrival at Sinai as a time of moral formation, much as Luke's Gospel described Jesus' work with the disciples in the weeks following his resurrection. Some Jewish sects in Luke's day also used this feast as a time to admit new members. Thus, we see how rich is the confluence of themes in Luke's narrative of the events in Jerusalem on the first Christian Pentecost: Babel's divisions are overcome, a new Law/Covenant is given, the life-giving Spirit promised of old is poured out on all people, and a rich period of formation culminates with the initiation of new members into life in the Spirit.

Reflecting on the Word

When Gary walked into the restaurant he had no idea that all his family and friends would be there to shout, "Surprise! Happy fiftieth birthday!" The party began with lots of kidding about his fading youth and failing manhood. But as the evening progressed he realized how lucky he was to celebrate so much growth in his first fifty years. There was a sense of fulfillment about turning fifty. He could happily let go of earlier notions of who he ought to be and embrace with gratitude the fruits of maturity.

Today's Scriptures overflow with a sense of fulfillment. In Luke's Pentecost account all God's promises seem to be "fulfilled." The disciples receive a level of maturity that allows them to leave behind their earlier fears and illusions. They can embrace with confidence "the fruit of the Spirit" that has ripened in them: "love, joy, peace, patience, kindness, generosity, faithfulness, gentleness, self-control."

**CONSIDER/
DISCUSS:** • What do you imagine the disciples were feeling when they were filled with the Holy Spirit?

• Would you say that you have you received the Holy Spirit? Explain.

• How has your faith matured over the years?

 Responding to the Word

The feast of Pentecost reminds us that the Lord is continually sending out the Spirit to "renew the face of the earth." That Spirit is available to help us let go of all that hinders us from "liv[ing] by the Spirit." This fiftieth day of Easter is a time to forget the mistakes we've made and the activities we've left behind. It's an opportunity to receive once again the fruits of the Spirit and put them to good use.

• During Sunday liturgy ask the Spirit to fill you with one of the fruits listed in Galatians.

• Become aware of how you use your greatest spiritual gift.

• Give thanks for one way in which you have matured as a Christian.

Introduction to Ordinary Time II

It has been more than three months since we left Ordinary Time for the Great Ninety Days of Lent-Easter. This week we resume the eleventh week of Ordinary Time. However, the Sundays of Ordinary Time are replaced for the next three weeks with special celebrations that take precedence over the Sunday observances. We celebrate first the solemnity of the Most Holy Trinity, then the Most Holy Body and Blood of Christ, and finally the feast of Saints Peter and Paul, Apostles. After that, we resume with the Fourteenth Sunday and then continue (except for the feasts of the Holy Cross and the Dedication of the Lateran Basilica, September 14 and November 9) with Sundays of Ordinary Time until the end of November.

We noted earlier in the year that Year B of the Lectionary cycle uses the Gospel of Mark as its anchor. We will resume reading from Mark's Gospel on the Fourteenth Sunday, but after only three weeks the Markan lections are interrupted by a five-week series of texts from Chapter 6 of John's Gospel (the Bread of Life discourse). After that, the readings from Mark continue to the end of the year. Throughout the remaining weeks of Year B the first reading will, as usual, be chosen in order to prepare for or support some theme found in the day's Gospel. The second reading will also follow the familiar pattern of an independent sequence of readings from the New Testament, first from the Pauline corpus (2 Corinthians and Ephesians), then from James and Hebrews. Thus does the Lectionary respond to the mandate of the Second Vatican Council that we should be given a richer diet of Scripture by readings that open up more of the treasures of the Bible on a regular basis.

The choice of semi-continuous readings for the New Testament and Gospel readings allows us to explore in more depth recurring themes and particular viewpoints of a specific author as we trace the development of ideas in a biblical book over a period of weeks. Some have regretted that a similar option (i.e., semi-continuous readings) was not made with regard to the selection of first readings. The Jewish Scriptures could then be similarly appreciated from the viewpoint of recurring themes and the unique perspectives of the various authors. One drawback to the current way of selecting the first reading in conjunction with the Gospel is that it might appear that the Jewish Scriptures only have value or meaning in relation to the Christian Scriptures. While it is true that we regard the Christ-event as the heart of all revelation, we also continue to respect the integrity and revelatory value of each and every book of the Bible, both Old and New Testaments. It is to be hoped that this esteem for the books of the Jewish Scriptures will be conveyed on those weeks when we choose to focus our commentaries and reflections on the first reading alone.

June 15, 2003

THE MOST HOLY TRINITY

Today's Focus: The Name of God

For most of us the concept of one God with three names is simply incomprehensible. Yet it is core to Christian faith and prayer. Perhaps the mystery of the Trinity that we celebrate today can only be grasped through a lifetime of experiencing the intimate love of God.

FIRST READING
Deuteronomy 4: 32–34, 39–40

Moses said to the people: "Ask now of the days of old, before your time, ever since God created man upon the earth; ask from one end of the sky to the other: Did anything so great ever happen before? Was it ever heard of? Did a people ever hear the voice of God speaking from the midst of fire, as you did, and live? Or did any god venture to go and take a nation for himself from the midst of another nation, by testings, by signs and wonders, by war, with strong hand and outstretched arm, and by great terrors, all of which the LORD, your God, did for you in Egypt before your very eyes? This is why you must now know, and fix in your heart, that the LORD is God in the heavens above and on earth below, and that there is no other. You must keep his statutes and commandments that I enjoin on you today, that you and your children after you may prosper, and that you may have long life on the land which the LORD, your God, is giving you forever."

PSALM RESPONSE
Psalm 33:12b

Blessed the people the Lord has chosen to be his own.

SECOND READING
Romans 8: 14–17

Brothers and sisters: Those who are led by the Spirit of God are sons of God. For you did not receive a spirit of slavery to fall back into fear, but you received a Spirit of adoption, through whom we cry, "Abba, Father!" The Spirit himself bears witness with our spirit that we are children of God, and if children, then heirs, heirs of God and joint heirs with Christ, if only we suffer with him so that we may also be glorified with him.

GOSPEL
Matthew 28: 16–20

The eleven disciples went to Galilee, to the mountain to which Jesus had ordered them. When they all saw him, they worshiped, but they doubted. Then Jesus approached and said to them, "All power in heaven and on earth has been given to me. Go, therefore, and make disciples of all nations, baptizing them in the name of the Father, and of the Son, and of the Holy Spirit, teaching them to observe all that I have commanded you. And behold, I am with you always, until the end of the age."

Understanding the Word

It is the business of theologians to speculate about the inner life of the Divinity, to make nuanced statements about categories such as persons, relationships, essence, and existence. But the language and *modus operandi* of the Scriptures is quite otherwise, as today's liturgical feast of the Holy Trinity amply demonstrates. Sacred Scripture, in addition to being the source of divine revelation, is a record of human experience, the faith-experience of our ancestors who encountered God in manifold ways, reflected on that encounter, and then committed to writing some measure of their experience.

Each of today's readings, then, is a written record of a human encounter with incomprehensible Mystery. Each in its own way puts into human words a faint reflection of the God whom we Christians have come to know and recognize and name as Father, Son, and Holy Spirit. The words of Jesus at the end of the Gospel of Matthew are a command to propagate throughout the world the three-fold experience of God that is uniquely ours as Christians. By commanding his disciples to baptize "in the name of the Father, and of the Son, and of the Holy Spirit," Jesus asks that what he has revealed about the inner life of the deity and has made available through our encounter with his humanity might be shared with people everywhere.

Paul's Letter to the Romans witnesses to the way that he, and we, have come to know this triune God. By virtue of our own inner experience of the Spirit, we have been put into intimate relationship with God, an intimacy expressed in the familiar term of endearment, "Abba," with which we dare to address God. In that intimate relationship we have experienced ourselves as God's children in solidarity with Christ. In fact, it is precisely our having been joined to Christ through receiving his Spirit in baptism that makes us know ourselves in a new way, as children of God.

Reflecting on the Word

If it takes a lifetime of intimacy to truly know the mystery of one's spouse, parent, or child, then surely it will take an eternity to get to know the mysterious God whom Christians name "Father, Son, and Holy Spirit." Yes, this God created and sustains the universe, and liberated and forms the chosen people, as today's first reading and psalm celebrate. But God also shared in our human life and death so that we might share in divine life here and now and forever. The full extent of God's identity with and intimate love for humanity was revealed on the cross.

God's desire for an intimate relationship with us is manifested again today in Christ's promise to be "with [us] always, even to the end of the age," and in the knowledge that we have received within ourselves "the Spirit of God" to lead us to our inheritance—an eternity of intimacy with God. Moses' questions could apply to us: "Did anything so great ever happen before? Was it ever heard of?" The name and the love of the Trinity cannot be fully understood, only experienced.

CONSIDER/ DISCUSS:
- When have you sensed God's presence with or within you?
- To which person of the Trinity do you pray most often? Why?
- Do you sometimes feel you keep God at arm's length? Explain.

 Responding to the Word

At the beginning and end of the Eucharist—and every prayer—Catholics make the sign of the cross, repeating the words with which we were baptized: "In the name of the Father and of the Son and of the Holy Spirit." When we make the sign of the cross we reclaim our inheritance as children of "Abba" and sisters and brothers of Christ through the Spirit that now dwells within us. We etch the mysterious name of God—and love of God—ever more deeply into our bodies and our lives.

- Let the name of God penetrate your being whenever you make the sign of the cross.
- Find a special way to honor your human father this week.
- Choose one of Christ's commands to observe more closely today.

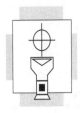

June 22, 2003

THE MOST HOLY
BODY AND BLOOD OF CHRIST

Today's Focus: Blood Sisters

Sometimes girlfriends will prick their fingers, touch them together and make a pact to be forever faithful "blood sisters." The feast of the Body and Blood of Christ reminds us of a solemn pact—the covenant Christ made with us and we make with Christ every time we share in the cup of the Eucharist.

FIRST READING
Exodus 24:3–8

When Moses came to the people and related all the words and ordinances of the LORD, they all answered with one voice, "We will do everything that the LORD has told us." Moses then wrote down all the words of the LORD and, rising early the next day, he erected at the foot of the mountain an altar and twelve pillars for the twelve tribes of Israel. Then, having sent certain young men of the Israelites to offer holocausts and sacrifice young bulls as peace offerings to the LORD, Moses took half of the blood and put it in large bowls; the other half he splashed on the altar. Taking the book of the covenant, he read it aloud to the people, who answered, "All that the LORD has said, we will heed and do." Then he took the blood and sprinkled it on the people, saying, "This is the blood of the covenant that the LORD has made with you in accordance with all these words of his."

PSALM RESPONSE
Psalm 116:13

I will take the cup of salvation, and call on the name of the LORD.

SECOND READING
Hebrews 9: 11–15

Brothers and sisters: When Christ came as high priest of the good things that have come to be, passing through the greater and more perfect tabernacle not made by hands, that is, not belonging to this creation, he entered once for all into the sanctuary, not with the blood of goats and calves but with his own blood, thus obtaining eternal redemption. For if the blood of goats and bulls and the sprinkling of a heifer's ashes can sanctify those who are defiled so that their flesh is cleansed, how much more will the blood of Christ, who through the eternal Spirit offered himself unblemished to God, cleanse our consciences from dead works to worship the living God.

For this reason he is mediator of a new covenant: since a death has taken place for deliverance from transgressions under the first covenant, those who are called may receive the promised eternal inheritance.

GOSPEL
Mark 14:
12–16, 22–26

On the first day of the Feast of Unleavened Bread, when they sacrificed the Passover lamb, Jesus' disciples said to him, "Where do you want us to go and prepare for you to eat the Passover?" He sent two of his disciples and said to them, "Go into the city and a man will meet you, carrying a jar of water. Follow him. Wherever he enters, say to the master of the house, 'The Teacher says, "Where is my guest room where I may eat the Passover with my disciples?"' Then he will show you a large upper room furnished and ready. Make the preparations for us there." The disciples then went off, entered the city, and found it just as he had told them; and they prepared the Passover.

While they were eating, he took bread, said the blessing, broke it, gave it to them, and said, "Take it; this is my body." Then he took a cup, gave thanks, and gave it to them, and they all drank from it. He said to them, "This is my blood of the covenant, which will be shed for many. Amen, I say to you, I shall not drink again the fruit of the vine until the day when I drink it new in the kingdom of God." Then, after singing a hymn, they went out to the Mount of Olives.

Understanding the Word

All three of today's readings refer to the blood of sacrifice, but each does so in its own particular way. In order to understand fully the feast of the Body and Blood of Christ, one must recognize that what we celebrate today is more than just our contemporary doctrine of the Real Presence. By exploring the Jewish roots of the notion of blood sacrifice, we should have a fuller understanding of the mystery of Jesus' blood shed for our salvation.

In the world of the ancient Jews, a covenant was a legally binding bilateral contract, often sealed with a ritual that bound the participants in a solemn fashion to the terms of the agreement. Today's reading from Exodus describes how the covenant between God and the Jewish people was ratified in blood. For the Jews, blood was the source of the life force, and to share blood was to share life. Thus, the ritual that involved blood sprinkled on both the altar (representing God) and the people indicated that the two shared a common life. The Covenant was not merely a legal contract, but a bond that had been forged between the Lord and the people at the deepest level. The decisive nature of the rite described in this passage is evident from the fact that it was not subsequently repeated, despite the fact that the Covenant was renewed at various times in Israel's history.

The blood ritual referred to in the second reading is the annual sacrifice performed on the Day of Atonement. On that day the high priest took the blood of a slaughtered animal and sprinkled it on the Ark of the Covenant in the holy of holies. The purpose of the ritual was to invoke God's forgiveness for the sins of the people and to renew their convenantal relationship with the Lord. The author of Hebrews uses this imagery to insist on the superiority of Christ's sacrificial death, through which the new covenant has been forged and our sins forgiven once and for all. The Gospel records Jesus' own words that portray his death as blood shed for the sake of the new and eternal covenant.

Jenna and Clarise ran away from the house, hand in hand, hoping no one would follow them into the woods to their secret place. Their hearts were pounding. "It's going to hurt. A lot." "I know. But it's worth it. Being friends just isn't enough. We need to be sisters." "Ready?" "Ouch!" "Now touch." And together they chanted, "Blood sisters. Faithful forever. You can always count on me."

Today's focus on blood sacrificed and the new covenant are enough to shake up our warm fuzzy notions about receiving Communion. When the disciples drank from the cup of Christ's blood they entered into a solemn pact with Jesus, a new covenant to love others as Jesus loved them. We do the same. Each time we drink in the Real Presence of Christ we recommit ourselves to sacrifice our lives for one another in Christ's name.

CONSIDER/
DISCUSS:

- How did you feel when you read today's Scriptures?
- Does receiving Communion comfort or challenge you? Explain.
- Do you receive Communion from the cup? Why or why not?

■ *Responding to the Word*

Who are the "many" for whom Christ's blood was shed? Maybe the "many" includes those who are suffering today, as Christ once suffered. Maybe the best way to be faithful to our covenant in Christ's blood is to sacrifice our comfort and reach out to the oppressed whom the psalmist calls "precious in the eyes of the Lord." Maybe we can't keep the covenant without recognizing our responsibility to all our "blood" brothers and sisters in Christ.

- As you watch people receive Communion, see them as your blood brothers and sisters.
- Sacrifice your own desires or comfort to meet someone else's needs.
- Recognize and respond to a specific case of human suffering in the world.

June 29, 2003

SAINTS PETER AND PAUL, APOSTLES

Today's Focus: Fraternal Twins

Fraternal twins may not look alike or always agree, but often they share a devotion to one another that binds them together throughout their lives. Saints Peter and Paul, our twin ancestors in faith, went separate ways and yet shared a lifelong devotion to Christ's Church that bound together the burgeoning Christian community.

FIRST READING
Acts 12:1–11

In those days, King Herod laid hands upon some members of the church to harm them. He had James, the brother of John, killed by the sword, and when he saw that this was pleasing to the Jews he proceeded to arrest Peter also. — It was the feast of Unleavened Bread. — He had him taken into custody and put in prison under the guard of four squads of four soldiers each. He intended to bring him before the people after Passover. Peter thus was being kept in prison, but prayer by the church was fervently being made to God on his behalf.

On the very night before Herod was to bring him to trial, Peter, secured by double chains, was sleeping between two soldiers, while outside the door guards kept watch on the prison. Suddenly the angel of the Lord stood by him and a light shone in the cell. He tapped Peter on the side and awakened him, saying, "Get up quickly ." The chains fell from his wrists. The angel said to him, "Put on your belt and your sandals." He did so. Then he said to him, "Put on your cloak and follow me." So he followed him out, not realizing that what was happening through the angel was real; he thought he was seeing a vision. They passed the first guard, then the second, and came to the iron gate leading out to the city, which opened for them by itself. They emerged and made their way down an alley, and suddenly the angel left him.

PSALM RESPONSE
Psalm 34:5b

The angel of the Lord will rescue those who fear him.

SECOND READING
2 Timothy 4: 6–8, 17–18

I, Paul, am already being poured out like a libation, and the time of my departure is at hand. I have competed well; I have finished the race; I have kept the faith. From now on the crown of righteousness awaits me, which the Lord, the just judge, will award to me on that day, and not only to me, but to all who have longed for his appearance.

The Lord stood by me and gave me strength, so that through me the proclamation might be completed and all the Gentiles might hear it. And I was rescued from the lion's mouth. The Lord will rescue me from every evil threat and will bring me safe to his heavenly kingdom. To him be glory forever and ever. Amen.

GOSPEL
Matthew 16:
13–19

When Jesus went into the region of Caesarea Philippi he asked his disciples, "Who do people say that the Son of Man is?" They replied, "Some say John the Baptist, others Elijah, still others Jeremiah or one of the prophets." He said to them, "But who do you say that I am?" Simon Peter said in reply, "You are the Christ, the Son of the living God." Jesus said to him in reply, "Blessed are you, Simon son of Jonah. For flesh and blood has not revealed this to you, but my heavenly Father. And so I say to you, you are Peter, and upon this rock I will build my church, and the gates of the netherworld shall not prevail against it. I will give you the keys to the kingdom of heaven. Whatever you bind on earth shall be bound in heaven; whatever you loose on earth shall be loosed in heaven."

Understanding the Word

It is not often that the observance of a saint's feast day replaces the Sunday celebration, but today's commemoration of Saints Peter and Paul has been given the rank of a solemnity in the liturgical calendar and thus has precedence over the Thirteenth Sunday in Ordinary Time. In the readings—as in the celebration generally—we remember and honor the greatness of the saints in order to praise the One whose power is the source of their triumph.

In the Gospel we hear the story of Peter's confession of faith at Caesarea Philippi. This is a decisive moment in the Gospel narrative, marking the first full recognition of the identity of Jesus as both Messiah and Son of God. So complete is this acknowledgment of Jesus' full identity that some scholars suggest it actually happened after the Resurrection but has been placed here, earlier in the narrative of Jesus' ministry, for literary purposes in the composition of the Gospel. Regardless of how one views that question, it is clear that this event marked a turning point in how Peter's role was to be regarded within the community of disciples. Jesus exercises a divine prerogative in changing the name of Simon to "Peter (Rock)," a designation hitherto unknown as a personal name. Jesus indicates that it is precisely Simon Peter's full and accurate profession of faith—which itself was a gift of God—that has won him his new name, role, and authority (represented by the symbolic "keys" bestowed upon him). Matthew intends this pronouncement of Jesus as an important statement about the Church, not just about Peter, since the successors of Peter in their role as head of the apostles continue to rely on the grace of God in order to lead the community in its profession of faith.

Most scholars regard the author of the Second Letter to Timothy as one of Paul's disciples, writing after the Apostle's death, but invoking his authority by attaching his name to the document. Such an explanation fits well with the excerpt read today that attests to Paul's fidelity to his ministry right up to the point of his death.

Reflecting on the Word

In Christian iconography, Saints Peter and Paul are almost always depicted together, rather like twins. That may seem odd because they probably looked nothing alike and they had very different personalities and temperaments. Peter worked largely with Jewish Christians and Paul with Gentile Christians. Peter has been connected to preserving the tradition and Paul is remembered for welcoming the freedom of the Spirit. However, both were committed to keeping all the members of Christ's Body united in faith and love. Their faith in Christ, love for the Church, and zeal for fostering the unity of the Christian community bind Peter and Paul together as no superficial resemblance could.

There is a lesson here for today's Church. We don't all agree about how much to stick to tradition and how much to allow the Spirit to guide the Church onto new paths. Yet both are necessary for continuing Jesus Christ's mission on earth. And Peter and Paul show us that remaining united in love as the one Body of Christ is more important than allowing differences of interpretation to divide us from one another.

CONSIDER/ DISCUSS:
- What comes into your mind when you think of Peter or Paul?
- How are preserving the tradition and following the Spirit both important to the future existence of the Church?
- What keeps the various factions in your parish from splitting apart?

Responding to the Word

Just as God rescued Peter from prison and Paul from "every evil," "the gates of hell shall not prevail against" Christ's Church. We believe that the fraternal love, faith, and work of these twin saints who died for Christ's Church will not be in vain. The God who was faithful to them will be faithful to the Church they loved, and preserve the faith and unity they worked so tirelessly to maintain.

- Go to a church event that you would not ordinarily attend. Bring an open mind.
- Help members of your parish understand each other's points of view.
- Pray for the unity of all Christians.

It's Time to Order
Living the Word 2004: Year C

By now you have found what a prayerful and valuable Scriptural resource *Living the Word* provides for you each Sunday of the year.

Don't miss a single week! Subscribe to *Living the Word 2004* today for yourself, your staff, parishioners, family and friends, and share the gift of God's Word.

The same low prices as 2003:

100 or more copies	$5.95 each
25-99 copies	$7.95 each
10-24 copies	$8.95 each
2-9 copies	$9.95 each
Single copies	$12.95

MAKE A COPY OF THIS ORDER FORM AND FAX IT TODAY TO 888-957-3291.
(This will keep your current book intact!)

OR, CALL WLP CUSTOMER CARE AT 800-566-6150 TO PLACE YOUR ORDER.

[ ] Yes, I'd like to order *Living the Word 2004: Year C*. Please send me _____ copies at _____ each, plus shipping, handling and any applicable sales tax.

NAME_____ POSITION _____

PARISH/INSTITUTION _____

ADDRESS _____

CITY _____ STATE _____ ZIP _____

PHONE _____ FAX_____ E-MAIL _____

Please keep a copy of your order for reference. *Living the Word 2004* will be shipped and billed after August 1, 2003.

Add $4.00 for orders up to $20.00. Add 15% of total for orders over $20.00. Payment in U.S. currency only. No cash or stamps, please. Make checks payable to World Library Publications. Prices subject to change without notice.

*Individuals in these states must add the following sales tax: CA 6.00%, FL 6.00%;IL 8.00%, IA 4.00%, MA 5.00%; MN 6.50%; NJ 6.00%; NY 4.00%; PA 6.00%; and TX 6.25%.

 World Library Publications
3825 North Willow Road, Schiller Park, IL 60176-2309
800-566-6150 Fax 888 957-3291
www.wlpmusic.com• wlpcs@jspaluch.com

LTWC04

July 6, 2003

FOURTEENTH SUNDAY IN ORDINARY TIME

Today's Focus: Political Resistance

The Scriptures for this weekend give an old meaning to the term "political resistance." All three prophets that we hear from—Ezekiel, Paul, and Jesus—warn us that those who dare to proclaim the Good News will encounter resistance from many people ("politikos," or citizens) to whom they speak.

FIRST READING
Ezekiel 2:2–5

As the LORD spoke to me, the spirit entered into me and set me on my feet, and I heard the one who was speaking say to me: Son of man, I am sending you to the Israelites, rebels who have rebelled against me; they and their ancestors have revolted against me to this very day. Hard of face and obstinate of heart are they to whom I am sending you. But you shall say to them: Thus says the LORD God! And whether they heed or resist — for they are a rebellious house — they shall know that a prophet has been among them.

PSALM RESPONSE
Psalm 123:2cd

Our eyes are fixed on the Lord, pleading for his mercy.

SECOND READING
2 Corinthians 12: 7–10

Brothers and sisters: That I, Paul, might not become too elated, because of the abundance of the revelations, a thorn in the flesh was given to me, an angel of Satan, to beat me, to keep me from being too elated. Three times I begged the Lord about this, that it might leave me, but he said to me, "My grace is sufficient for you, for power is made perfect in weakness." I will rather boast most gladly of my weaknesses, in order that the power of Christ may dwell with me. Therefore, I am content with weaknesses, insults, hardships, persecutions, and constraints, for the sake of Christ; for when I am weak, then I am strong.

GOSPEL
Mark 6:1–6

Jesus departed from there and came to his native place, accompanied by his disciples. When the sabbath came he began to teach in the synagogue, and many who heard him were astonished. They said, "Where did this man get all this? What kind of wisdom has been given him? What mighty deeds are wrought by his hands! Is he not the carpenter, the son of Mary, and the brother of James and Joses and Judas and Simon? And are not his sisters here with us?" And they took offense at him. Jesus said to them, "A prophet is not without honor except in his native place and among his own kin and in his own house." So he was not able to perform any mighty deed there, apart from curing a few sick people by laying his hands on them. He was amazed at their lack of faith.

Understanding the Word

In popular language today the term prophet is associated with the ability to foretell the future. In the Scriptures, however, the ability to predict future events was not at all the major focus of a prophet's mission. More often than not, the emphasis of a prophet's message was on interpretation of contemporary events. Since there were numerous individuals who claimed for themselves the role of prophet (i.e., interpreter and spokesperson for God's will), the question of authenticity was an important one. That is why the narrative of a prophet's call from God became such a significant literary feature in the Scriptures. In fact, stories of a prophet's call became stylized to the point that there were certain features that were an expected aspect of the narrative.

Today's reading from the Book of Ezekiel is part of the longer narrative of his call. He has described an ecstatic vision, and now he narrates what he experienced and heard. Scholars note that there is a fundamental experience of the prophet being possessed by a force outside of and beyond the prophet ("the spirit entered into me"). The call to be a prophet is never self-generated. It always has its origin in the divine initiative. Frequently, in fact, there is resistance on the part of the prophet, a reluctance that emphasizes the external origin of the call.

In the divine commission there is an explicit sending forth to deliver a message. Most often, as the prophet is told where to go, there is a warning that both the prophet and the message will be resisted but that the message will ultimately prevail. The strength of God's word is such that it has a force superior to any human power, whether that resistance is the prophet's reluctance to accept the call, or the resistance the message will encounter in the prophet's audience! The prophet knows that the word to be delivered will ultimately be successful precisely because it is God's word, not the prophet's own, that is proclaimed.

Reflecting on the Word

On this Fourth of July weekend Americans feel very patriotic. Most express their patriotism by displaying flags and condoning the policies of our government. However, a few express their patriotism by displaying placards and marching in protest against the policies of our government. Chances are the protesters will encounter stiff political resistance from the majority. The flag wavers will be "astonished" by the words of the protesters and the protesters will be "amazed" at their resistance.

Today's readings make no judgments about American politics, but politics and protesters may supply us with some insight into the motivation and experience of prophets. All those who accept God's call to proclaim the Good News are likely to encounter "insults" and "persecutions," and people who "resist," show "contempt," take "offense" at their words. They—we—are spurred on by our conviction that it is God's word we speak and "the power of Christ" that dwells in us.

• Why might the people in these readings have resisted the
words of Ezekiel, Paul, and Jesus?

• What Christians do you know who stand up for their convictions even when they are in the minority?

• When have you encountered resistance to your unpopular words?

Responding to the Word

In today's Gospel we see Jesus struggling in his ministry in his native place. There's something comforting about knowing that Jesus didn't always succeed. All of us have felt a sense of failure in our lives. Sometimes we feel we are not accomplishing what God intends us to do. At times like these we are called to persevere despite whatever internal or external resistance we may encounter. Like Jesus and the psalmist, we must keep "our eyes are fixed on the Lord, pleading for his mercy."

• Discover how Christ is calling you to "prophesy" this week.

• Go to God with any fears you have about resistance or failure in some aspect of your life.

• Say something difficult that you believe needs to be heard.

July 13, 2003

FIFTEENTH SUNDAY IN ORDINARY TIME

Today's Focus: Crystal Ball

Fortunetellers might see a glorious future for you in a crystal ball, but they won't do anything to bring that future about. The prophets we encounter today and in these few weeks also seem to see the future, and they do everything they can to make God's vision for the world come true.

FIRST READING
Amos 7:12–15

Amaziah, priest of Bethel, said to Amos, "Off with you, visionary, flee to the land of Judah! There earn your bread by prophesying, but never again prophesy in Bethel; for it is the king's sanctuary and a royal temple." Amos answered Amaziah, "I was no prophet, nor have I belonged to a company of prophets; I was a shepherd and a dresser of sycamores. The LORD took me from following the flock, and said to me, Go, prophesy to my people Israel."

PSALM RESPONSE
Psalm 85:8

Lord, let us see your kindness, and grant us your salvation.

In the shorter form of the reading, the passage in brackets is omitted.

SECOND READING
Ephesians 1: 3–14 or 1:3–10

Blessed be the God and Father of our Lord Jesus Christ, who has blessed us in Christ with every spiritual blessing in the heavens, as he chose us in him, before the foundation of the world, to be holy and without blemish before him. In love he destined us for adoption to himself through Jesus Christ, in accord with the favor of his will, for the praise of the glory of his grace that he granted us in the beloved. In him we have redemption by his blood, the forgiveness of transgressions, in accord with the riches of his grace that he lavished upon us. In all wisdom and insight, he has made known to us the mystery of his will in accord with his favor that he set forth in him as a plan for the fullness of times, to sum up all things in Christ, in heaven and on earth.

[In him we were also chosen, destined in accord with the purpose of the One who accomplishes all things according to the intention of his will, so that we might exist for the praise of his glory, we who first hoped in Christ. In him you also, who have heard the word of truth, the gospel of your salvation, and have believed in him, were sealed with the promised holy Spirit, which is the first installment of our inheritance toward redemption as God's possession, to the praise of his glory.]

GOSPEL
Mark 6:7–13
Jesus summoned the Twelve and began to send them out two by two and gave them authority over unclean spirits. He instructed them to take nothing for the journey but a walking stick — no food, no sack, no money in their belts. They were, however, to wear sandals but not a second tunic. He said to them, "Wherever you enter a house, stay there until you leave. Whatever place does not welcome you or listen to you, leave there and shake the dust off your feet in testimony against them." So they went off and preached repentance. The Twelve drove out many demons, and they anointed with oil many who were sick and cured them.

Understanding the Word

Last week we looked at certain features that are classic elements of the prophetic call narratives in the Jewish Scriptures. This week, again, the readings for the day present us with themes of being called and sent forth on mission. In the first reading, the prophet Amos defends his ministry to the priest Amaziah by pointing out that his preaching was initiated by God, not himself. Amos, an unlettered peasant, found himself confronting the cultured, well-educated ruling class, represented here by Amaziah, but including even the king himself. His sole defense of his mission is that he is not a professional prophet, merely God's messenger who had no option but to deliver the message with which he was entrusted.

The Gospel text today shows how the notion of prophetic call evolved in the ministry of Jesus and the early Christian community of Mark. Still present is the clear call-sending motif, but this time it is Jesus himself who initiates both. Exercising this divine prerogative, Jesus entrusts a share of his own prophetic ministry to the community he has chosen. Without making any explicit statement regarding the divinity of Jesus, Mark subtly shows him acting in a way that was reserved to God alone. The disciples' success in their mission that Mark reports at the end of the passage is consistent with the Jewish understanding that God's word exercises inexorable power and always triumphs.

The reading from Ephesians today shows how the notion of being called by God has been taken and reflected upon in the early community and applied to the entirety of our Christian lives. The author praises God who has "blessed us in Christ ... [and] chose[n] us in him ... to be holy and without blemish before him." Just as God revealed to prophets of old the message of salvation, so God "has made known to us the mystery of his will ..." This passage wonderfully illuminates the prayer said at every baptism, where the newly baptized is pronounced a "prophet."

Reflecting on the Word

Ezekiel, Amos, Jeremiah, Elisha, Moses, Elijah, Joshua, Isaiah, Paul, Jesus, Mark, the disciples of Jesus—these are some of the prophets we are hearing from in these summer Sundays of Ordinary Time. They may not be fortunetellers, but each in his own way seems to be propelled by a common vision of the future. It's as though they share the same crystal ball that gives them insight into the glorious future that God has in mind for the people.

Having seen what's possible, these prophets go out and use their specific talents to try to make that vision a reality. One preaches, one writes. One warns, another comforts. One gathers the people, another feeds them. One inspires, one prays, one cures. All encounter doubt and resistance, yet all persevere. And Jesus does all these things. These prophets not only see God's future, they say and do whatever they can to make it happen.

CONSIDER/ DISCUSS:
- What vision for their lives did Amos and the apostles have to let go of?
- Are your choices more often based on your past experience or your vision of the future? Explain.
- How have you gotten in touch with and worked toward God's vision for the future?

Responding to the Word

Today's psalm and selection from Ephesians allow us to glimpse the vision that the prophets "see" in their crystal ball. It is a vision of kindness and truth springing up under the warm sun of God's justice. It's a vision of God's glory triumphing in Christ. We, the baptized, are those who are "chosen," "adopted," given "insight," "sealed," and "destined in accord with the purpose" of God. We, the baptized, are to devote our words, deeds, and lives to bringing about God's vision for the world.

- Close your eyes and take your time seeing yourself, where you are and what you are doing, in God's crystal ball.
- Take one step to make God's vision for the world come true.
- Thank someone for his or her "prophetic" words or actions.

July 20, 2003

SIXTEENTH SUNDAY IN ORDINARY TIME

Today's Focus: Leadership Training

This week we see the apostles receiving leadership training under the mentorship of the one Good Shepherd. All the readings highlight aspects of good—and bad—leadership. While the Scriptures seem to focus on the leader as shepherd, they also bring out many other tasks and roles that good leaders share.

FIRST READING
Jeremiah 23: 1–6

Woe to the shepherds who mislead and scatter the flock of my pasture, says the LORD. Therefore, thus says the LORD, the God of Israel, against the shepherds who shepherd my people: You have scattered my sheep and driven them away. You have not cared for them, but I will take care to punish your evil deeds. I myself will gather the remnant of my flock from all the lands to which I have driven them and bring them back to their meadow; there they shall increase and multiply. I will appoint shepherds for them who will shepherd them so that they need no longer fear and tremble; and none shall be missing, says the LORD.

Behold, the days are coming, says the LORD,
    when I will raise up a righteous shoot to David;
as king he shall reign and govern wisely,
    he shall do what is just and right in the land.
In his days Judah shall be saved,
    Israel shall dwell in security.
This is the name they give him:
    "The LORD, our justice."

PSALM RESPONSE
Psalm 23:1

The Lord is my shepherd; there is nothing I shall want.

SECOND READING
Ephesians 2: 13–18

Brothers and sisters: In Christ Jesus you who once were far off have become near by the blood of Christ.

For he is our peace, he who made both one and broke down the dividing wall of enmity, through his flesh, abolishing the law with its commandments and legal claims, that he might create in himself one new person in place of the two, thus establishing peace, and might reconcile both with God, in one body, through the cross, putting that enmity to death by it. He came and preached peace to you who were far off and peace to those who were near, for through him we both have access in one Spirit to the Father.

GOSPEL
Mark 6:30–34

The apostles gathered together with Jesus and reported all they had done and taught. He said to them, "Come away by yourselves to a deserted place and rest a while." People were coming and going in great numbers, and they had no opportunity even to eat. So they went off in the boat by themselves to a deserted place. People saw them leaving and many came to know about it. They hastened there on foot from all the towns and arrived at the place before them.

When he disembarked and saw the vast crowd, his heart was moved with pity for them, for they were like sheep without a shepherd; and he began to teach them many things.

Understanding the Word

Last week in the Gospel we read about the mission of the Twelve. Today's Gospel reports how they returned and reported to Jesus "all they had done and taught." For the first and only time in his Gospel, Mark here refers to the Twelve as "apostles," possibly because here they have met with an initial success by faithfully fulfilling the mandate the Lord had given them. Some scholars have suggested that there is a notion of accountability for one's ministry that is being introduced here as the apostles report back to Jesus on how well they have fulfilled his mandate. Henceforth in the Gospel, Mark has Jesus direct his teaching less to the crowds and more to the Twelve.

In one of our commentaries earlier this year, we noted that whenever Mark uses the phrase that the disciples "went off by themselves" with Jesus, they are about to be given some special revelation. What follows this transitional passage is the story of the multiplication of the loaves. Together with the crowds, the disciples are about to be taught and fed. Mark was writing for a Christian community that regularly gathered as a liturgical assembly to be taught (in the Liturgy of the Word) and fed (in the Liturgy of the Eucharist). One suspects that he intends the readers to recognize themselves in the narrative and to realize that their gathering for worship is always a special moment of revelation as they "go off by themselves" with the Lord in the celebration of the liturgy.

In the next section of his Gospel, Mark tells the story of the multiplication of the loaves in two versions. Instead of using Mark's descriptions of this miracle, next week the Lectionary begins a five-week series of readings from Chapter 6 of John's Gospel, where John recounts the story of the multiplication of the loaves and the teaching of Jesus about the Bread of Life.

What does a good leader look like, act like? What do you value in a leader? Leadership is a hot topic in management circles. Corporate managers read magazines about leadership and go to leadership training seminars. People discuss different models and images of good leadership. They talk about the value of authoritative leadership, collaborative leadership, and even servant leadership.

Today's Scriptures give us a miniature leadership training session. The reading from Jeremiah depicts the good leader as a wise judge and a protector of the weak. The psalm shows a conscientious shepherd and perfect host. The writer of Ephesians describes Christ's leadership as that of a peacemaker who brings people together. In the Gospel Jesus trains the apostles to reflect on and be accountable for their choices and continually seek nourishment and support for their leadership. Jesus himself then leads the people by "teach[ing] them many things."

CONSIDER/ DISCUSS:
- Which leadership image or role in today's Scriptures strikes you as most surprising or significant? Why?
- Who do you know who is a good leader? Describe what you value in this person's leadership.
- How are you called to show good leadership in your life?

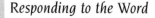 *Responding to the Word*

In our Catholic tradition we call parish priests "pastors" and diocesan bishops "shepherds" of Christ's flock. Both titles suggest that the non-ordained might only be required to follow these human shepherds like sheep. Yet, today's Scriptures invite us to consider what leadership role each of us has to play. And they invite us always to follow the one Good Shepherd who is with us to protect and guide, to reconcile and support, to teach and to nourish us.

- Use Psalm 23 as a prayer at least twice this week.
- During Mass allow Christ to teach and feed you.
- Look for a way to exercise good leadership in your faith community.

July 27, 2003

SEVENTEENTH SUNDAY IN ORDINARY TIME

Today's Focus: Leftovers

Do leftovers go to waste in your house? This Sunday both Elisha and Jesus feed hungry crowds with the paltry offerings of one of their disciples. And after each miraculous feeding there is bread left over. Today's Scriptures suggest that we not waste the leftovers after we have had our fill of Christ's love.

FIRST READING
2 Kings 4: 42–44

A man came from Baal-shalishah bringing to Elisha, the man of God, twenty barley loaves made from the firstfruits, and fresh grain in the ear. Elisha said, "Give it to the people to eat." But his servant objected, "How can I set this before a hundred people?" Elisha insisted, "Give it to the people to eat. For thus says the Lord, 'They shall eat and there shall be some left over.'" And when they had eaten, there was some left over, as the Lord had said.

PSALM RESPONSE
Psalm 145:16

The hand of the Lord feeds us; he answers all our needs.

SECOND READING
Ephesians 4: 1–6

Brothers and sisters: I, a prisoner for the Lord, urge you to live in a manner worthy of the call you have received, with all humility and gentleness, with patience, bearing with one another through love, striving to preserve the unity of the spirit through the bond of peace: one body and one Spirit, as you were also called to the one hope of your call; one Lord, one faith, one baptism; one God and Father of all, who is over all and through all and in all.

GOSPEL
John 6:1–15

Jesus went across the Sea of Galilee. A large crowd followed him, because they saw the signs he was performing on the sick. Jesus went up on the mountain, and there he sat down with his disciples. The Jewish feast of Passover was near. When Jesus raised his eyes and saw that a large crowd was coming to him, he said to Philip, "Where can we buy enough food for them to eat?" He said this to test him, because he himself knew what he was going to do. Philip answered him, "Two hundred days' wages worth of food would not be enough for each of them to have a little." One of his disciples, Andrew, the brother of Simon Peter, said to him, "There is a boy here who has five barley loaves and two fish; but what good are these for so many?" Jesus said, "Have the people recline." Now there was a great deal of grass in that place. So the men reclined, about five thousand in number. Then Jesus took the loaves, gave thanks, and distributed them to those who were reclining, and also as much of the fish as they wanted. When they had had their fill, he said to his disciples, "Gather the fragments left over, so that nothing will be wasted." So they collected them, and filled twelve wicker baskets with fragments from the five barley loaves that had been more than

155

they could eat. When the people saw the sign he had done, they said, "This is truly the Prophet, the one who is to come into the world." Since Jesus knew that they were going to come and carry him off to make him king, he withdrew again to the mountain alone.

Understanding the Word

Once every three years, in the dog days of August, the Lectionary allows us to feast on a series of readings from chapter 6 of John's Gospel, the Bread of Life discourse. One hopes that for those on vacation during this time—as well as for those who remain hard at work—there will be special nourishment and refreshment in this opportunity to reflect on Jesus as the Bread of Life and on our participation in the Eucharist as a foretaste of the banquet with the Lord that lasts forever.

For the next five weeks we continue to read from the Letter to the Ephesians. Although not chosen specifically to match the Gospel, these selections are certainly compatible with the themes that we will follow each week from the Gospel texts. The first readings, on the other hand, have been very carefully chosen to support the Gospel passages. Four of the five weeks are stories of miraculous feedings. The fifth is a call to decide whether or not we will cast our lot with the God who has nourished us so lavishly.

This entire series of readings hinges on today's Gospel account of the multiplication of the loaves, the one miracle story that is told in all four Gospels. The importance of this miracle and the Johannine commentary on it that forms the remainder of the chapter is supported by the fact that in John's Gospel there is no separate narrative of the Last Supper. Scholars suggest that this section serves as a functional equivalent to what the institution narrative contributes to the other three Gospels. John further signals the importance of this miracle by calling it a "sign," the technical term he uses in his Gospel to signal an action that is a moment of special revelation and encounter with Jesus. Those who recognize the "sign" are challenged to commit themselves to Jesus, the one whom it reveals as Savior and Lord.

Reflecting on the Word

In many homes, meals begin with grace and end with putting away the leftover food. Those leftovers are either eaten later by someone who missed dinner or added to tomorrow's meals. The meal in today's Gospel is somewhat similar. Before the meal Jesus "gave thanks." After all had eaten he asked that the leftovers be gathered "so that nothing will be wasted."

It's not a stretch to see the similarity to our Liturgy of the Eucharist, which begins with a prayer of thanksgiving. It ends with the remaining Eucharist being reserved for those who couldn't be present and the "crowd" being sent to share Christ's sacrificial love. It's miraculous enough that all who are present can eat and have their fill. That is something to be truly grateful for. Yet, the miracle extends beyond the table. "The hand of the Lord feeds us" with leftover love to spare. The abundant "leftovers" are meant not to be wasted, but to be shared with all those in need of Christ's love.

- What happens to leftover food at your house?
- What do you think happened to the leftovers in today's miracle stories?
- When have you felt that you were given so much love that you had "leftovers" to share with others?

 ## Responding to the Word

Each of the miracles in these Scriptures begins with someone contributing what little they have to others. It's easy to belittle our paltry gifts and let them go to waste—like leftovers that are too little to save. Today's Scriptures encourage us to offer whatever we have to give and watch in gratitude as the Lord turns it into something miraculous.

- At Communion, open your heart to receive so much love that you have leftovers to share.
- Give thanks for the gift of the Eucharist.
- Share some of your gifts with those who are spiritually or physically hungry.

August 3, 2003

EIGHTEENTH SUNDAY IN ORDINARY TIME

Today's Focus: Bread of Angels

If angels needed to take nourishment they might eat what today's Psalm calls "the bread of angels." In this week's Gospel Jesus tells us that he himself is the heavenly bread that brings eternal life. Like the angels, those who believe in him will live forever and never be hungry or thirsty again.

FIRST READING
Exodus 16:2–4, 12–15

The whole Israelite community grumbled against Moses and Aaron. The Israelites said to them, "Would that we had died at the LORD's hand in the land of Egypt, as we sat by our fleshpots and ate our fill of bread! But you had to lead us into this desert to make the whole community die of famine!"

Then the LORD said to Moses, "I will now rain down bread from heaven for you. Each day the people are to go out and gather their daily portion; thus will I test them, to see whether they follow my instructions or not.

"I have heard the grumbling of the Israelites. Tell them: In the evening twilight you shall eat flesh, and in the morning you shall have your fill of bread, so that you may know that I, the LORD, am your God."

In the evening quail came up and covered the camp. In the morning a dew lay all about the camp, and when the dew evaporated, there on the surface of the desert were fine flakes like hoarfrost on the ground. On seeing it, the Israelites asked one another, "What is this?" for they did not know what it was. But Moses told them, "This is the bread that the LORD has given you to eat."

PSALM RESPONSE
Psalm 78:24b

The Lord gave them bread from heaven.

SECOND READING
Ephesians 4: 17, 20–24

Brothers and sisters: I declare and testify in the Lord that you must no longer live as the Gentiles do, in the futility of their minds; that is not how you learned Christ, assuming that you have heard of him and were taught in him, as truth is in Jesus, that you should put away the old self of your former way of life, corrupted through deceitful desires, and be renewed in the spirit of your minds, and put on the new self, created in God's way in righteousness and holiness of truth.

GOSPEL
John 6:24–35
When the crowd saw that neither Jesus nor his disciples were there, they themselves got into boats and came to Capernaum looking for Jesus. And when they found him across the sea they said to him, "Rabbi, when did you get here?" Jesus answered them and said, "Amen, amen, I say to you, you are looking for me not because you saw signs but because you ate the loaves and were filled. Do not work for food that perishes but for the food that endures for eternal life, which the Son of Man will give you. For on him the Father, God, has set his seal." So they said to him, "What can we do to accomplish the works of God?" Jesus answered and said to them, "This is the work of God, that you believe in the one he sent." So they said to him, "What sign can you do, that we may see and believe in you? What can you do? Our ancestors ate manna in the desert, as it is written:

He gave them bread from heaven to eat."

So Jesus said to them, "Amen, amen I say to you, it was not Moses who gave the bread from heaven; my Father gives you the true bread from heaven. For the bread of God is that which comes down from heaven and gives life to the world."

So they said to him, "Sir, give us this bread always." Jesus said to them, "I am the bread of life; whoever comes to me will never hunger, and whoever believes in my will never thirst."

Understanding the Word

In John's Gospel a familiar pattern is often followed to develop progressively deeper insights in the reader. First a miracle is narrated, then a dialogue with Jesus ensues, and finally a monologue/discourse unfolds the deepest meaning of the teaching. Last week's Gospel contained a description of the miracle, the multiplication of the loaves. In today's reading we are presented with the dialogue between Jesus and the crowds. As is customary in such Johannine dialogues, the technique of misunderstanding is used very effectively to allow the conversation to go forward on two levels. Each time the crowd misunderstands what Jesus is saying, the opportunity opens up for a deeper explanation. That explanation, in turn, only reveals an even deeper misunderstanding, which in turn evokes an answer that is progressively revelatory of the deeper truth that John wishes his readers to grasp.

Today's dialogue has the crowd asking Jesus three questions. First, "When did you get here," to which Jesus responds by rebuking them for their failure to grasp his miracle as a "sign," an occasion to put faith in him. Their second question about accomplishing the "works of God" has Jesus respond that faith is the "work" that God wishes. Many scholars believe this is John's answer to the faith-works dichotomy emerging in the early Christian community. Faith is the work of God in the believer, John would have us understand. The third question asked by the crowd is a request for a "sign" that would allow them to put faith in Jesus, as the manna in the desert allowed the Israelites to put faith in the Lord God. Jesus answers by revealing himself as the "bread of life" that "comes down from heaven and gives life to the world," a truth that the crowd still fails to grasp.

159

The brilliance of John's composition is evident in the way he has woven so many themes of the Jewish Scriptures into a dialogue that goes forward on multiple levels. In a Passover/messianic context, Jesus is revealed as the new Sophia, surpassing Wisdom herself, whose disciples grew hungry again, because Jesus refreshes with food that satisfies all (spiritual) hunger and thirst forever.

Reflecting on the Word

Unlike mortals, angels do not die. Nor do they need to eat or drink. Without corruptible bodies, they live eternally with God. But the psalm for today describes the manna that the Israelites ate in the desert as "the bread of angels." As the first reading tells us, it seemed to them that it came down from heaven every night. Through the manna, God gave them life when death seemed imminent. Through the manna, their faith in God's eternal care for them was revived.

In the case of the Israelites, they received life by eating the bread from heaven. And the life they were given allowed them to believe. In the case of the disciples of Jesus it's the other way around. We must believe in Jesus as "the true bread from heaven" in order to receive the eternal life that he provides. No wonder the people who followed him were confused!

CONSIDER/
DISCUSS:
- Can you sympathize with the Israelites or the crowd in today's Scriptures? Explain.

- How do you envision eternal life in heaven?

- How has believing in Christ satisfied your hunger or thirst?

Responding to the Word

The Eucharist has also been called the "bread of angels." It, too, is a free gift from God. It, too, is offered to give us eternal life because through it we receive the life of Christ, "the true bread from heaven." Jesus promised that those who believe and eat it will resemble the angels—they will hunger and thirst for nothing throughout all eternity.

- When you receive the Eucharist, ask Christ to quench your thirst or satisfy a friend's hunger.

- Take action to ease the physical hunger and thirst in the world.

- Greet and talk with someone new after Mass this weekend.

August 10, 2003

NINETEENTH SUNDAY IN ORDINARY TIME

Today's Focus: Bread for the Journey

In this Sunday's first reading we find Elijah emotionally and physically spent and the angel of the Lord nourishes him. He is given bread for the journey. Like manna, Passover bread, and the Eucharist, like the Torah and like Jesus himself, it supplies Elijah with the strength and the courage to journey on.

FIRST READING
1 Kings 19:4–8

Elijah went a day's journey into the desert, until he came to a broom tree and sat beneath it. He prayed for death, saying: "This is enough, O LORD! Take my life, for I am no better than my fathers." He lay down and fell asleep under the broom tree, but then an angel touched him and ordered him to get up and eat. Elijah looked and there at his head was a hearth cake and a jug of water. After he ate and drank, he lay down again, but the angel of the LORD came back a second time, touched him, and ordered, "Get up and eat, else the journey will be too long for you!" He got up, ate, and drank; then strengthened by that food, he walked forty days and forty nights to the mountain of God, Horeb.

PSALM RESPONSE
Psalm 34:9a

Taste and see the goodness of the Lord.

SECOND READING
Ephesians 4: 30 — 5:2

Brothers and sisters: Do not grieve the Holy Spirit of God, with which you were sealed for the day of redemption. All bitterness, fury, anger, shouting, and reviling must be removed from you, along with all malice. And be kind to one another, compassionate, forgiving one another as God has forgiven you in Christ.

So be imitators of God, as beloved children, and live in love, as Christ loved us and handed himself over for us as a sacrificial offering to God for a fragrant aroma.

GOSPEL
John 6:41–51

The Jews murmured about Jesus because he said, "I am the bread that came down from heaven," and they said, "Is this not Jesus, the son of Joseph? Do we not know his father and mother? Then how can he say, 'I have come down from heaven'?" Jesus answered and said to them, "Stop murmuring among yourselves. No one can come to me unless the Father who sent me draw him, and I will raise him on the last day. It is written in the prophets:

They shall all be taught by God.

Everyone who listens to my Father and learns from him comes to me. Not that anyone has seen the Father except the one who is from God; he has seen the Father. Amen, amen, I say to you, whoever believes has eternal life. I am the bread of life. Your ancestors ate the manna in the desert, but they died; this is the bread that comes down from heaven so that one may eat it and not die. I am the living bread that came down from heaven; whoever eats this bread will live forever; and the bread that I will give is my flesh for the life of the world."

Understanding the Word

The imagery that John uses in his Gospel is always fluid and evocative on multiple levels. For our Western mindset that desires clarity and precision, this can be frustrating. We want to ask, "What, exactly, is John/Jesus referring to here?" But the answer is usually that his meanings are multiple and many-layered. Scholars who comment on the section of chapter 6 that we read today tend to emphasize that the bread mentioned here seems to allude more to Jesus' wisdom/teaching than to any sacramental/eucharistic symbolism.

The rabbis often referred to the Torah metaphorically as "bread" that nourishes, gives life, and so forth. It was also rabbinical usage to speak of being "drawn to" the Torah. Evidently, John wishes for his readers to recall this strain of Jewish tradition when Jesus says no one can come to him "unless the Father who sent me draw him." Here, Jesus is offering himself as Torah-bread that comes down from heaven and nourishes unto eternal life. Clearly, the bread/nourishment/revelation that Jesus offers is superior to the Torah! John's contrast between the manna that perished in the desert and the heavenly, imperishable bread that Jesus offers is deliberate and provocative. For one who wishes to be "taught by God" (verse 45), it is necessary to "come to" Jesus in faith. That—and that alone—is the key to eternal life. For one who remains on an earthly, physical plane, faith is impossible. It is only when one lets go of the earthly level of existence and allows oneself to be "drawn by God" to faith in Jesus that eternal life is possible.

In the final verse of today's reading, Jesus speaks of his "flesh for the life of the world." Scholars suggest that here the implicit allusion seems more sacramental/eucharistic than wisdom/teaching. A subtle shift begins here and, as next week's reading will show, becomes progressively more explicitly eucharistic.

Reflecting on the Word

The Passover bread that the Israelites made when leaving Egypt had no leaven in it so that it would not spoil and could continue to provide nourishment to them on the road. Thus it is sometimes called bread for the journey. Of course manna also sustained them on their journey through the desert. And so did the Torah. So deliciously nourishing is the Word of God that some young Jewish children begin learning the Hebrew alphabet by licking honey placed on each letter so that the Torah should always be "sweet on the tongue."

The story of Elijah being nourished in the desert beautifully epitomizes the many ways in which God provides bread for the journey. For Christians, Jesus' words, works, and life given for us are the bread we crave. He alone gives us the strength and courage to "be kind ... forgive one another ... and live in love." And, oddly enough, we can find this ample nourishment from the Eucharist when all we taste is a sip and a crumb.

CONSIDER/ DISCUSS:

- Which words of Jesus confuse you or hit home for you today?
- When have you felt like Elijah? Have you received bread for the journey? Explain.
- How might God be urging you to get up, eat, and journey on?

 Responding to the Word

The nourishment Jesus gives is meant not to put us to sleep but to fuel us for action. Another image from today's Scripture urges us to action. The selection from Ephesians seems to refer to the perfumed chrism with which the baptized "were sealed for the day of redemption." We can imagine the "fragrant aroma" of the chrism arising from Christ's "sacrificial offering" of himself on the altar of the cross. Will others smell the heavenly aroma of Christ's love on us and be drawn to him?

- Pray for strength and courage in some aspect of your life.
- Write to a relative or friend about a time when you received "bread for the journey" when you needed it most.
- "Be kind" in some unexpected way this week.

August 15, 2003

THE ASSUMPTION
OF THE BLESSED VIRGIN MARY

Today's Focus: Happy Birthday!

Today, just as with most of the saints' days, we celebrate the end of Mary's life on earth as her birthday into eternal life with God. What makes Mary's "birthday" all the happier is that we believe she has already experienced the fullness of the Resurrection that we hope to enjoy together on the last day.

FIRST READING
Revelation 11: 19a; 12:1–6a, 10ab

God's temple in heaven was opened, and the ark of his covenant could be seen in the temple.

A great sign appeared in the sky, a woman clothed with the sun, with the moon beneath her feet, and on her head a crown of twelve stars. She was with child and wailed aloud in pain as she labored to give birth. Then another sign appeared in the sky; it was a huge red dragon, with seven heads and ten horns, and on its heads were seven diadems. Its tail swept away a third of the stars in the sky and hurled them down to the earth. Then the dragon stood before the woman about to give birth, to devour her child when she gave birth. She gave birth to a son, a male child, destined to rule all the nations with an iron rod. Her child was caught up to God and his throne. The woman herself fled into the desert where she had a place prepared by God.

Then I heard a loud voice in heaven say: "Now have salvation and power come, and the kingdom of our God and the authority of his Anointed One."

PSALM RESPONSE
Psalm 45:10bc

The queen stands at your right hand, arrayed in gold.

SECOND READING
1 Corinthians 15: 20–27

Brothers and sisters: Christ has been raised from the dead, the firstfruits of those who have fallen asleep. For since death came through man, the resurrection of the dead came also through man. For just as in Adam all die, so too in Christ shall all be brought to life, but each one in proper order: Christ the firstfruits; then, at his coming, those who belong to Christ; then comes the end, when he hands over the kingdom to his God and Father, when he has destroyed every sovereignty and every authority and power. For he must reign until he has put all his enemies under his feet. The last enemy to be destroyed is death, for "he subjected everything under his feet."

Mary set out and traveled to the hill country in haste to a town of Judah, where she entered the house of Zechariah and greeted Elizabeth. When Elizabeth heard Mary's greeting, the infant leaped in her womb, and Elizabeth, filled with the Holy Spirit, cried out in a loud voice and said, "Blessed are you among women, and blessed is the fruit of your womb. And how does this happen to me, that the mother of my Lord should come to me? For at the moment the sound of your greeting reached my ears, the infant in my womb leaped for joy. Blessed are you who believed that what was spoken to you by the Lord would be fulfilled."

And Mary said:

> "My soul proclaims the greatness of the Lord;
>   my spirit rejoices in God my Savior
>   for he has looked upon his lowly servant.
> From this day all generations will call me blessed:
>   the Almighty has done great things for me,
>   and holy is his Name.
> He has mercy on those who fear him
>   in every generation.
> He has shown the strength of his arm,
>   and has scattered the proud in their conceit.
> He has cast down the mighty from their thrones,
>   and has lifted up the lowly.
> He has filled the hungry with good things,
>   and the rich he has sent away empty.
> He has come to the help of his servant Israel
>   for he has remembered his promise of mercy,
>   the promise he made to our fathers,
>   to Abraham and his children for ever."

Mary remained with her about three months and then returned to her home.

Understanding the Word

The Book of Revelation is perhaps one of the most misunderstood books of the Bible. In order to understand it and how it must be interpreted in the context of a liturgical celebration, one must first have a sense of what kind of literature the author of this book intended to create. First of all, the fantastic visions and imagery of Revelation are not meant to be a prediction of far-distant events, predictions of exactly how it will happen when the world ends in the year 2003, in 3002, or whenever. The author had no more idea about the end of the world than you or I!

The overriding purpose of the Book of Revelation was to offer encouragement and hope to Christians undergoing persecution at the hands of the Roman state. This kind of literature, called apocalyptic, is meant to console those for whom it was first written (and, of course, subsequent readers in similar situations). The "apocalypse," or revelation, that is in question here discloses that God is in charge of heaven and earth and all human history, and the outcome of the present struggle is certain to be victory for God's faithful ones. This message, however, is coded by the use of imagery and allusions that would have been understood by the early Christian community, but missed by pagan Roman authorities who might come upon it.

Thus, for example, the image of a dragon attempting to devour an infant at its birth would seem to the Roman authorities as harmless as their own myth of Apollo pursued by Python but rescued by Zeus. For the Christian, however, the woman in labor would have evoked the image of Israel, giving birth to the Messiah, or perhaps Mary giving birth to Jesus, or even Mother Church begetting new Christian believers. When the liturgy selects a passage like this and places it in a specific context such as today's feast, it encourages us to see in this imagery how Mary's Assumption is her own victory over evil, her "rescue" from sin and death.

Reflecting on the Word

It is an ancient tradition in the Church to commemorate saints on the anniversary of their death because that was the day on which they were born into eternal life. We celebrate the same reality in our funeral liturgies and on the anniversaries of the death of our own loved ones. In Mary's case, her "birthday" has been celebrated on August 15 for approximately 1500 years.

Throughout most of that time, theologians commonly thought that both Mary's body and her soul were taken up into glory. This is the same glory that we believe all Christians await on the last day. Her perfect cooperation with God in her lifetime and her honored place as mother of the Messiah made her the first to enjoy the fullness of the Resurrection. In answer to a century of calls to proclaim this opinion as a doctrine of the Church, Pope Pius XII defined Mary's assumption as doctrine in 1950.

CONSIDER/ DISCUSS:
- Is Mary's assumption difficult for you to believe? Explain.
- How do you envision the fullness of the Resurrection on the last day?
- What words from today's Scriptures touch you most deeply or give you hope? Why?

Responding to the Word

Commemorating the death of someone we love can bring bittersweet emotions, at best. We hope that they are happy. We hope that they are with God. We hope that they have forgiven us. We hope we will be with them again someday. Today's feast should bolster all our hopes. Yes, Christ was raised from the dead, but he was divine as well as human. Today we confirm our belief that a human being, Mary, shares in Christ's total victory over death. So can our loved ones, and so can we.

- Pray aloud the words of Mary from today's Gospel.
- Remember a happy story or beautiful image of a loved one who has died.
- Entrust the eternal happiness of your loved ones to God.

August 17, 2003

TWENTIETH SUNDAY IN ORDINARY TIME

Today's Focus: Eat, Drink, and Live Forever

"Eat, drink and be merry, for tomorrow we die!" So goes the old adage. It suggests that life is short and pointless so we should spend it pleasing ourselves while we can. Christians believe otherwise. This week both Wisdom and Jesus beckon us to "Eat, drink, and live forever!"

FIRST READING
Proverbs 9:1–6

Wisdom has built her house,
    she has set up her seven columns;
she has dressed her meat, mixed her wine,
    yes, she has spread her table.
She has sent out her maidens; she calls
    from the heights out over the city:
"Let whoever is simple turn in here;
    to the one who lacks understanding, she says,
Come, eat of my food,
    and drink of the wine I have mixed!
Forsake foolishness that you may live;
    advance in the way of understanding."

PSALM RESPONSE
Psalm 34:9a

Taste and see the goodness of the Lord.

SECOND READING
Ephesians 5: 15–20

Brothers and sisters: Watch carefully how you live, not as foolish persons but as wise, making the most of the opportunity, because the days are evil. Therefore, do not continue in ignorance, but try to understand what is the will of the Lord. And do not get drunk on wine, in which lies debauchery, but be filled with the Spirit, addressing one another in psalms and hymns and spiritual songs, singing and playing to the Lord in your hearts, giving thanks always and for everything in the name of our Lord Jesus Christ to God the Father.

GOSPEL
John 6:51–58

Jesus said to the crowds: "I am the living bread that came down from heaven; whoever eats this bread will live forever; and the bread that I will give is my flesh for the life of the world."

The Jews quarreled among themselves, saying, "How can this man give us his flesh to eat?" Jesus said to them, "Amen, amen, I say to you, unless you eat the flesh of the Son of Man and drink his blood, you do not have life within you. Whoever eats my flesh and drinks my blood has eternal life, and I will raise him on the last day. For my flesh is true food, and my blood is true drink. Whoever eats my flesh and drinks my blood remains in me and I in him. Just as the living Father sent me and I have life because of the Father, so also the one who feeds on me will have life because of me. This is the bread that came down from heaven. Unlike your ancestors who ate and still died, whoever eats this bread will live forever."

Understanding the Word

Several weeks ago we noted the absence of any institution narrative in John's account of the Last Supper, and we recalled the view of many scholars that chapter 6 offers a functional equivalent to that scene as it is described in the synoptic Gospels. The verses that are read this week form the heart of what many scholars regard as John's version of Jesus' institution of the Eucharist. While earlier verses are unclear about whether the "bread" being spoken of is primarily Jesus' teaching/revelation or the Eucharist, in the verses read today it seems much more likely that the reference is sacramental and eucharistic in nature.

Once again, as in previous readings, it is the misunderstanding of the crowd that offers the occasion for Jesus to explain in more depth the true meaning of what he is saying. The Jews question how he can give them his flesh to eat. Jesus' response is deliberately insistent about the realism of what it is that he offers— his own body and blood. Common sense rejects a cannibalistic interpretation of these verses in favor of a sacramental realism. Later tradition in Paul and the synoptics used the term "body" instead of the more shocking "flesh," but John here probably reflects earlier usage. It is not a merely spiritual encounter with Jesus that gives life, much less an intellectual grasp of the revelation he offers as Wisdom incarnate. Rather, John presses for a sacramental/eucharistic participation in the life of Jesus that is real and true.

The liturgical context suggested by the fact that this scene is set at the Passover time, with its references to manna, offers the key to interpreting Jesus' words as the sacramental meal of the early Christians. Just as the Jews ate the Passover lamb in remembrance of God's saving deeds on Israel's behalf, so the community of Jesus' disciples consumes the new paschal lamb, whose body and blood have been given over "for the life of the world."

Reflecting on the Word

"Eat, drink, and be merry, for tomorrow we die." Such a philosophy might characterize the "foolish persons" in today's selection from Ephesians who "continue in ignorance" and "get drunk on wine." Obsessed with enjoying mortal life while it lasts, they are oblivious to Wisdom and Jesus, who are inviting them to "eat, drink, and live forever."

With what great care does Wisdom prepare the banquet hall and the meat (flesh?) and wine for the meal. With what great care does she lay the table and make certain that all feel welcome to feast on God's word that alone gives life. How foolish anyone must be to turn her down!

With what great care has Jesus prepared his disciples for his death. With what great care has he laid out the truth of God's limitless love and made certain that all feel welcome to believe and know lasting life in the Spirit. With what great care does Jesus give his "flesh and blood"—his mortal life—"for the life of the world." How foolish anyone must be to turn away.

CONSIDER/ DISCUSS:
- In what way do you sometimes fit in with the foolish people described today?
- How might you have responded to Jesus' words about eating his flesh and drinking his blood?
- How do you feel when you think of Christ giving his "flesh and blood" for us?

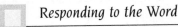

Responding to the Word

The reading from Ephesians bids us to get drunk—not on wine, but on the Spirit. What does that mean? Perhaps it is the normal response when we imbibe the Blood of Christ. As we accept the gift of Christ's life we would have to be foolish not to sing for joy and give thanks. Forgetting our mortality, we are freed to let Christ's eternal life in us pour out "for the life of the world."

- Accept and give thanks for the gift of Christ's flesh and blood.
- Get drunk on the Spirit at Mass this Sunday.
- Take action "for the life of the world."

August 24, 2003

TWENTY-FIRST SUNDAY IN ORDINARY TIME

Today's Focus: "I do!"

When a woman and man stand before their friends and family and say "I do!" in the sacrament of marriage, they know that they are making a lifetime commitment to each other. What about us? Do we know what commitment we are making each time we say "Amen" to the Body and Blood of Christ?

FIRST READING
Joshua 24:1–2a, 15–17, 18b

Joshua gathered together all the tribes of Israel at Shechem, summoning their elders, their leaders, their judges, and their officers. When they stood in ranks before God, Joshua addressed all the people:

"If it does not please you to serve the LORD, decide today whom you will serve, the gods your fathers served beyond the River or the gods of the Amorites in whose country you are now dwelling. As for me and my household, we will serve the LORD."

But the people answered, "Far be it from us to forsake the LORD for the service of other gods. For it was the LORD, our God, who brought us and our fathers up out of the land of Egypt, out of a state of slavery. He performed those great miracles before our very eyes and protected us along our entire journey and among the peoples through whom we passed. Therefore we also will serve the LORD, for he is our God."

PSALM RESPONSE
Psalm 34:9a

Taste and see the goodness of the Lord.

In the shorter form of the reading, the passage in brackets is omitted

SECOND READING
Ephesians 5: 21–32 or 5:2a, 25–32

Brothers and sisters: [Be subordinate to one another out of reverence for Christ. Wives should be subordinate to their husbands as to the Lord. For the husband is head of his wife just as Christ is head of the church, he himself the savior of the body. As the church is subordinate to Christ, so wives should be subordinate to their husbands in everything.] Husbands, love your wives, even as Christ loved the church and handed himself over for her to sanctify her, cleansing her by the bath of water with the word, that he might present to himself the church in splendor, without spot or wrinkle or any such thing, that she might be holy and without blemish. So also husbands should love their wives as their own bodies. He who loves his wife loves himself. For no one hates his own flesh but rather nourishes and cherishes it, even as Christ does the church, because we are members of his body.

*For this reason a man shall leave his father and his mother
and be joined to his wife,
and the two shall become one flesh.*

This is a great mystery, but I speak in reference to Christ and the church.

GOSPEL
John 6:60–69
Many of Jesus' disciples who were listening said, "This saying is hard; who can accept it?" Since Jesus knew that his disciples were murmuring about this, he said to them, "Does this shock you? What if you were to see the Son of Man ascending to where he was before? It is the spirit that gives life, while the flesh is of no avail. The words I have spoken to you are Spirit and life. But there are some of you who do not believe." Jesus knew from the beginning the ones who would not believe and the one who would betray him. And he said, "For this reason I have told you that no one can come to me unless it is granted him by my Father."

As a result of this, many of his disciples returned to their former way of life and no longer accompanied him. Jesus then said to the Twelve, "Do you also want to leave?" Simon Peter answered him, "Master, to whom shall we go? You have the words of eternal life. We have come to believe and are convinced that you are the Holy One of God."

Understanding the Word

Today we complete the five-week series of readings from chapter 6 of John's Gospel. The past several weeks' focus on Jesus as the Bread of Life gives way today to an emphasis on the response of his hearers—those who have seen the miracles he has worked. These people have heard his claims regarding his identity and his offer of unending life to whoever is willing to participate in the food he offers. Jesus provides no further defense or explanation of his claim. Rather, in these verses he challenges his audience to make a decision.

It is Peter who speaks on behalf of the disciples. His answer reveals a number of things about faith: it flows from a personal relationship with Jesus, it must be embodied in a commitment to cast one's lot with Jesus Christ and the credibility of his claim, and it has a public dimension to its witness. John's intent in this passage is clearly to summarize for his readers the meaning of discipleship and to drive home the importance of committed belonging as a condition of eucharistic participation. For those who accept the claim of Jesus that he is the Bread of Life, the only adequate response is a faith commitment. That commitment is embodied in the dual realities of eucharistic sharing and a life of discipleship.

The first reading today from the Book of Joshua also contains the theme of faith as commitment to a personal relationship and a life of participation in a covenant community. This passage forms the climax not only of the Book of Joshua, but also of the entire drama narrated in the Pentateuch. The Chosen People have finally arrived in the Promised Land, and there they renew their commitment to live in an exclusive relationship with the Lord as their sole God and protector. As the people say, the Lord God has performed "great miracles ... and protected us," and as a consequence they pledge themselves to "serve the LORD, for he is our God."

It was three days before the wedding and Alexis just couldn't hide her fears from her sister any longer. "Therese, I'm not sure I can say 'I do.' So many of our friends' marriages have failed. And Mom and Dad haven't always modeled marital bliss. Once we say those two little words we've bound our future together, whatever comes. It's 'Alexis and Don,' 'Don and Alexis' forever in the eyes of God, you, everybody. I'm not sure I'm ready to make that commitment."

Like the life-changing commitment a couple makes in marriage, in today's Gospel Jesus' disciples must choose whether to commit themselves to him and his way of life. He has offered them a new kind of life that comes only through him. Yet receiving this life is not a decision to be made lightly, for it requires Christ's followers to turn their backs every day on whatever might hinder their new life together in Christ, to recommit themselves continually to one another and the Lord.

CONSIDER/ DISCUSS:
- What life-changing decision have you made? Explain.
- How does the first or second reading help you grasp the commitment Christ asks of us?
- When do you recall being especially aware of the faith commitment involved in receiving the Eucharist?

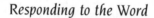 Responding to the Word

We don't say "I do" when we receive communion but we do express our faith in and commitment to Christ by saying "Amen!"—meaning both "So it is!" and "So be it!" St. Augustine explained: "It is your own mystery that you are receiving! You are saying Amen to what you are—your response is a personal signature, affirming your faith. Be a member of Christ's body, then, so that your Amen may ring true!"

- Make a conscious faith commitment when you say "Amen" to the Body of Christ.
- After communion ask Christ to feed your love for those with whom you worship.
- Choose a specific way to witness your commitment to Christ this week.

August 31, 2003

TWENTY-SECOND SUNDAY IN ORDINARY TIME

Today's Focus: Back to School

It's that time of year again! Many of us are getting ready to go back to school. Even in church this Sunday we find ourselves returning to "school." We begin a series of Scriptures that will teach us what it means—and what it costs—to be a disciple of Jesus.

FIRST READING
Deuteronomy 4: 1–2, 6–8

Moses said to the people: "Now, Israel, hear the statutes and decrees which I am teaching you to observe, that you may live, and may enter in and take possession of the land which the LORD, the God of your fathers, is giving you. In your observance of the commandments of the LORD, your God, which I enjoin upon you, you shall not add to what I command you nor subtract from it. Observe them carefully, for thus will you give evidence of your wisdom and intelligence to the nations, who will hear of all these statutes and say, 'This great nation is truly a wise and intelligent people.' For what great nation is there that has gods so close to it as the LORD, our God, is to us whenever we call upon him? Or what great nation has statutes and decrees that are as just as this whole law which I am setting before you today?"

PSALM RESPONSE
Psalm 15:1a

The one who does justice will live in the presence of the Lord.

SECOND READING
James 1:17–18, 21b–22, 27

Dearest brothers and sisters: All good giving and every perfect gift is from above, coming down from the Father of lights, with whom there is no alteration or shadow caused by change. He willed to give us birth by the word of truth that we may be a kind of firstfruits of his creatures.

Humbly welcome the word that has been planted in you and is able to save your souls.

Be doers of the word and not hearers only, deluding yourselves.

Religion that is pure and undefiled before God and the Father is this: to care for orphans and widows in their affliction and to keep oneself unstained by the world.

When the Pharisees with some scribes who had come from Jerusalem gathered around Jesus, they observed that some of his disciples ate their meals with unclean, that is, unwashed, hands. — For the Pharisees and, in fact, all Jews, do not eat without carefully washing their hands, keeping the tradition of the elders. And on coming from the marketplace they do not eat without purifying themselves. And there are many other things that they have traditionally observed, the purification of cups and jugs and kettles and beds. — So the Pharisees and scribes questioned him, "Why do your disciples not follow the tradition of the elders but instead eat a meal with unclean hands?" He responded, "Well did Isaiah prophesy about you hypocrites, as it is written:

> *This people honors me with their lips,*
> > *but their hearts are far from me;*
> *in vain do they worship me,*
> > *teaching as doctrines human precepts.*

You disregard God's commandment but cling to human tradition." He summoned the crowd again and said to them, "Hear me, all of you, and understand. Nothing that enters one from outside can defile that person; but the things that come out from within are what defile.

"From within people, from their hearts, come evil thoughts, unchastity, theft, murder, adultery, greed, malice, deceit, licentiousness, envy, blasphemy, arrogance, folly. All these evils come from within and they defile."

Understanding the Word

After more than a month of readings from the Gospel of John, today we resume a series of readings from Mark. Our focus today, however, is on the second reading from the Epistle of James. Today's text begins a five-week series of selections from James, a letter that is classified among the so-called "catholic" (or universal) epistles because they are addressed to a general audience rather than to one particular community. The authorship of this letter is unclear, although the rather refined Greek style in which it is written would argue against one of the original Twelve. The letter itself makes no specific claim, and so it could simply be that authorship has been attributed to a renowned Christian leader as a way of honoring the tradition of his teaching.

Scholars point out that the literary genre most closely resembles moral exhortation from the Jewish Wisdom tradition. Various discrete topics are treated in the course of the letter, and the author seems conversant with a number of issues that the early Christian community was dealing with. It has been suggested that today's excerpt is the second in a pattern of twelve exhortations inspired by the twelve patriarchs of Genesis 49. Be that as it may, today's text offers important advice for Christians of every generation. God is first cited as the author of all gifts, and in particular reference is made to the gift of baptism by which we have been made the "first fruits" of the new creation.

What follows is advice based on a very Jewish understanding of the "word" as an active force, operative in the world. We are reminded that unless we, too, become "doers" of the word, our claim to faith is empty. Scholars point out that this is a necessary corrective that balances Paul's emphasis on salvation by means of faith. Today and in subsequent weeks the author reminds us that it is equally important to do the "works" of love, for example, by caring for the "orphans and widows in their affliction."

Reflecting on the Word

Is someone in your house going back to school? If so there are books and supplies to buy, schedules to plan, transportation to be arranged. There is the worry over new teachers and whether everything that was learned last year has been forgotten. But no matter. Most of the time the school year begins with a review. That's good because sometimes we understand things better the second or third time we learn them.

With the Scriptures this Sunday all of us are going back to school. The series of selections from the Gospel of Mark and the letter of James that we begin this week will teach us one more time what it means to be a disciple. Lucky for us, since most of us can only learn this lesson if we hear and apply it on a daily basis. Today's first reading also instructs us to "hear" and "observe" "the commandments of the Lord" "that [we] may live." And the psalm reviews the basics: "The one who does justice will live in the presence of God."

CONSIDER/ DISCUSS:
- Do you like it when teachers review what you have already learned? Why?
- Do today's readings feel like a review? Explain.
- What do you understand better about discipleship as you reflect on these Scriptures?

Responding to the Word

They say we learn more from example than we do from words. Some teachers are better than others in this regard. Today we are blessed to be going back to school with the very best of teachers, Jesus, who was the model "doer of the word." If we want to know how to "do justice," all we need to do is look to the front of the classroom and imitate our favorite teacher.

- Examine your life for ways in which you are and are not doing the word.
- Volunteer your help to a local orphanage, foster care, or adoption program.
- Spend time with an elderly member of your faith community after Mass.

September 7, 2003

TWENTY-THIRD SUNDAY IN ORDINARY TIME

Today's Focus: 911 Call

This coming week marks the second anniversary of 9/11/2001. Today's Scriptures, including Jesus' cure of a deaf man, seem to call out to us to adhere to our faith in a God who is with us to save those who are most desperate, to lift up humanity from even the worst of disasters.

FIRST READING
Isaiah 35:4–7a

Thus says the LORD:
　　Say to those whose hearts are frightened:
　　　　Be strong, fear not!
　　Here is your God,
　　　　he comes with vindication;
　　with divine recompense
　　　　he comes to save you.
　　Then will the eyes of the blind be opened,
　　　　the ears of the deaf be cleared;
　　then will the lame leap like a stag,
　　　　then the tongue of the mute will sing.
　　Streams will burst forth in the desert,
　　　　and rivers in the steppe.
　　The burning sands will become pools,
　　　　and the thirsty ground, springs of water.

PSALM RESPONSE
Psalm 146:1b

Praise the Lord, my soul!

SECOND READING
James 2:1–5

My brothers and sisters, show no partiality as you adhere to the faith in our glorious Lord Jesus Christ. For if a man with gold rings and fine clothes comes into your assembly, and a poor person in shabby clothes also comes in, and you pay attention to the one wearing the fine clothes and say, "Sit here, please," while you say to the poor one, "Stand there," or "Sit at my feet," have you not made distinctions among yourselves and become judges with evil designs?

Listen, my beloved brothers and sisters. Did not God choose those who are poor in the world to be rich in faith and heirs of the kingdom that he promised to those who love him?

GOSPEL
Mark 7:31–37

Again Jesus left the district of Tyre and went by way of Sidon to the Sea of Galilee, into the district of the Decapolis. And people brought to him a deaf man who had a speech impediment and begged him to lay his hand on him. He took him off by himself away from the crowd. He put his finger into the man's ears and, spitting, touched his tongue; then he looked up to heaven and groaned, and said to him, *"Ephphatha!"* — that is, "Be opened!" — And immediately the man's ears were opened, his speech impediment was removed, and he spoke plainly. He ordered them not to tell anyone. But the more he ordered them not to, the more they proclaimed it. They were exceedingly astonished and they said, "He has done all things well. He makes the deaf hear and the mute speak."

Understanding the Word

The Gospel narratives can appear deceptively simple and straightforward. On the surface, they may appear simply to be an account of a sequence of events that took place in the life of Jesus. However, Scripture scholars have helped us to look more closely at these narratives and to uncover the often highly sophisticated literary effort they represent. By techniques such as overall structure, sequence of ideas, word association, and subtle allusion, the author is usually inferring much more than he appears to be saying on the surface.

Today's story of the cure of a deaf man with a speech impediment is a good example of how much is contained in a simple miracle story. The Greek word *mogilalos* appears only here in all of the New Testament. It is a technical term referring to someone with a stammer. It is also used only once in the entire Jewish Scriptures, in the passage that we read today as our first reading from Isaiah. Clearly, by his choice of this precise word Mark wants us to recognize that what Jesus is doing is the fulfillment of what Isaiah had predicted centuries earlier. In fact, Mark wants us to recognize that Jesus is the Messiah foretold by Isaiah and the other Jewish prophets of old.

The word *ephphatha*, "be opened," used to describe the restoration of the man's speech, is another example of a subtle allusion to an earlier prophecy. This time the prophecy in question is from Ezekiel, when he foretells that in the messianic age, "your mouth shall be opened to speak" (24:26). The sophistication of Mark's narrative is further revealed when we realize that there are multiple levels within a single reference. Mark not only draws our attention back to Israel's prophetic past, he also points to the initiatory practice of his contemporaries by his mention of such things as spittle, touching of ears, and the use of the word *ephphatha*, all of which were practices incorporated into the early Church's baptismal ritual.

Reflecting on the Word

The expression "911 call" will always remind her of that morning. At 8:37 a.m. Central Time the telephone rang. It was Mark calling from Brooklyn. "Hi, Mom." "Mark! How sweet of you to call me on my birthday!" "Oh, yeah. Happy birthday. Are you watching the news?" "No, why?" "I'm looking out my apartment window. I can see—and smell—the World Trade Center towers burning."

Even now, two years later, it is all too easy for us to feel afraid and vengeful when we think of the lives that were lost on 9/11/2001. Yet, today's Scriptures simply will not allow it. The first reading calls out to us: "Be strong, fear not! Here is your God ... [who] comes to save you." The psalm praises the Lord who "sets free ... raises up ... protects ... and sustains" all who are in need. In the Gospel God's glorious power works through Jesus. Finally, the letter of James issues a 911 call to all of us. God saved us through baptism; now we must "adhere to the faith" and come to the rescue of all the "poor ones" in our midst.

CONSIDER/ DISCUSS:
- What feelings emerge when you remember 9/11/2001?
- How have you found hope in a time of disaster? Explain.
- How does God save, set free, heal, and protect the "poor ones" today?

Responding to the Word

If you have ever made a 911 call you might understand the fear and helplessness that witnesses of the 9/11 disasters felt. Perhaps you have been in danger, someone you love has had a heart attack, or you have seen a car accident. Whatever the cause, most of us have experienced real fear at some time in our lives. We are blessed to be able to call out in faith to "our glorious Lord Jesus Christ" in times of trial and "fear not."

- Reach out to someone you would normally hesitate to greet.
- Contribute to a health-related global charity.
- Tutor or read aloud with a child this week.

September 14, 2003

THE EXALTATION OF THE HOLY CROSS

Today's Focus: Tree of Life

Have you seen depictions of the cross covered with leaves and flowers? Sometimes they even show birds sucking nectar from the flowers. This feast and such representations of the cross remind us that the "tree" of Christ's death became the source of abundant life for all the world.

FIRST READING
Numbers 21: 4b–9

With their patience worn out by the journey, the people complained against God and Moses, "Why have you brought us up from Egypt to die in this desert, where there is no food or water? We are disgusted with this wretched food!"

In punishment the LORD sent among the people saraph serpents, which bit the people so that many of them died. Then the people came to Moses and said, "We have sinned in complaining against the LORD and you. Pray the LORD to take the serpents from us." So Moses prayed for the people, and the LORD said to Moses, "Make a saraph and mount it on a pole, and if any who have been bitten look at it, they will live." Moses accordingly made a bronze serpent and mounted it on a pole, and whenever anyone who had been bitten by a serpent looked at the bronze serpent, he lived.

PSALM RESPONSE
Psalm 78:7b

Do not forget the works of the Lord!

SECOND READING
Philippians 2: 6–11

Brothers and sisters:
Christ Jesus, though he was in the form of God,
    did not regard equality with God
    something to be grasped.
Rather, he emptied himself,
    taking the form of a slave,
    coming in human likeness;
    and found human in appearance,
    he humbled himself,
    becoming obedient to the point of death,
    even death on a cross.
Because of this, God greatly exalted him
    and bestowed on him the name
    which is above every name,
    that at the name of Jesus
    every knee should bend,
    of those in heaven and on earth and under the earth,
    and every tongue confess that
    Jesus Christ is Lord,
    to the glory of God the Father.

GOSPEL

John 3:13–17 Jesus said to Nicodemus: "No one has gone up to heaven except the one who has come down from heaven, the Son of Man. And just as Moses lifted up the serpent in the desert, so must the Son of Man be lifted up, so that everyone who believes in him may have eternal life."

For God so loved the world that he gave his only Son, so that he who believes in him might not perish but might have eternal life. For God did not send his Son into the world to condemn the world, but that the world might be saved through him.

Understanding the Word

To understand today's readings properly, one must read them in the context of the day's liturgical feast. The Exaltation (or, as it is sometimes called, the Triumph) of the Cross is celebrated on September 14 because on that day in the year 325 the Empress Helena displayed to the faithful in Jerusalem the wood of the true cross that she had discovered the previous day. Later ages observed the custom of showing a relic of that cross to the faithful on the same day in a ceremony called the Exaltatio ("lifting up"). The earliest Christian community did not make the cross an important object of veneration, probably because of the immediacy of their experience of it as an instrument of terror. Later generations, however, were able to reflect on the cross's role in the drama of salvation and to transform it from an object of horror to a focal point of piety.

The way Jesus' attitude toward his suffering and death on the cross is portrayed in the Gospel of John is quite different from that of the synoptic Gospels. In the latter, Jesus approaches with dread and a sense of resignation the inevitability of his terrible death. In the former, the image of Jesus presented by John is one of a God-man completely in control of his destiny who goes to the cross freely, with no hint of human reluctance. While for the synoptics Jesus hangs on the cross suffering, in John's Gospel Jesus reigns triumphant from the cross. The conversation with Nicodemus in chapter three of John's Gospel is one way that the author introduces and prepares his readers for this focal point of Jesus' redemptive ministry. John has Jesus use the language of a royal coronation ("lifted up") when foretelling his eventual glorification on the cross. That language is also chosen to recall the passage in the Book of Numbers that is today's first reading. The reference is chosen because that which is "lifted up" (the serpent/cross) becomes a source of salvation for those who encounter it.

Reflecting on the Word

On Easter morning, as Delphine's godmother watched her receive communion, she couldn't have been more proud. After Mass Emma had one more gift for Delphine. It was a cross covered with green branches and leaves, and hummingbirds drawing nectar from bright red flowers. "That's you, Delphine. You are a new shoot that has sprouted from the wood of the cross. Like these flowers, you'll draw others to Christ and share with them the new life that you found in baptism."

This feast gives us an opportunity to honor the wood of the cross as the tree of everlasting life. In the words of the preface for today, it is "the tree of victory; where life was lost, there life has been restored through Christ our Lord." The wood on which Jesus was lifted up to die also lifted him to eternal life, and lifts us with him. Through the centuries millions of new shoots of life (neophytes) have sprouted from the wood of the cross to share life and nourishment with a thirsty, hungry world.

CONSIDER/ DISCUSS:
- Describe a cross that you love.
- What new life are the neophytes in your parish sharing with your community? How might you encourage their "growth?"
- How do these Scriptures call you to respond to Christ's cross today?

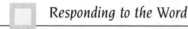

Responding to the Word

In some parts of the world this feast comes during the return of spring. New shoots are budding forth from trees that have looked dead all winter long. Birds build nests to cradle the new chicks that are emerging from their eggs. Flowers are opening to share life with the birds and the bees. For those who continually return to the wood of the cross on bended knee, the tree of life provides an eternal spring of abundant life in Christ.

- Talk with someone who was recently initiated. Thank them for their participation in the Church.
- Pray before an image of Christ's cross. Tell Christ what he has saved you from. Thank him for his love.
- Resolve to share with others the life that Christ has shared with you.

September 21, 2003

TWENTY-FIFTH SUNDAY IN ORDINARY TIME

Today's Focus: King of the Hill

As children we played a game called King of the Hill. It was simple. Everyone piled on the ground. Then each child tried to get—and stay—on top of the pile. In today's Gospel the disciples appear to be playing the same game and Jesus teaches them how to win.

FIRST READING
Wisdom 2:12, 17–20

The wicked say:
    Let us beset the just one, because he is obnoxious to us;
      he sets himself against our doings,
reproaches us for transgressions of the law
    and charges us with violations of our training.
Let us see whether his words be true;
    let us find out what will happen to him.
For if the just one be the son of God, God will defend him
    and deliver him from the hand of his foes.
With revilement and torture let us put the just one to the test
    that we may have proof of his gentleness
    and try his patience.
Let us condemn him to a shameful death;
    for according to his own words, God will take care of him.

PSALM RESPONSE
Psalm 54:6b

The Lord upholds my life.

SECOND READING
James 3:16 — 4:3

Beloved: Where jealousy and selfish ambition exist, there is disorder and every foul practice. But the wisdom from above is first of all pure, then peaceable, gentle, compliant, full of mercy and good fruits, without inconstancy or insincerity. And the fruit of righteousness is sown in peace for those who cultivate peace.

Where do the wars and where do the conflicts among you come from? Is it not from your passions that make war within your members? You covet but do not possess. You kill and envy but you cannot obtain; you fight and wage war. You do not possess because you do not ask. You ask but do not receive, because you ask wrongly, to spend it on your passions.

GOSPEL
Mark 9:30–37

Jesus and his disciples left from there and began a journey through Galilee, but he did not wish anyone to know about it. He was teaching his disciples and telling them, "The Son of Man is to be handed over to men and they will kill him, and three days after his death the Son of Man will rise." But they did not understand the saying, and they were afraid to question him.

They came to Capernaum and, once inside the house, he began to ask them, "What were you arguing about on the way?" But they remained silent. They had been discussing among themselves on the way who was the greatest. Then he sat down, called the Twelve, and said to them, "If anyone wishes to be first, he shall be the last of all and the servant of all." Taking a child, he placed it in their midst, and putting his arms around it, he said to them, "Whoever receives one child such as this in my name, receives me; and whoever receives me, receives not me but the One who sent me."

Understanding the Word

The geography of today's Gospel is significant. Jesus is completing his ministry in Galilee and beginning his journey to Jerusalem, where he will meet both death and resurrection. The prediction of his death placed here is the second of three in Mark's Gospel, and as usual it is the occasion for an important teaching on the part of Jesus. The literary technique Mark uses to set up this teaching is reminiscent of that used by John in his Gospel. Last month, when we read from the Bread of Life discourse in John's Gospel, we saw how the author used the technique of misunderstanding as an occasion for Jesus to clarify and take his teaching to an even deeper level. Mark does something similar here and in the other passages where Jesus predicts his death. The disciples fail to grasp the meaning of Jesus' prediction, and so he must explain further just what his ministry (and his death) is all about.

Today that explanation is tied to Jesus' teaching on the need for his disciples to embrace a ministry of service. A play on words in Aramaic would have linked the words "child" and "servant," thus turning Jesus' gesture of placing a child in their midst into an illustration of his own self-understanding as the Servant of the Lord. It is that same awareness of the meaning of their ministry that Jesus (and Mark) wishes to instill in the disciples. Theirs must be a ministry of service if they are to follow in the footsteps of Jesus. And that service might even require of them that they be "handed over" to death. What would have been—in the culture of Jesus' day—an ordinary discussion of social status ("who was the greatest") becomes in Mark's context a key insight into the meaning of discipleship. The link that is made here between the suffering/death of Jesus and the disciples' own ministry of service is another key insight that Mark does not want lost on his readers.

Reflecting on the Word

King of the Hill was a lot of fun until someone took the game seriously. Then it got ugly. The problem was that the only way to stay on top was to keep pushing others down. Anyone who was really serious about staying on top of the pile had to keep kicking and tromping on those of us who were down below.

The Scriptures for this week depict four scenes in which people push others down in order to be king of the hill. In the reading from the book of Wisdom "the wicked ... beset the just one" and "condemn him to a shameful death." The psalmist cries out to God: "Haughty men have risen up against me, the ruthless seek my life." James chides those who act out of "jealousy and selfish ambition" and the disciples argue about "who was the greatest." Jesus tells the Twelve to lift others up, not to push them down. He says this knowing that those who serve others will surely suffer and may end up—as he did—on the bottom of the pile.

CONSIDER/ DISCUSS:
- In what ways do we adults play King of the Hill?
- How did "the just one" in the first reading serve others? How did the author of the letter of James serve the Church?
- What wisdom from these Scriptures could you apply to your life? Explain.

Responding to the Word

Usually when we played King of the Hill my eldest brother ended up at the bottom of the pile even though he was the biggest and strongest. We all looked up to him as our real leader despite, or perhaps because of, his losing ways. Like Jesus, he seemed to know that the real way to win was to lift others up, not to push them down. In the process he taught us a lot about wisdom, peacemaking, suffering, and service.

- Serve someone you love in an unexpected way.
- Pray for an end to violence and oppression in our world.
- Work toward a peaceful solution to a combative situation.

September 28, 2003

TWENTY-SIXTH SUNDAY IN ORDINARY TIME

Today's Focus: Gated Community

While a gated community can provide a great sense of security, it can also foster discrimination against those who don't meet the entrance requirements. In today's Scriptures people want to exclude some suspicious characters. We are reminded that there are no gates excluding anyone from the community of God's chosen people.

FIRST READING
Numbers 11: 25–29

The LORD came down in the cloud and spoke to Moses. Taking some of the spirit that was on Moses, the LORD bestowed it on the seventy elders; and as the spirit came to rest on them, they prophesied.

Now two men, one named Eldad and the other Medad, were not in the gathering but had been left in the camp. They too had been on the list, but had not gone out to the tent; yet the spirit came to rest on them also, and they prophesied in the camp. So, when a young man quickly told Moses, "Eldad and Medad are prophesying in the camp," Joshua, son of Nun, who from his youth had been Moses' aide, said, "Moses, my lord, stop them." But Moses answered him, "Are you jealous for my sake? Would that all the people of the LORD were prophets! Would that the LORD might bestow his spirit on them all!"

PSALM RESPONSE
Psalm 19:9a

The precepts of the Lord give joy to the heart.

SECOND READING
James 5:1–6

Come now, you rich, weep and wail over your impending miseries. Your wealth has rotted away, your clothes have become moth-eaten, your gold and silver have corroded, and that corrosion will be a testimony against you; it will devour your flesh like a fire. You have stored up treasure for the last days. Behold, the wages you withheld from the workers who harvested your fields are crying aloud; and the cries of the harvesters have reached the ears of the Lord of hosts. You have lived on earth in luxury and pleasure; you have fattened your hearts for the day of slaughter. You have condemned; you have murdered the righteous one; he offers you no resistance.

At that time, John said to Jesus, "Teacher, we saw someone driving out demons in your name, and we tried to prevent him because he does not follow us." Jesus replied, "Do not prevent him. There is no one who performs a mighty deed in my name who can at the same time speak ill of me. For whoever is not against us is for us. Anyone who gives you a cup of water to drink because you belong to Christ, amen, I say to you, will surely not lose his reward.

"Whoever causes one of these little ones who believe in me to sin, it would be better for him if a great millstone were put around his neck and he were thrown into the sea. If your hand causes you to sin, cut it off. It is better for you to enter into life maimed than with two hands to go into Gehenna, into the unquenchable fire. And if your foot causes you to sin, cut it off. It is better for you to enter into life crippled than with two feet to be thrown into Gehenna. And if your eye causes you to sin, pluck it out. Better for you to enter into the kingdom of God with one eye than with two eyes to be thrown into Gehenna, where 'their worm does not die, and the fire is not quenched.'"

Understanding the Word

We have mentioned before how the interpretation of the Sunday readings is often influenced by the liturgical cycle, a special feast day, or even the other readings chosen for a particular Sunday. This Sunday's texts are a good example of how the latter example operates. Today's Gospel selection is made up of four sayings of Jesus that appear totally unrelated. Knowledge of Greek, however, reveals the key to their association. Each of the sayings is connected to the one that follows by a Greek catchword (which is lost in translation), no doubt as a way to foster memorization of material that first existed only in oral form. But the choice of today's reading from the Book of Numbers concentrates our attention on only one of those four sayings, and thus highlights a dominant theme for the day's liturgy.

The issue addressed in the reading from Numbers was whether the gift of prophecy could be authentic in persons who had not been part of an earlier foundational event in which God had shared with seventy elders a portion of Moses' prophetic spirit. Moses authenticates the prophetic gift given to the two latecomers, appealing to the fact that God is not limited by human institutions when choosing who will receive the spirit of prophecy. Scholars suggest that this incident has been preserved and incorporated into the book of Numbers because subsequent generations also were wrestling with the issue of how to discern authentic prophets in a religious culture where many false prophets also claimed divine legitimacy.

The Gospel passage reflects a similar situation in Mark's Christian community. Apparently there were those not officially designated to do so who were exorcising demons, and so the evangelist incorporates into his Gospel this incident in which Jesus faced a similar situation during his ministry. Like Moses, the response of Jesus points to God's freedom to bestow the Spirit on anyone, regardless of institutional religious affiliation.

Reflecting on the Word

The word "discriminate" actually means to divide or distinguish differences. In that sense of the word, we can say that gated communities "discriminate." They literally divide the worlds of residents and nonresidents. They also distinguish the difference between those who are and are not wealthy enough to live there. The same gates that protect the possessions and lifestyle of the residents also exclude (or discriminate against) those who don't meet the entrance requirements.

In today's Scriptures people try to exclude those whom they suspect of not meeting the "entrance requirements" for God's people. Moses and Jesus challenge their discriminating view of who can and cannot receive the Spirit. Jesus even goes so far as to say that "whoever is not against us is for us," thus opening wide the gates that distinguished God's chosen ones. Those wandering the streets have no less claim to God's favor than longtime residents whose mortgages are paid.

CONSIDER/ DISCUSS:
- What feelings do you have about gated communities?
- Can you empathize with Joshua and John in these Scriptures? Explain.
- How might our discriminating tendencies "cause one of these little ones"—or us ourselves—to sin?

Responding to the Word

While gated communities exclude most of the needy, some of the poor slip in past the gates by working in the homes and yards of the rich. That's when a second method of discrimination can set in. We might wonder whether the residents treat their workers with dignity or pay them wages that meet their human needs. The fact is that all of us discriminate against some vulnerable "little ones" of the world. The warnings in this week's Scriptures apply to us all.

- Ask God to open your mind and heart to rejoice in the Lord's limitless mercy.
- Treat those of a different socioeconomic status with dignity and respect.
- Consider before you act how your choices will affect those who are poor or vulnerable.

October 5, 2003

TWENTY-SEVENTH SUNDAY IN ORDINARY TIME

Today's Focus: Paradise Found

In paradise every creature was in right relationship with the Creator. Man and woman harmonized with each other perfectly. All things fit naturally into the plan of God. Today's readings retrieve this vision of our origins and our destiny as a model for all our relationships here and now.

FIRST READING
Genesis 2: 18–24

The LORD God said: "It is not good for the man to be alone. I will make a suitable partner for him." So the LORD God formed out of the ground various wild animals and various birds of the air, and he brought them to the man to see what he would call them; whatever the man called each of them would be its name. The man gave names to all the cattle, all the birds of the air, and all wild animals; but none proved to be the suitable partner for the man.

So the LORD God cast a deep sleep on the man, and while he was asleep, he took out one of his ribs and closed up its place with flesh. The LORD God then built up into a woman the rib that he had taken from the man. When he brought her to the man, the man said:

"This one, at last, is bone of my bones
    and flesh of my flesh;
this one shall be called 'woman,'
    for out of 'her man' this one has been taken."

That is why a man leaves his father and mother and clings to his wife, and the two of them become one flesh.

PSALM RESPONSE
Psalm 128:5

May the Lord bless us all the days of our lives

SECOND READING
Hebrews 2:9–11

Brothers and sisters: He "for a little while" was made "lower than the angels," that by the grace of God he might taste death for everyone.

For it was fitting that he, for whom and through whom all things exist, in bringing many children to glory, should make the leader to their salvation perfect through suffering. He who consecrates and those who are being consecrated all have one origin. Therefore, he is not ashamed to call them "brothers."

GOSPEL
Mark 10:2–16
or 10:2–12

The Pharisees approached Jesus and asked, "Is it lawful for a husband to divorce his wife?" They were testing him. He said to them in reply, "What did Moses command you?" They replied, "Moses permitted a husband to write a bill of divorce and dismiss her." But Jesus told them, "Because of the hardness of your hearts he wrote you this commandment. But from the beginning of creation,

> *God made them male and female. For this reason a man shall leave his father and mother and be joined to his wife, and the two shall become one flesh.*

So they are no longer two but one flesh. Therefore what God has joined together, no human being must separate." In the house the disciples again questioned Jesus about this. He said to them, "Whoever divorces his wife and marries another commits adultery against her; and if she divorces her husband and marries another, she commits adultery."

[And people were bringing children to him that he might touch them, but the disciples rebuked them. When Jesus saw this he became indignant and said to them, "Let the children come to me; do not prevent them, for the kingdom of God belongs to such as these. Amen, I say to you, whoever does not accept the kingdom of God like a child will not enter it." Then he embraced them and blessed them, placing his hands on them.]

Understanding the Word

Our focus today is on the Gospel and Jesus' teaching on marriage. We are familiar with the running conflict between Jesus and the Jewish religious authorities that appears in all four Gospels. Sensing the larger implications of his claim to teach with authority, the Pharisees were eager to discredit him in the eyes of the people. Today's question about divorce probably reflects a contemporary dispute among the Pharisees of Jesus' day. Two rival Pharisee groups, the disciples of Hillel and those of Shammai, argued over whether divorce was permitted only in cases of adultery (Shammai) or for a number of other lesser reasons (Hillel). Jesus answers in the customary manner of a rabbinic disputation by asking a question of those who question him. His answer then proceeds to resolve the issue by citing the one source considered more authoritative than Moses, that is, God. Jesus appeals to the divine will revealed in the Book of Genesis to support his claim that divorce is not permitted at all. The dispute among the Pharisees was over the interpretation of a passage in the Mosaic Law (Deuteronomy 24:1–4). Mark shows how clever Jesus was by his return to the Book of Genesis. Time and again, Jesus confounds his adversaries by shifting the conversation to a higher plane and revealing how limited and inadequate their thinking is.

This is also a good example of how Jesus often developed his moral teaching in light of the advent of the Reign of God and the radical stance that is required by the disciples who wish to be part of God's Reign. Just as the seemingly impossible demands of the Beatitudes are presented by Jesus as a real possibility for those who live within the dynamic of God's Reign, so the seemingly impossible teaching on the permanency of marriage must be understood as an expression of the grace available to those who live within the new dispensation of God's Reign.

Reflecting on the Word

The creation story paints a picture of a blessed garden called paradise where all creatures are at peace with one another and with God. Man and woman are equal partners. Then something happens. Sin, discord. Paradise is lost, but not forever. The story of our origins also describes our destiny. We believe that we are destined to find that paradise again when the Reign of God is fully realized on the last day. In the meantime we are called to let that incredible vision transform every relationship we have here on earth.

The second reading today points to the dignity of all human beings as brothers and sisters of Christ. In the Gospel passage, Jesus overturns societal norms by emphasizing the equal rights and responsibilities of men and women in marriage. Then he embraces children not as the third-class citizens they were, but as precious models for all those who would find "paradise" here and now. Radical equality and dignity, trust in God and harmony with one another bless the relationships of those who see Christ in all their brothers and sisters.

CONSIDER/ DISCUSS:
- What part of the vision of these Scriptures attracts you? Does anything bother you? Explain.
- What interferes with our ability to find paradise here on earth?
- In what ways would you like to improve one of your relationships?

Responding to the Word

While Jesus' words challenge those who are married not to give up the pursuit of "paradise," that certainly doesn't mean people should spend their lives searching for the perfect mate! Nor should anyone live in shame and blame for hurting or "failed" relationships. Recognizing that the perfection of paradise will be found only in eternity, we all can still open our hearts to the possibility of seeing Christ in one another despite our differences. Such openness is a vital step toward finding blessing within our far-from-perfect human relationships.

- Name three good things about the person with whom you share your primary relationship or about a person with whom you have a significant relationship.
- Name one way in which you could improve your relationship.
- Ask God to bless all your relationships with an increase in harmony and peace.

October 12, 2003

TWENTY-EIGHTH SUNDAY IN ORDINARY TIME

Today's Focus: Prize Possessions

Most of us can name a few prize possessions—things we display in our homes, things that give us joy and pride. Today's Scriptures showcase a cornucopia of heavenly treasures. Unlike the rich young man in the Gospel, perhaps we will give up everything to obtain these prize possessions.

FIRST READING
Wisdom 7:7–11

I prayed, and prudence was given me;
    I pleaded, and the spirit of wisdom came to me.
I preferred her to scepter and throne,
and deemed riches nothing in comparison with her,
    nor did I liken any priceless gem to her;
because all gold, in view of her, is a little sand,
    and before her, silver is to be accounted mire.
Beyond health and comeliness I loved her,
and I chose to have her rather than the light,
    because the splendor of her never yields to sleep.
Yet all good things together came to me in her company,
    and countless riches at her hands.

PSALM RESPONSE
Psalm 90:14

Fill us with your love, O Lord, and we will sing for joy!

SECOND READING
Hebrews 4:12–13

Brothers and sisters: Indeed the word of God is living and effective, sharper than any two-edged sword, penetrating even between soul and spirit, joints and marrow, and able to discern reflections and thoughts of the heart. No creature is concealed from him, but everything is naked and exposed to the eyes of him to whom we must render an account.

In the shorter form of the reading, the passage in brackets is omitted.

GOSPEL
Mark 10:17–30 or 10:17–27

As Jesus was setting out on a journey, a man ran up, knelt down before him, and asked him, "Good teacher, what must I do to inherit eternal life?" Jesus answered him, "Why do you call me good? No one is good but God alone. You know the commandments:

You shall not kill; you shall not commit adultery; you shall not steal; you shall not bear false witness; you shall not defraud; honor your father and your mother."

He replied and said to him, "Teacher, all of these I have observed from my youth." Jesus, looking at him, loved him and said to him, "You are lacking in one thing. Go, sell what you have, and give to the poor and you will have treasure in heaven; then come, follow me." At that statement his face fell, and he went away sad, for he had many possessions.

Jesus looked around and said to his disciples, "How hard it is for those who have wealth to enter the kingdom of God!" The disciples were amazed at his words. So Jesus again said to them in reply, "Children, how hard it is to enter the kingdom of God! It is easier for a camel to pass through the eye of a needle than for one who is rich to enter the kingdom of God." They were exceedingly astonished and said among themselves, "Then who can be saved?" Jesus looked at them and said, "For human beings it is impossible, but not for God. All things are possible for God." [Peter began to say to him, "We have given up everything and followed you." Jesus said, "Amen, I say to you, there is no one who has given up house or brothers or sisters or mother or father or children or lands for my sake and for the sake of the gospel who will not receive a hundred times more now in this present age: houses and brothers and sisters and mothers and children and lands, with persecutions, and eternal life in the age to come."]

Understanding the Word

Scripture scholars have suggested that one way to deepen our understanding of Mark's Gospel is to read it from the perspective of the particular concerns that apparently motivated the evangelist in the composition of his work. One of his major concerns, they point out, was to drive home to his readers the true meaning and cost of discipleship. Mark's Gospel is written for those (perhaps like us?) who have finally begun to ask themselves just what it means and implies to give oneself over to Jesus as Lord and Master.

The passage chosen for today's Gospel reading contains a narrative of an encounter between Jesus and a would-be disciple (verses 17–22), followed by two dialogues (verses 23–27, 28–31) in which Mark has Jesus explain more fully to his inner circle the meaning of what has just transpired. This is a familiar technique of Mark when he wishes his readers to understand the deeper implications of something that has been narrated in the Gospel.

The basic thrust of the entire passage is that "something more" is required of those who would be Jesus' followers, but "something more" will be given them as well. The man in question is a follower of the law, but Jesus invites him to enter a personal relationship of love that goes beyond mere fulfillment of one's legal obligations under the Torah. This is the only place in Mark's Gospel where it is explicitly said that Jesus "loved" someone. The gratuitous nature of the love that characterizes discipleship is further highlighted in Jesus' words that indicate that is it God who enables the disciple to give up all possessions for the sake of following Jesus ("All things are possible for God"). The paradoxical nature of discipleship is even clearer in the final segment where Jesus promises rewards that are "hundredfold," as well as persecutions! For the community to whom Mark addressed his Gospel, already undergoing active persecution, these would have been words of great reassurance.

What is your prize possession? Is it a pet? A recent survey found that most Americans would not trade their pets for a million dollars. Maybe it's a diamond necklace. Maybe it's a car. It could be a family business, a work of art, or a savings account; a lock of baby hair, a photograph, or a letter from a loved one. Maybe it's beauty or status, or even a grudge. Whatever they might be, most of us have some prize possessions that we would be very reluctant to give up for anything in the world.

As we watch the rich man in today's Gospel go away sad, we can't help but wonder if we, too, have any prize possessions that are making it difficult for us "to enter the kingdom of God." Would we give those possessions in trade for the heavenly treasures displayed in this week's Scriptures—prudence and wisdom (Wisdom); God's love, kindness, and care (Psalm 90); the living and effective word of God (Hebrews); the law, the kingdom of God, the Gospel, persecutions, eternal life (Mark)?

CONSIDER/ DISCUSS:
- Can you empathize with the unnamed man in today's Gospel? Explain.
- What might be your prize possessions? What makes them so valuable to you?
- Which of the treasures in today's Scriptures would you most like to possess? What would you give for it?

Responding to the Word

Perhaps you think it's impossible to "give up everything and follow" Christ. And yet Jesus says, "All things are possible for God." The truth of the matter is that Jesus himself wants to be our prize possession. When we treasure his love above all else, our other possessions just might lose their hold over us. And those who prize their relationship with the Lord will be given all the treasures of heaven besides.

- Take some quiet time to treasure the love Christ has for you.
- Ask Christ, "What must I do to inherit eternal life?" Listen for the answer.
- Give away some of your possessions or wealth this week.

October 19, 2003

TWENTY-NINTH SUNDAY IN ORDINARY TIME

Today's Focus: Human Nature

Often you will hear people excuse an error, a weakness, or a sin by attributing it to "human nature." The Scriptures for this week suggest a more lofty view of humanity. With Jesus as our model, we see what it might mean for us to embrace our true human nature.

FIRST READING
Isaiah 53:10–11

The LORD was pleased
    to crush him in infirmity.

If he gives his life as an offering for sin,
    he shall see his descendants in a long life,
    and the will of the LORD shall be accomplished through him.

Because of his affliction
    he shall see the light in fullness of days;
through his suffering, my servant shall justify many,
    and their guilt he shall bear.

PSALM RESPONSE
Psalm 33:22

Lord, let your mercy be on us, as we place our trust in you.

SECOND READING
Hebrews 4:14–16

Brothers and sisters: Since we have a great high priest who has passed through the heavens, Jesus, the Son of God, let us hold fast to our confession. For we do not have a high priest who is unable to sympathize with our weaknesses, but one who has similarly been tested in every way, yet without sin. So let us confidently approach the throne of grace to receive mercy and to find grace for timely help.

In the shorter form of the reading, the passage in brackets is omitted.

GOSPEL
Mark 10:35–45 or 10:42–45

[James and John, the sons of Zebedee, came to Jesus and said to him, "Teacher, we want you to do for us whatever we ask of you." He replied, "What do you wish me to do for you?" They answered him, "Grant that in your glory we may sit one at your right and the other at your left." Jesus said to them, "You do not know what you are asking. Can you drink the cup that I drink or be baptized with the baptism with which I am baptized?" They said to him, "We can." Jesus said to them, "The cup that I drink, you will drink, and with the baptism with which I am baptized, you will be baptized; but to sit at my right or at my left is not mine to give but is for those for whom it has been prepared." When the ten heard this, they became indignant at James and John.] Jesus summoned

[them] the Twelve and said to them, "You know that those who are recognized as rulers over the Gentiles lord it over them, and their great ones make their authority over them felt. But it shall not be so among you. Rather, whoever wishes to be great among you will be your servant; whoever wishes to be first among you will be the slave of all. For the Son of Man did not come to be served but to serve and to give his life as a ransom for many."

Understanding the Word

All three readings today support—each in its own way, of course—a reflection on the humanity of Jesus Christ and how that humanity played a key role in the drama of our salvation. The first reading is taken from one of Isaiah's so-called "Servant Songs," poems about a mysterious figure whose innocent sufferings have redemptive value for the people at large. These portions of the Book of Isaiah were to provide an important basis for later Christian understandings of the mystery of Jesus' own suffering and death.

Although not chosen specifically to coordinate with the other two readings, today's second reading does in fact carry forward the theme of Christ's humanity in a remarkable way. The author of the Letter to the Hebrews highlights the solidarity that exists between Jesus and us, precisely because in his human nature Jesus has known the same sufferings and testing that are our own experience. Because he can "sympathize with our weaknesses," we can "approach the throne of grace to receive mercy." For the author of Hebrews, the humanity of Jesus was an essential requirement for his redemptive death, as well as an invitation to us to find in Jesus someone with whom we can identify in our daily struggles.

The Gospel story today tells about the disciples arguing over who would be most important in the Reign of God, and Jesus' rebuke and reminder that his disciples will find their greatness in suffering and service. Mark here is highlighting the blindness of the disciples who still do not "get it," namely that the Messiah is destined to suffer. The message of this episode is highlighted by being placed between Jesus' third and final prediction of his death and the cure of the blind man in Jericho. There is deliberate irony in the fact that the blind man is the one who "sees" Jesus and willingly follows him "on the way" to Jerusalem (and suffering). Mark wants his readers, followers of the Way (i.e., Christian disciples), to recognize that their current sufferings are part of the divine plan as well.

Reflecting on the Word

While some religions assert humanity's "utter depravity" or inability to do what is good, Catholicism is not one of them. We believe humans are good by nature and Jesus is the epitome of that goodness. In the *Vatican II Constitution on the Church in the Modern World* #22 we read: "It is only in the mystery of the Word made flesh that the mystery of man truly becomes clear. ... Christ ... fully reveals man to himself and brings to light his most high calling."

What does the portrait of Jesus Christ in this week's Scriptures reveal to us about our true human nature? First, we are not alone in our suffering; Jesus suffered and died like us. Second, through Christ we have the grace to be like him, "the perfect man"—to choose freely what is good and to know, love, and serve God and one another. Third, thanks to Jesus Christ's sacrifice we are destined to live forever with him beyond the grave. The humanity of Jesus invites us to identify with, to emulate, and to place our trust in him.

<table>
<tr><td>CONSIDER/
DISCUSS:</td><td>• How do you usually understand or use the phrase "human nature?"</td></tr>
</table>

- How do you usually understand or use the phrase "human nature?"

- Do you feel it is human nature to trust in God and to sacrifice for others? Explain.

- How does Jesus' humanity in these Scriptures offer you empathy, example, or hope today?

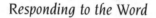

Responding to the Word

Can you drink the cup that Jesus drank? The cup we bless and share in the Eucharist is the cup of Christ's life poured out on behalf of others. He invites us to "do this in memory of me." It takes courage to accept this invitation to claim our true human nature. Maybe that's the real reason so many of us refuse the cup when receiving communion.

- During the Eucharistic Prayer at Mass, listen prayerfully to the words over the cup.

- Serve someone who least expects it.

- Notice when you are acting out of your true human nature this week.

October 26, 2003

THIRTIETH SUNDAY IN ORDINARY TIME

Today's Focus: The Panhandler

We usually think of the leading character in this Gospel story as a pitiful blind man. He was also a ragged beggar, sitting on the street asking passersby for spare change—in short, a panhandler. And it is he—not the Twelve—whom we take as a model of discipleship.

FIRST READING
Jeremiah 31: 7–9

Thus says the LORD:
Shout with joy for Jacob,
    exult at the head of the nations;
    proclaim your praise and say:
The LORD has delivered his people,
    the remnant of Israel.
Behold, I will bring them back
    from the land of the north;
I will gather them from the ends of the world,
    with the blind and the lame in their midst,
the mothers and those with child;
    they shall return as an immense throng.
They departed in tears,
    but I will console them and guide them;
I will lead them to brooks of water,
    on a level road, so that none shall stumble.
For I am a father to Israel,
    Ephraim is my first-born.

PSALM RESPONSE
Psalm 126:3

The Lord has done great things for us; we are filled with joy.

SECOND READING
Hebrews 5:1–6

Brothers and sisters: Every high priest is taken from among men and made their representative before God, to offer gifts and sacrifices for sins. He is able to deal patiently with the ignorant and erring, for he himself is beset by weakness and so, for this reason, must make sin offerings for himself as well as for the people. No one takes this honor upon himself but only when called by God, just as Aaron was. In the same way, it was not Christ who glorified himself in becoming high priest, but rather the one who said to him:

You are my son:
    this day I have begotten you;
just as he says in another place:
You are a priest forever
    according to the order of Melchizedek.

GOSPEL
Mark 10:46–52

As Jesus was leaving Jericho with his disciples and a sizable crowd, Bartimaeus, a blind man, the son of Timaeus, sat by the roadside begging. On hearing that it was Jesus of Nazareth, he began to cry out and say, "Jesus, son of David, have pity on me." And many rebuked him, telling him to be silent. But he kept calling out all the more, "Son of David, have pity on me." Jesus stopped and said, "Call him." So they called the blind man, saying to him, "Take courage; get up, Jesus is calling you." He threw aside his cloak, sprang up, and came to Jesus. Jesus said to him in reply, "What do you want me to do for you?" The blind man replied to him, "Master, I want to see." Jesus told him, "Go your way; your faith has saved you." Immediately he received his sight and followed him on the way.

Understanding the Word

Scholars have called one of the literary techniques used by Mark in his Gospel the "Messianic Secret." This refers to the fact that Mark portrays Jesus making attempts to keep secret his identity as the Messiah. The attempts are meant to be seen by the reader as ineffective and doomed to fail. This motif is woven into another theme, the blindness of those closest to Jesus, a blindness that is contrasted with the fact that those farthest from him (such as the demons) are the first to "recognize" his true identity. For Mark, it is only in his suffering and death that Jesus is "seen" by all for who he really is—the Messiah of God.

Today's story of the cure of a blind man is highly symbolic. It forms the end of a unit of material that begins with another story of a cure of a blind man (8:22–26). That first story happens at the beginning of Jesus' journey to Jerusalem; this cure marks the end of the journey, since Jesus enters Jerusalem immediately after healing Bartimaeus. In between these two stories, there is a growing sense of irony, as Jesus progressively reveals by word and deed what he is about, while his disciples continuously miss the point. Finally, Mark shows what a true disciple looks like in the story of Bartimaeus.

That the blind man can "see" better than the disciples is shown by his use of the messianic title "Son of David," which he proclaims in a loud voice. The word Mark uses here for "call out" is also associated elsewhere in the Gospel with the revelation of Jesus' messianic power. Breaking the expected behavior of the Messianic Secret, Jesus on this occasion tells those who try to silence Bartimaeus to allow him to come forward. Then, after his cure, the man is described as following Jesus "on the way," an obvious reference to the life of discipleship (see Acts 9:2, 19:9, etc., where "followers of the way" is an early Christian term used for disciples).

Reflecting on the Word

We've all done it—passed street people without seeming to see, hear, or smell them sitting on the sidewalk begging. I usually encounter them when I'm dressed up to go to the theater or on vacation in a strange city. I'm slightly out of my comfort zone. I might catch sight of their shoeless feet or sunglasses or hear the thin request, "Spare change?" Immediately my guard goes up and I pretend not to notice their existence, let alone their need. Chances are they aren't really blind, anyway, and they'd probably just spend the money on liquor.

The star of today's Gospel is a panhandler. Bartimaeus is blind, yes, but he is probably also homeless and filthy, a real nuisance to respectable citizens. Even so it is Bartimaeus who recognizes Jesus as the Messiah, places all his faith in him, throws aside everything he has (his cloak), begs him for mercy, receives new vision, and follows Jesus on the way to suffering and death in Jerusalem. How desperate will we have to get before we can do the same?

CONSIDER/
DISCUSS:
- What experience do you have with street people or panhandlers?
- How did you feel when you heard today's readings? Explain.
- What aspect of discipleship is most difficult for you?

Responding to the Word

Panhandlers are utterly dependent on charity for their daily bread. They have nothing of real value, so they have nothing to lose. They seem to be so insignificant as to be invisible to most of society. Might our self-sufficiency, self-defensiveness, and self-importance blind us to something that their poverty reveals? Like Bartimaeus, if we would follow Jesus we must depend utterly on him for mercy, vision, direction, and daily bread.

- Pray the "Our Father" fervently each morning this week.
- Approach the bread of the Eucharist with utter faith and dependence on Christ.
- Contribute to a homeless shelter in your community.

November 1, 2003

THE SOLEMNITY OF ALL SAINTS

Today's Focus: Holy Communion

The solemnity of All Saints reminds us that we are not alone in the pursuit of holiness. The Body of Christ includes throngs of holy men and women who have gone before us and who assemble with us to praise the Lamb of God and sustain us on our journey to the kingdom.

FIRST READING
Revelation 7: 2–4, 9–14

I, John, saw another angel come up from the East, holding the seal of the living God. He cried out in a loud voice to the four angels who were given power to damage the land and the sea, "Do not damage the land or the sea or the trees until we put the seal on the foreheads of the servants of our God." I heard the number of those who had been marked with the seal, one hundred and forty-four thousand marked from every tribe of the Israelites.

After this I had a vision of a great multitude, which no one could count, from every nation, race, people, and tongue. They stood before the throne and before the Lamb, wearing white robes and holding palm branches in their hands. They cried out in a loud voice:

"Salvation comes from our God,
who is seated on the throne,
and from the Lamb."

All the angels stood around the throne and around the elders and the four living creatures. They prostrated themselves before the throne, worshiped God, and exclaimed:

"Amen. Blessing and glory, wisdom and thanksgiving,
honor, power, and might
be to our God forever and ever. Amen."

Then one of the elders spoke up and said to me, "Who are these wearing white robes, and where did they come from?" I said to him, "My lord, you are the one who knows." He said to me, "These are the ones who have survived the time of great distress; they have washed their robes and made them white in the blood of the Lamb."

PSALM RESPONSE
Psalm 24:6

Lord, this is the people that longs to see your face.

SECOND READING
1 John 3:1–3

Beloved: See what love the Father has bestowed on us that we may be called the children of God. Yet so we are. The reason the world does not know us is that it did not know him. Beloved, we are God's children now; what we shall be has not yet been revealed. We do know that when it is revealed we shall be like him, for we shall see him as he is. Everyone who has this hope based on him makes himself pure, as he is pure.

GOSPEL
Matthew 5:
1–12a

When Jesus saw the crowds, he went up the mountain, and after he had sat down, his disciples came to him. He began to teach them, saying:

"Blessed are the poor in spirit,
for theirs is the kingdom of heaven.
Blessed are they who mourn,
for they will be comforted.
Blessed are the meek,
for they will inherit the land.
Blessed are they who hunger and thirst for righteousness,
for they will be satisfied.
Blessed are the merciful,
for they will be shown mercy.
Blessed are the clean of heart,
for they will see God.
Blessed are the peacemakers,
for they will be called children of God.
Blessed are they who are persecuted for the sake of righteousness,
for theirs is the kingdom of heaven.
Blessed are you when they insult you and persecute you and utter every kind of evil against you falsely because of me. Rejoice and be glad, for your reward will be great in heaven."

Understanding the Word

One of the things that All Saints Day celebrates is our conviction that there exists a solidarity between us and the countless holy men and women who have passed from this life to the next. These holy ones, the saints, are with God in a mysterious communion of love, yet they remain in relationship with us as well. Today's first reading from the Book of Revelation expresses this conviction in exotic imagery taken over from a kind of writing called "apocalyptic."

Apocalyptic writing uses fantastic images to convey truths beyond human perception, much as poetry finds its creativity in the juxtaposition of familiar images in fresh ways. The author offers a series of visions, highly symbolic in nature, using images that often would have had special meaning to his audience of Christian believers, while for the uninitiated appearing no more exceptional than the familiar pagan mythology of Roman society. The ultimate purpose of this literature was to comfort, console, and encourage those undergoing persecution.

Thus, in today's text the author portrays a scene of victory on the part of those who have remained faithful under persecution. All who have gathered around the divine throne singing victory songs are wearing white robes, reminiscent of their baptismal garments, and they sing of the Lamb who is with God—an obvious reference to Jesus, whom the early believers honored under the title "Lamb of God" for the sacrificial nature of his death.

It was popularly believed that the Messiah would return at the end of time from the east, whence comes the dawn. The fact that the angel in the vision also comes from the east is significant, since he is ushering in the age of the Messiah. The act of placing a royal seal on an object to claim it for a king was widely understood, and so the direction to the angel to place the seal on the multitude (144,000 is a "perfect" number) would have been understood as an act of protection. The "servants of God" belong to the divine king, and none shall touch them.

Reflecting on the Word

We may believe in the communion of saints, but the Orthodox churches celebrate it constantly. In each Divine Liturgy it is understood that a spiritual doorway connects the living to the liturgy of praise that the angels and saints celebrate eternally in heaven. Their church buildings are often circular, capped by a large dome to symbolize heaven. Often, too, the interiors are covered with icons of saints and angels and an icon of Christ in the dome. This emphasizes the communion of all God's holy people, in heaven and on earth, around Christ's altar.

It shouldn't surprise us, then, to find many similarities to our eucharistic liturgy in today's reading from Revelation as it describes the heavenly liturgy of the saints and angels. The Constitution on the Church #50 states: "Our communion with the saints joins us to Christ. ... It is especially in the sacred liturgy that our union with the heavenly Church is best realized."

**CONSIDER/
DISCUSS:**
- Describe an Orthodox church or liturgy that you have attended.
- How many similarities or references to our liturgy can you find in the selection from Revelation?
- How have saints supported you in your life?

Responding to the Word

The Constitution on the Church #49 states: "Being more closely united to Christ, those who dwell in heaven fix the whole Church more firmly in holiness ... So by their brotherly concern is our weakness greatly helped." The people on earth "that longs to see [God's] face" and struggles to live as "children of God" can look with real hope to this holy communion of saints. They, the "righteous" and the "persecuted," have received their "reward in heaven." The support they gave the Church when they were on earth is even more available now that they are in close communion with the Lord.

- Listen to the Eucharistic Prayer for connections with the heavenly liturgy.
- When you receive "Holy Communion," become aware of all those with whom you are in communion.
- Open your heart to the spiritual support of the saints.

November 2, 2003

THE COMMEMORATION OF ALL
THE FAITHFUL DEPARTED (ALL SOULS)

Today's Focus: Rest in peace

The feast of All Souls commemorates all the baptized who have died in the hope of eternal life. We hope and pray that our loved ones will be eternally rewarded for their faith, receive mercy for their sins, and "rest in peace" from their sufferings and labors here on earth.

The readings printed here are chosen from the broad selection available for the Mass on this day.

FIRST READING
Wisdom 3:1-9

The souls of the just are in the hand of God,
and no torment shall touch them.
They seemed, in the view of the foolish, to be dead;
and their passing away was thought an affliction
and their going forth from us utter destruction.
But they are in peace.
For if in the sight of others, indeed, they be punished,
yet is their hope full of immortality;
chastised a little, they shall be greatly blessed,
because God tried them
and found them worthy of himself.
As gold in the furnace, he proved them,
and as sacrificial offerings he took them to himself.
In the time of their visitation they shall shine,
and shall dart about as sparks through stubble;
they shall judge nations and rule over peoples,
and the LORD shall be their King forever.
Those who trust in him shall understand the truth,
and the faithful shall abide with him in love:
because grace and mercy are with his holy ones,
and his care is with his elect.

PSALM RESPONSE
Psalm 23:1

The Lord is my shepherd; there is nothing I shall want.

SECOND READING
Romans 6:3-9

Brothers and sisters: Are you unaware that we who were baptized into Christ Jesus were baptized into his death? We were indeed buried with him through baptism into his death, so that, just as Christ was raised from the dead by the glory of the Father, we too might live in newness of life.

For if we have grown into union with him through a death like his, we shall also be united with him in the resurrection. We know that our old self was crucified with him, so that our sinful body might be done away with, that we might no longer be in slavery to sin. For a dead person has been absolved from sin. If, then, we have died with Christ, we believe that we shall also live with him. We know that Christ, raised from the dead, dies no more; death no longer has power over him.

GOSPEL
John 11:17-27

When Jesus arrived in Bethany, he found that Lazarus had already been in the tomb for four days. Now Bethany was near Jerusalem, only about two miles away. Many of the Jews had come to Martha and Mary to comfort them about their brother. When Martha heard that Jesus was coming, she went to meet him; but Mary sat at home. Martha said to Jesus, "Lord, if you had been here, my brother would not have died. But even now I know that whatever you ask of God, God will give you." Jesus said to her, "Your brother will rise." Martha said to him, "I know he will rise, in the resurrection on the last day." Jesus told her,

"I am the resurrection and the life;
whoever believes in me, even if he dies, will live,
and everyone who lives and believes in me will never die.

Do you believe this?" She said to him, "Yes, Lord. I have come to believe that you are the Christ, the Son of God, the one who is coming into the world."

Understanding the Word

The passages we read from Sacred Scripture never come to us as isolated units of text, devoid of context or history. We frequently indicate here how important it is to understand the context in which the original author lived and wrote or spoke in order to interpret the text appropriately. In addition, we often point out the importance of the relationship of a particular text to the other readings on a given Sunday, since certain themes and ideas can be highlighted or contrasted by their juxtaposition with other passages.

These issues of context are highly relevant in any attempt to interpret the meaning of a specific reading within the liturgical cycle of the Lectionary. Today's selection of Romans 6:3–9 as the second reading for All Souls offers us yet another opportunity to appreciate how the use of a given passage within the liturgical cycle "layers" it with meaning whenever it is read in other contexts. This passage from Romans, of course, is read every year at the Easter Vigil, the night on which we celebrate the Paschal Mystery of Christ and in a particular way focus our attention on his resurrection from the dead. It is impossible, therefore, to ignore this primary use of the text when it appears in Masses for the Dead or on the celebration of All Souls.

We can and should take note of Paul's original concerns in writing to the Christians in Rome, balancing what he said earlier in this letter about salvation by grace with a reminder that baptism should mark the end (death) of sin for the believer. Paul's use of the past tense in verbs that refer to the death of the Christian in baptism highlights that as an event already achieved, while his choice of the future tense in verbs that speak of the Resurrection is a pointed reminder that we still await the fullness of glory. The focus is on baptism as the decisive turning point for the Christian when this text is read at the Easter Vigil; but, today as well, baptism is suggested as an important foundation of our prayer for sisters and brothers who have died in the Lord.

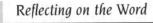

Reflecting on the Word

Tom stood staring at the letters R.I.P. on his grandfather's gravestone. "Rest in peace, Grampa." He wanted nothing more for this beleaguered old man. Grampa had seen so much hardship and was always good to Tom. But would he rest in peace? His love for the bottle was well known. No one had ever seen him in church. Tom just couldn't shake his fears about the fate of his grandfather's immortal soul.

Today's feast gathers up all our hopes and fears about the eternal destiny of our loved ones. We may hope that their faith and love will be rewarded. We may be relieved that their suffering is over, or afraid they did not merit heaven. For all these reasons we pray: "Eternal rest grant unto them, O Lord, and let perpetual light shine upon them. May their souls and the souls of all the faithful departed, through the mercy of God, rest in peace. Amen."

CONSIDER/ DISCUSS:
- Who do you hope will rest in peace? Tell their story.
- How does each of these Scriptures give you hope for your deceased loved ones?
- Does the idea of "purgatory" increase your hopes or your fears for your loved ones? Why?

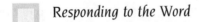

Responding to the Word

Throughout the month of November, as we move toward the end of the liturgical year, the Scriptures continue to focus our attention on the final hope of all baptized disciples of Christ. What about us? Will we "abide with the Lord in love" and "live in newness of life?" Will we join our deceased loved ones and rest in peace?

- Pray for someone who has died in need of God's mercy.
- Light a vigil candle at home or in church in prayerful memory of your friends and family who have died.
- Send a note to someone who has lost a loved one this past year.

November 9, 2003

THE DEDICATION OF THE LATERAN BASILICA

Today's Focus: Mother Church

Why does the whole Church celebrate a church dedication that happened long ago and far away? The Lateran Basilica is the cathedral of the bishop of Rome. Honoring it allows us to reflect on and give thanks for the life, nourishment, and healing that flow from the one Church, our mother.

FIRST READING
Ezekiel 47: 1–2, 8–9, 12

The angel brought me back to the entrance of the temple, and I saw water flowing out from beneath the threshold of the temple toward the east, for the facade of the temple was toward the east; the water flowed down from the southern side of the temple, south of the altar. He led me outside by the north gate, and around to the outer gate facing the east, where I saw water trickling from the southern side. He said to me, "This water flows into the eastern district down upon the Arabah, and empties into the sea, the salt waters, which it makes fresh. Wherever the river flows, every sort of living creature that can multiply shall live, and there shall be abundant fish, for wherever this water comes the sea shall be made fresh. Along both banks of the river, fruit trees of every kind shall grow; their leaves shall not fade, nor their fruit fail. Every month they shall bear fresh fruit, for they shall be watered by the flow from the sanctuary. Their fruit shall serve for food, and their leaves for medicine."

PSALM RESPONSE
Psalm 46:5

The waters of the river gladden the city of God, the holy dwelling of the Most High.

SECOND READING
1 Corinthians 3: 9c–11, 16–17

Brothers and sisters: You are God's building. According to the grace of God given to me, like a wise master builder I laid a foundation, and another is building upon it. But each one must be careful how he builds upon it, for no one can lay a foundation other than the one that is there, namely, Jesus Christ.

Do you not know that you are the temple of God, and that the Spirit of God dwells in you? If anyone destroys God's temple, God will destroy that person; for the temple of God, which you are, is holy.

Since the Passover of the Jews was near, Jesus went up to Jerusalem. He found in the temple area those who sold oxen, sheep, and doves, as well as the money changers seated there. He made a whip out of cords and drove them all out of the temple area, with the sheep and the oxen, and spilled the coins of the money changers and overturned their tables, and to those who sold doves he said, "Take these out of here, and stop making my Father's house a marketplace." His disciples recalled the words of Scripture, *Zeal for your house will consume me.* At this the Jews answered and said to him, "What sign can you show us for doing this?" Jesus answered and said to them, "Destroy this temple and in three days I will raise it up." The Jews said, "This temple has been under construction for forty-six years, and you will raise it up in three days?" But he was speaking about the temple of his body. Therefore, when he was raised from the dead, his disciples remembered that he had said this, and they came to believe the Scripture and the word Jesus had spoken.

Understanding the Word

On the feast of the Dedication of St. John Lateran we celebrate the "mother church" of all Christendom. This building is still considered the cathedral church of the bishop of Rome, and just as the bishop of Rome enjoys primacy among all bishops, so the Lateran Basilica enjoys primacy among all the churches throughout the world. By observing the anniversary of its dedication, we have the opportunity to reflect on the symbolic importance of every place of worship.

Recognition of the symbolic role played by the place where people of faith gather to worship is an ancient and venerable part of our tradition. Today's first reading from the Book of Ezekiel is a reminder that the Temple in Jerusalem assumed an enormously important role in the lives of our Jewish ancestors as a symbol of the Lord's presence and power in their midst. Its destruction at the time of the Exile was seen as a catastrophe of immense proportions, a sign that God had abandoned the people and was no longer their protector and guide. Tempted to despair of their future as the Chosen People, the Jews in Babylon were in desperate need of a message of hope for the future. The prophet Ezekiel saw as his primary mission the proclamation of that message of hope, and with it, encouragement to remain faithful to God and the Covenant.

Today's vision of miraculous water flowing out from the Temple would have been a wondrous word of consolation to the Jewish people. Not only was the Temple to be rebuilt, but it would also become a source of life beyond the people's wildest imaginings. In a desert land, even ordinary water was life-giving. But Ezekiel foresaw a river of water whose properties were incredibly miraculous: salt water is turned into fresh water, trees nourished by this river never fade, they constantly bear fruit, and their leaves serve as medicinal herbs with healing properties. The use of this text today encourages our Christian imagination to recognize the building we call "church" as a symbol of the community we call "Church." Both are the "place/source" from which life flows in abundance.

"Congratulations on your new baby, Katrine! How was childbirth for you?" "It was easy! Once my water broke everything happened smoothly. Actually, pregnancy and childbirth were a snap compared to the way I have to care for her constantly now. Nursing her every two hours; changing and bathing her; keeping her warm, content, and healthy; and, of course, doing laundry. I have no life of my own anymore. It must be really hard to have three or four children!"

While the dominant image in today's readings is that of a temple, the preface for this feast also calls the Church "the joyful mother of a great company of saints." Like a mother, each generation of the Church passes on the Spirit of God that dwells within them, "giving birth" to new Christians in the waters of baptism. Like a mother, the Church "nurses" her children with the Eucharist and heals them with the sacraments of reconciliation and anointing. Like a mother, the Church community constantly cares for the faith of its "offspring."

CONSIDER/ DISCUSS:
- What experience do you have with the work of mothering?
- How has the Church "mothered" you?
- What images of the Church from these Scriptures do you like best? Why?

Responding to the Word

Apparently it's not enough to see ourselves only as a temple, a place where the Spirit of God dwells. We must also always be "mothering"—allowing that Spirit to come to birth and nurturing it in the world. Jesus did not keep the Spirit within him. Nor did Mary. The Spirit within the Church that mothered each of us is to flow through us like water out into the parched earth and give life to all the living.

- Reread the first reading with the image of Mother Church in mind.
- Reflect on how you have given life, nourishment, care, or healing to someone's faith.
- Discover how you might help with the work of Mother Church.

November 16, 2003

THIRTY-THIRD SUNDAY IN ORDINARY TIME

Today's Focus: Safe Harbor

In a dark and turbulent thunderstorm a ship relies on the piercing beacon of the lighthouse to lead it safely to shore. Just so, this week's Scriptures depict the tribulations of the Barque of Peter and assure us that, with Christ as our light and our guide, we can find safe harbor.

FIRST READING
Daniel 12:1–3

In those days, I, Daniel,
    heard this word of the Lord:
"At that time there shall arise
    Michael, the great prince,
    guardian of your people;
it shall be a time unsurpassed in distress
    since nations began until that time.
At that time your people shall escape,
    everyone who is found written in the book.

Many of those who sleep in the dust of the earth shall awake;
    some shall live forever,
    others shall be an everlasting horror and disgrace.

But the wise shall shine brightly
    like the splendor of the firmament,
and those who lead the many to justice
    shall be like the stars forever."

PSALM RESPONSE
Psalm 16:1

You are my inheritance, O Lord!

SECOND READING
Hebrews 10:11–14, 18

Brothers and sisters: Every priest stands daily at his ministry, offering frequently those same sacrifices that can never take away sins. But this one offered one sacrifice for sins, and took his seat forever at the right hand of God; now he waits until his enemies are made his footstool. For by one offering he has made perfect forever those who are being consecrated.

Where there is forgiveness of these, there is no longer offering for sin.

GOSPEL
Mark 13:24–32

Jesus said to his disciples:

"In those days after that tribulation
  the sun will be darkened,
    and the moon will not give its light,
  and the stars will be falling from the sky,
    and the powers in the heavens will be shaken.

"And then they will see 'the Son of Man coming in the clouds' with great power and glory, and then he will send out the angels and gather his elect from the four winds, from the end of the earth to the end of the sky.

"Learn a lesson from the fig tree. When its branch becomes tender and sprouts leaves, you know that summer is near. In the same way, when you see these things happening, know that he is near, at the gates. Amen, I say to you, this generation will not pass away until all these things have taken place. Heaven and earth will pass away, but my words will not pass away.

"But of that day or hour, no one knows, neither the angels in heaven, nor the Son, but only the Father."

Understanding the Word

Despite the fact that the entire Bible is considered inspired revelation, God's word of truth, many of the ideas in the Bible reflect a particular, limited stage of religious development of the people for whom and by whom the text was written. One of the most marked examples of how the Bible contains theological reflections that matured over time is in the concept of life after death. There are only a handful of places in the Jewish Scriptures that reflect a belief in personal survival beyond the grave. Those passages tend to be written late in Israel's history, and even so they do not present a refined notion of the afterlife.

Today's first reading from the Book of Daniel is one of those places in the Jewish Scripture where the author seems to hold a firm conviction that those who die will survive death and continue to exist in a personal way that allows them to experience a fate that is either positive or negative. This is an important element in the attempt that the author of Daniel makes to encourage his audience to hold fast in the face of persecution. The Book of Daniel was written during the Maccabean revolt and persecution of the Jews by Antiochus Epiphanes IV (ca. 167–164 B.C.), a time of fierce persecution aimed at intimidating the Jewish population into abandoning its ancestral faith. The author here presents a vision of the final times. In the end, he insists, God's people will triumph over their persecutors, and those who have remained faithful will enjoy a fullness of life, while those who have defected from their faith will awake to "everlasting horror and disgrace."

Apocalyptic literature, such as the Book of Daniel, is misinterpreted if it is presented as a source book of prophecies about future historical and political events. In order to interpret such a text properly today, it is important to know that the author did not intend to foretell specific details of the future, but rather to reassure his readers of the eventual victory of God's faithful ones and console them in their present suffering.

210

Occasionally the Church is depicted in art as a boat being tossed on a rough sea. It is called the Barque (or boat) of Peter. Like the Ark of Noah during the flood, the Barque of Peter provides temporary haven to those brave enough to stay on board until they reach the safety of shore. Like the boat in the familiar Gospel story, Christ has the power to keep the Barque of Peter safe through all the rough weather it will encounter.

Today's readings focus on the last days and the "distress" and "tribulation" that we will certainly endure before the end. We are assured that all the "elect" who are "found written in the book" will escape the raging storms and be gathered into safe harbor. "The Son of Man" will be "near" as a beacon to "lead the many to justice." Once safely on shore they will receive their "inheritance"—which is the Lord.

**CONSIDER/
DISCUSS:**
- Where might you find yourself in a painting of the Barque of Peter? What would you be doing? Thinking? Feeling?
- What "persecutions" has the Church survived?
- When have you been tempted to "jump ship" and abandon your faith?

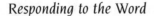

Responding to the Word

Each of us will encounter our own personal end of time on the day we die. "Of that day or hour, no one knows ... but only the Father." In our lifetimes we are sure to experience the distress of suffering, doubts, and temptations that will lure us to abandon Christ's guiding light and head for the rocks. Will we be on board the Barque of Peter at the time of our death or will we have jumped ship? Will we find safe harbor?

- Pray for courage and strength in the hour of your death.
- Support someone whose faith is being shaken by rough seas.
- Help your faith community weather its current storm.

November 23, 2003

THE SOLEMNITY OF OUR LORD JESUS CHRIST THE KING

Today's Focus: Here and Now

It's easy to think of the Scriptures as dealing with things that happened long ago and far away. It's also easy to think of them as stories of things that will happen somewhere, some day. But today's feast invites us to claim Christ as our King right here and right now.

FIRST READING
Daniel 7:13–14

As the visions during the night continued, I saw
   one like a Son of man coming,
     on the clouds of heaven;
   when he reached the Ancient One
     and was presented before him,
   the one like a Son of man received dominion, glory, and kingship;
     all peoples, nations, and languages serve him.
His dominion is an everlasting dominion
   that shall not be taken away,
     his kingship shall not be destroyed.

PSALM RESPONSE
Psalm 93:1a

The Lord is king; he is robed in majesty.

SECOND READING
Revelation 1: 5–8

Jesus Christ is the faithful witness, the firstborn of the dead and ruler of the kings of the earth. To him who loves us and has freed us from our sins by his blood, who has made us into a kingdom, priests for his God and Father, to him be glory and power forever and ever. Amen.

Behold, he is coming amid the clouds,
   and every eye will see him,
     even those who pierced him.
All the peoples of the earth will lament him.
   Yes. Amen.

"I am the Alpha and the Omega," says the Lord God, "the one who is and who was and who is to come, the almighty."

GOSPEL
John 18:33b–37

Pilate said to Jesus, "Are you the King of the Jews?" Jesus answered, "Do you say this on your own or have others told you about me?" Pilate answered, "I am not a Jew, am I? Your own nation and the chief priests handed you over to me. What have you done?" Jesus answered, "My kingdom does not belong to this world. If my kingdom did belong to this world, my attendants would be fighting to keep me from being handed over to the Jews. But as it is, my kingdom is not here." So Pilate said to him, "Then you are a king?" Jesus answered, "You say I am a king. For this I was born and for this I came into the world, to testify to the truth. Everyone who belongs to the truth listens to my voice."

Understanding the Word

Last week we discussed the Book of Daniel as an example of apocalyptic literature, a very specific kind of writing that was produced during a time of religious persecution. By means of a series of narratives and exotic visions of the future, the author attempts to reassure his readers that it is worth their while to remain faithful in the face of persecution, since in the end God's people will surely triumph.

The selection from the Book of Daniel presented in today's first reading was part of that attempt to weave a vision of ultimate success for the Jews under persecution. Exactly whom the author had in mind when he refers to "one like a Son of Man" is hotly disputed by scholars today. The fact is, we simply do not know if the author meant anyone in particular or if this is a collective, figurative image of Israel's triumph. What we do know is that the early Christian community seized upon this passage and recognized it as a messianic prophecy, a foretelling of the ultimate triumph of Jesus as the Christ of God. The Lectionary's juxtaposition of this text with today's Gospel narrative of Jesus before Pilate is a wonderful example of how the liturgy "layers" passages with new meaning by inserting them in a particular context.

The celebration of Christ the King allows us to hear these passages with a new depth of meaning in light of our contemporary understanding of how, in Jesus and his resurrection and ascension, we have seen the fulfillment of Daniel's vision of ultimate deliverance. The veiled admission of Jesus before Pilate that he did indeed have a kingdom "not here" takes on new meaning against the cosmic vision of Daniel, who allows us to glimpse the "Ancient One" on his heavenly throne. The Book of Revelation from which our second reading is taken today is also an example of apocalyptic literature, and it allows us to see how that literary tradition was continued in the Christian era. As the author of the Book of Daniel had consoled his contemporaries, so the author of Revelation consoles fellow Christians by reminding them that Christ is indeed "coming amid the clouds."

Reflecting on the Word

In ancient cultures the gods ruled people's lives minute by minute. They were believed to control every natural, political, economic, and social event. The deities were blamed for a thunderstorm and thanked for the return of spring. They were rulers of the here and now.

At first glance the Scriptures for this solemnity of Christ the King seem to speak of a deity who will rule somewhere, someday. His "kingdom is not here"— but somewhere. He "is coming amid the clouds and every eye will see him"—not now but someday. On closer examination, however, we discover a king who reigns here and now. He has already "received dominion" and "all peoples serve him." "The Lord is king" right now and "has made us into a kingdom" right here. Christ rules all times and all places, as "the one who is and who was and who is to come, the almighty."

- Are these Scriptures about the end of time or here and now? Explain.

- Does Christ's kingdom "belong to this world?" Why or why not?

- How does Christ rule your life here and now?

Responding to the Word

Next Sunday is the first Sunday of Advent. We will remember the birth of the King of Kings some two thousand years ago in the Middle East. But we will also "remember" the fulfillment of his kingdom at the end of time and its effective presence in the world today. For us, the Kingship of Christ is an ever-present reality that bridges the end of time with the beginning of the story. Christ wants to rule our lives minute by minute, here and now, and forever.

- Pledge your allegiance to Christ who bought your freedom with his blood.

- Serve Christ in the poor of your community.

Notes

Rev. Robert D. Duggan is a priest in the Archdiocese of Washington, D.C., where he currently ministers as pastor of St. Rose of Lima parish in Gaithersburg, Maryland. He holds a License in Sacred Theology from the Gregorian University in Rome and a doctorate from the Catholic University of America. In addition to his work in parish ministry, Father Duggan has been actively involved since 1980 in the implementation of the Rite of Christian Initiation of Adults on both the national and international levels. He has served on the board and as a team member for the North American Forum on the Catechumenate and is a frequent speaker on liturgical and sacramental topics. Father Duggan is also an author of books and articles on a variety of topics in the fields of liturgical, sacramental, and pastoral theology.

Virginia Stillwell has worked for fifteen years in various parish ministries, including liturgy, music, initiation, and adult education. She possesses a Master of Divinity degree and a Master of Arts in Theology (Liturgy) from St. John's University School of Theology and Seminary in Collegeville, Minnesota. Virginia has taught in undergraduate theology and diaconal training programs and has led workshops on many liturgical topics. A past team member for the North American Forum on the Catechumenate, she is currently writing, teaching, and enjoying the friendship of her four adult children. Virginia lives in the Twin Cities area with her husband of twenty-nine years.